LITERACY INSTRUCTION FOR
ENGLISH LANGUAGE LEARNERS, PRE-K–2

Solving Problems in the Teaching of Literacy

Cathy Collins Block, *Series Editor*

Recent Volumes

Literacy Instruction for English Language Learners, Pre-K–2

DIANE M. BARONE
SHELLEY HONG XU

THE GUILFORD PRESS
New York   London

Printed in the United States of America

This book is printed on acid-free paper.

Last digit is print number: 9 8 7 6 5 4 3 2 1

We are grateful to the following publishers for allowing us to reprint extracts from their books:

Baa Baa Black Sheep by Iza Trapani, copyright 2001 by Iza Trapani. Used with permission of
Charlesbridge Publishing, Inc.

The Cloud Book by Tomie dePaola, copyright 1975 by Tomie dePaola. Reprinted by permission of
Holiday House, Inc.

Corduroy by Don Freeman, copyright 1968 by Don Freeman. Used by permission of Viking
Penguin, A Division of Penguin Young Readers Group, A Member of Penguin Group (USA).

Swimmy by Leo Lionni, copyright 1963 by Leo Lionni. Copyright renewed 1991 by Leo Lionni.
Used by permission of Alfred A. Knopf, an imprint of Random House Children's Books, a
division of Random House, Inc.

Library of Congress Cataloging-in-Publication Data

Literacy instruction for English language learners, Pre-K–2 / Diane M. Barone, Shelley
Hong Xu.
    p. cm. — (Solving problems in the teaching of literacy)
Includes bibliographical references and index.
ISBN-10: 1-59385-602-4 ISBN-13: 978-1-59385-602-1 (pbk. : alk. paper)
ISBN-10: 1-59385-603-2 ISBN-13: 978-1-59385-603-8 (cloth: alk. paper)
    1. English language—Study and teaching—Foreign speakers.   2. English language—
Study and teaching (Primary)   3. Bilingualism.   4. Language acquisition.   I. Barone,
Diane M.   II. Xu, Shelley Hong, 1964–
    PE1128.A2L533 2008
    372.652′1—dc22
                                                                            2007028818

About the Authors

Diane M. Barone, EdD, is Professor of Literacy at the University of Nevada, Reno, where she teaches courses in literacy and qualitative research methods and conducts research on young children's literacy development and instruction in high-poverty schools. She has directed two longitudinal studies of literacy development: a 4-year study of children prenatally exposed to crack/cocaine, and a 7-year study of children, predominantly English language learners, in a high-poverty school. Dr. Barone has published numerous articles and book chapters as well as several books, including *Developing Literacy: An Integrated Approach to Assessment and Instruction* (with Donald R. Bear), *Resilient Children: Stories of Poverty, Drug Exposure, and Literacy Development*, *The National Board Handbook* (with National Board Teachers), and *Teaching Early Literacy: Development, Assessment, and Instruction* (with Marla H. Mallette and Shelley Hong Xu). She served as Editor of *Reading Research Quarterly* for 8 years and is currently a board member of the International Reading Association. In addition, Dr. Barone is the principal investigator of the Reading First grant in Nevada.

Shelley Hong Xu, EdD, is Professor of Teacher Education at the California State University, Long Beach, where she teaches literacy courses in a graduate reading program and a teaching credential program. She previously taught English as a foreign language and as a second language. Dr. Xu's research includes preparing teachers for teaching English language learners and integrating multimedia texts into literacy curriculum. Her work has appeared in literacy journals and edited books, and she is also the coauthor (with Diane M. Barone and Marla H. Mallette) of *Teaching Early Literacy: Development, Assessment, and Instruction*, and *Trading Cards to Comic Strips: Popular Culture Texts and Literacy Learning in Grades K–8*.

Preface

> The process of English language learners acquiring English literacy is not a mere process of learning the linguistic codes. Rather, the process is dynamic, cultural, and social, and it involves not just the learner but, equally important, the teacher, the text, and the context.
>
> —Xu (2003, p. 67)

This quote by Xu frames the content of *Literacy Instruction for English Language Learners, Pre-K–2*. We believe there is a synergy required among English language learners (ELLs), teachers, text support, and the context of classrooms and schools that is essential for the academic success of ELLs. Not one of these elements can stand alone as the most critical to achievement. For instance, an ELL cannot succeed in U.S. classrooms without the support of his or her teacher in bridging home and school cultures and facilitating the learning of academic content.

Throughout this book, we describe the connections among instruction, materials, assessment, and student support. Each chapter adds to a multilayered, comprehensive approach for the literacy learning and instruction of young ELLs—students, we believe, who are capable of matching the learning expectations of their monolingual counterparts.

Each chapter focuses on a particular aspect of the comprehensive approach we believe supports ELLs' learning. Chapter 1, "Creating Classrooms to Engage Learners," centers on the context of learning. The chapter includes numerous suggestions about arranging the physical space to support learning. There are recommendations for the social and emotional environment with an extensive discussion centered on the importance of the teacher.

Chapter 2, "Working with Families," shares numerous opportunities to involve families in essential ways to support the learning of their children. This chapter offers suggestions for learning about families and language so that teachers can better support the in-class learning of ELLs. The chapter concludes with many practical suggestions for welcoming families to classrooms.

Chapter 3, "Assessment," discusses the important role that classroom-based assessment plays in identifying ELLs' strengths and needs. The chapter also provides teachers with specific details on the use of classroom-based assessment, ranging from selecting an assessment focus to identifying assessment materials to reporting assessment results to families.

Chapter 4, "Oral Language Development and Instruction," provides the foundation of oral language and its importance to other literacy learning. The chapter describes elements of language structure and then explores the requirements necessary to learn a new language. The chapter suggests many activities that support oral language in classrooms and provides instruction centered on phonemic awareness.

Chapter 5, "Encouraging All Students to Become Writers," moves from oral language to a discussion of how children learn to write. From this foundation, we build an extensive discussion about writing development and how children come to learn to represent words. We then present readers with multiple strategies and activities to support ELL writers. The chapter concludes with the importance of having ELLs write about the content they are learning.

Chapter 6, "Instructional Materials Supportive of Student Learning," tackles the issue of providing appropriate materials for ELLs. This chapter is unique to many books written about ELLs in that it addresses the challenges presented by text, both narrative and informational, to the comprehension of ELLs.

Chapter 7, "Phonics, Spelling, and Vocabulary," targets word-level knowledge. Throughout this chapter we share language-rich activities that support the word learning of ELLs.

Chapter 8, "Engaging English Language Learners in the Comprehension Process," focuses on the meaning aspects of literacy. Teachers are presented with a multitude of ways to support the comprehension process in narrative and informational texts before, through, and after reading. We share book examples to show the complexity of text and the difficulties that ELLs have in acquiring meaning.

Chapter 9, "Visits to Classrooms and Schools," brings the book's discussion to life by focusing on teachers and schools in action. There are classroom examples for each level targeted in this book (pre-K through second grade). Finally, we elaborate on an entire school's goal of increasing parent involvement in their children's literacy. These examples allow readers to see the application of many of the ideas presented in this book.

We wrote this book so that teachers can see the possibilities for supporting ELLs in their classrooms and schools. We believe that teachers can enhance the learning of all students in a classroom or school. We value teachers who recognize the strengths ELLs bring from their home experiences, including their language. We know that exemplary teachers of ELLs

> do not wallow in the demographics associated with their students; rather, they identify and extend the personal and academic potential within each student. Students achieve the highest literacy expectations when they are in a classroom with a caring teacher who has high expectations and uses exemplary literacy practices. The synergy between a teacher and exemplary strategies is what makes a difference in student learning. (Barone, 2006, p. 9)

Exemplary teachers of ELLs understand that their students' literacy achievement may be differentially affected by multiple factors such as their family's economic circumstances, immigration status, education, social community, bilingualism, and/or level of acculturation (Garcia & Willis, 2001). Moreover, they understand that learning to read in English, a new language, offers challenges and opportunities for students and their teachers. They know that ELLs do not constitute a homogeneous group; rather, they can range from students who are emergent literacy learners to proficient readers and writers in their first language.

This unique book features:

- Discussions of the processes of becoming literate, such as oral language comprehension, phonics, and orthographic knowledge.
- Discussion questions to guide reading or to use in discussion groups.
- Classroom examples.
- A chapter devoted to assessment, as well as examples integrated throughout the text.
- Online resources in addition to print resources.
- Inclusion of teacher and student voices.
- "Take-a-moment" boxes that allow readers to reflect and make connections to classroom practice.

We offer these features so that reading this book provides ways for teachers to enrich their knowledge about the instruction and learning of ELLs. They are meant to support discussion and reflection and to extend this conversation through connections to classrooms and through online resources. It is our hope that these discussions and explorations result in enhanced learning for ELLs.

Contents

CHAPTER 1

Creating Classrooms to Engage Learners

> Instead of looking at educational settings . . . as having
> clear boundaries and identifiable contents, I look at
> them as extensive in space and time, fluid in form and
> content; as intersections of multiple networks shaping
> cities, communities, schools, pedagogies, and teacher
> and student practices.
>
> —NESPOR (1997, p. xiii)

Just as Nespor (1997) views schools as having fluid boundaries, we describe preschool, kindergarten, and first- and second-grade classrooms as also having fluid boundaries where the home lives of students influence their school lives and their school lives influence their home lives. This chapter is grounded in this perspective and provides examples that demonstrate what these permeable boundaries might look like in practice. We feel this first chapter in a book about English language learners (ELLs) is critical to future discussions of teaching and learning in literacy. We believe that the physical and emotional spaces created by teachers are central to the literacy learning of all students and in particular ELLs.

ELLs are the fastest-growing student population in the United States. According to the U.S. Department of Education (2002), between 2001 and 2002 the total K–12 enrollment growth was 12% whereas ELLs' enrollment growth was 95%. In 2000, more than 3 million school-age children were ELLS with 57% of them Spanish speakers and 18% Asian/Pacific Islanders (*www.ncela.gwu/edu/ellcensus90s.pdf*). In 16 states there has been more than a 200% enrollment growth of ELLs between 1992 and 2002. California, Florida, Illinois, New York, and Texas have experienced the greatest growth of all states. However, even in states like North Dakota and Rhode Island, 10% of their students are learning English as a new language (Freeman & Freeman, 2000).

Although there are certainly many configurations to support ELLS, such as bilingual education classes or English-language learning support outside the classroom, most mainstream classroom teachers have the primary responsibility for developing students' competence in English as they teach these students to read and write (Au, 2002; Neufeld & Fitzgerald, 2001). Perhaps not surprising is that most teachers have had little or no professional training in facilitating English learning and literacy development for ELLs (Hadaway, Vardell, & Young, 2004). For this reason and others, many teachers find meeting their ELLs' learning needs a challenge. They worry about how to teach a student who does not speak the language of the school. ELLs experience a similar challenge as they are often required to leave their home identity, experiences, and literacy knowledge at the classroom door. Once they cross the threshold of the classroom, their home language and literacy experiences are frequently not valued or are ignored as teachers attempt to build oral competence and literacy knowledge in English (Smagorinsky & Smith, 2002).

In this chapter, we discuss the physical and social/emotional environment of the classroom. We share ways to build connections between home and school cultures (see Chapter 2 to learn about more extensive ways to engage parents), and we provide examples of activities that support a students' home culture and language even when all or the majority of instruction is in English.

At the end of this chapter, you will be able to:

- Describe the critical aspects of creating the physical environment of a classroom.
- Describe the importance of the emotional/social environment of the classroom.
- Describe the important characteristics of exemplary teachers of ELLs.
- Describe the intersections of physical and emotional/social environments.
- Describe strategies to support ELLs in classrooms.

THE PHYSICAL ENVIRONMENT

Why begin a book focused on ELLs' literacy with a section on the physical environment? We believe that the environment of the classroom facilitates the comfort level of students who are learning English as they enter school. As they come to school for the first time, they rely on the structure of the classroom to provide clues as to what they are expected to do and where. They learn that when in centers, they can quietly chat with fellow students, for instance.

Teachers should think about the classroom environment long before school actually begins. Teachers plan the orientation of tables or desks in the primary grades. Just where will they place all the furniture? They then consider the other spaces within the room. How will students access computers and where will the computers be? How will materials be placed so that students have easy access? Organizing a classroom space may sound very simple—just look at a room and decide what goes where—but it isn't. The physical organization of a classroom can result in a structure that supports learning or interferes with it.

First, teachers need to think about the instruction they will provide students and how the physical structure of the classroom will support it. Instruction guides the placement of furniture and supplies. In preschool and primary grades, teachers need spaces for whole-class instruction, small-group instruction, and centers. Whole-group instruction often occurs either on the carpet or with students at their desks. Teachers need to consider where they will configure:

- Whole-class instruction with space at tables or desks and on the carpet.
- Small-group instruction, typically at a small table.
- Centers for students.

As these places are determined, it is also important to not have centers near the location for small-group instruction. When students work together in centers, they can get noisy and interfere with small-group instruction. In addition, centers in preschool often take more space than those in first and second grades. In preschool, students may engage in a housekeeping area or other dramatic play areas, block areas, and so on. These require room for movement. In first and second grade, and often kindergarten as well, centers are located on tables.

TAKE A MOMENT

Use a paper that represents the configuration of your classroom or a rectangular shape if you are unsure or do not yet have a classroom. Plan where whole-class instruction, small-group instruction, and centers (plan for five) might be located. Be mindful of noise level in centers. You might want to think about the fixed aspects of the room, such as a sink, bathrooms, and so on.

Once the big areas for instruction are planned, a teacher can tailor each area so that needed materials are included. Following are some considerations for organization.

1. There should be an easel and an overhead projector near the large-group instruction area. Often teachers have storage on the back of the easel or on the overhead cart for letter cards, books, and so on.

2. The small-group instruction area needs storage for white boards (for individual student writing), paper, books, pencils, chart paper, and so on.

3. Centers need supporting materials where students can store them efficiently. For example, in preschool, students know where to put blocks when they are finished constructing with them. In primary grades, students know where to place writing materials when they have finished. Storage and organization vary as to the type of center. Play centers require different organization than do literacy centers. Play centers may have tubs for large blocks whereas literacy centers may have trays for papers and small containers for pencils and crayons.

The physical structure of a classroom is very important to all young learners, and in particular to ELLs. The structure of the room provides predictability for students. They know where activities occur and what is expected during each activity. By having these parts of their classrooms as established places with predictable routines, they are able to focus on instruction and learning.

Literacy Center

The literacy center or area is a very important place for young learners. Here they can explore books and other reading materials. Guthrie

(2002) notes that an inviting space in the room focused on literacy results in students more interested in books and writing. Sometimes teachers combine the more traditional reading center with a writing center. They portion out a part of the literacy center with writing materials. However this space is configured, it is important for students, even as young as 2 or 3, to have a special place to explore books and writing. A goal for the literacy center is that it easily accommodates five to six children at one time.

In our experience, we have seen teachers frame off this space. They may have a bookshelf against the back wall and lower shelves to the side, resulting in a U-shaped space. Thus they can observe children in this center as they instruct or chat with children in other parts of the room. They also find comfortable pillows or a sofa for children to relax in as they read. And in some rooms we have seen teachers who place stuffed animals in the literacy center so that small children can read to their favorite bear. A stuffed animal helps make the center a safe structure for ELLs to practice newly developed English oral language.

Once the physical space of the literacy center is established, teachers collect books for students to explore. It is important to provide a great variety of texts. These texts might include:

■ *Board or cloth books.* These are appropriate for our youngest students. They also are engaging for students who are learning English as they often center on simple concepts.

■ *Concept books.* These books generally have no storyline. They just identify pictures with words. They help ELLs learn English equivalents for objects with which they may already be familiar.

■ *Environmental print.* This is text that children see in their world, home, and classroom. Students might create their own environmental print books in English or their home language or a combination of both for exploration.

■ *Wordless books.* These books have storylines without words to support them. The young child creates a story to match the illustrations.

■ *Catalogues, television guides, and newspaper advertising.* Although not typically on the list of materials for a literacy center, we consider them important. They are frequently in homes and thus familiar. Students can also identify the pictures within them. With the advertising from newspapers they can pretend to shop for food for home.

■ *Children's magazines.* Magazines like *Zoo Books* or *Your Big Backyard* engage students in discussions centered on the illustrations.

■ *Alphabet books.* These books focus children's attention on the alphabet and often extend vocabulary as ELLs learn about items that begin with each letter.

■ *Number books.* These books target children's attention to numbers.

■ *Books connected to television shows.* These books again connect television watching at home with a print extension. Children will be familiar with the characters and this familiarity should stimulate conversation, especially for ELLs.

■ *Traditional literature.* Although many ELLs may not be familiar with nursery rhymes or fairytales, these serve as reading for teachers to students who then revisit the stories and rhymes in the literacy center. It is helpful to have multiple copies so that small groups of students can explore the same book. Moreover, once the teacher has shared a book, it often becomes a favorite that children clamor to read.

■ *Easy-to-read books.* These are books that students with sufficient literacy knowledge can read on their own. There should be predictable text available as well as decodable text for independent practice.

■ *Informational books.* Such books serve as a stimulus for discussion and are often the preferred books of young children. Similar to traditional literature, once read by teachers, they offer opportunities for students to revisit them.

Teachers generally feature some of these books on bookshelves so that children can see the covers for easy selection. Other books may be organized in tubs marked by category (animals, alphabet books, etc.) where students can explore those they want to investigate. Later in the year, the teacher might break the animal books up into groupings such as pets, zoo animals, or farm animals. Later the books might be reconfigured into mammals, reptiles, or insects. Each successive grouping recognizes the more sophisticated knowledge of students.

Within the literacy center or in another location in the room, teachers also display books and materials related to the current theme, author, or illustrator study. Students are welcome to explore these books independently. It is important that many books focus on the same topic or theme so ELLs can constantly revisit similar content to develop their knowledge base, vocabulary, oral language, and reading and writing competence.

Other parts of the literacy center include a listening center, with a selection of nursery rhymes and books for students to listen to. Within this center is a computer or two for reading, exploring, and writing. Students may engage with the computer to listen to a story, they may explore a website, or they may create a story using a program to support young students' writing. Finally, to support writing, there would be an area with pencils, crayons, and paper for student writing.

Play and Dramatic Play Centers

Although these centers are not frequently seen in first and second grades, they are very important for preschool and kindergarten children. If teachers organize the center around a theme, they increase children's opportunities for language and literacy play (Neuman & Roskos, 1993). For example, if the instructional theme is transportation, the teacher might create an airport or a garage. Here children would dress as flight attendants or mechanics. They would have props that support literacy but are tied to the theme. They may have repair slips or plane tickets (see Figure 1.1). They may have to list all the passengers on the plane. They may need to take drink orders. As a mechanic, they would note repairs and the costs of repairs. They jot down phone numbers so they can contact the client when the work is complete. We include pictures so that children who cannot read or do not know English have clues to what is expected.

Teachers also want a supply of books related to the theme available for students. They include realia (real objects) in the center, like a toy wrench or hammer, so that students can pretend to repair a truck, for example. Other examples of literacy-enriched dramatic play centers might be a post office, a doctor's office, a veterinarian's office, a supermarket, and a restaurant, among others.

To extend the theme to home, teachers create boxes or plastic bags with a book and artifacts related to the theme inside. For example, there may be a book about trucks and a small truck with paper to record repairs. Through these collections, parents and students are connected in literacy-based activities that may not be typical experiences in their homes. As students mature in their literacy knowledge, these containers

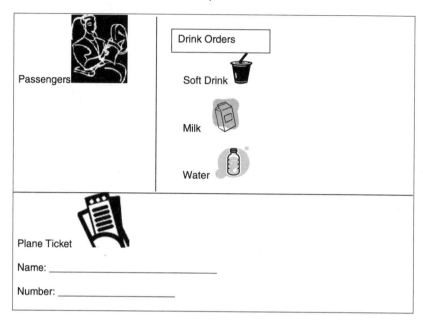

FIGURE 1.1. Airport forms.

include text that they read to their parents as well as a book that a parent would read or discuss with them (Neuman, 1999). Figure 1.2 shows a child and her teacher as they investigate a collection that will be going home. In this case, the school purchased these collections from a publisher (Lakeshore) to save preparation time.

These centers and take-home activities support students in literacy play that is engaged in by adults. As students participate, teachers can keep informal records of the conversation and activities of students. They might also ask parents to record interesting observations about their child's engagement with these materials at home.

Labeling the Room and Activities

After the room is physically organized, teachers want to stand back and think about other text support for young learners. They may develop a bulletin board to support the first theme and they may also create a bulletin board or sign to indicate the literacy and writing areas.

FIGURE 1.2. Take-home collection.

Once students arrive, it is important to engage them in labeling important parts of the room. We recommend that teachers participate in this process with their students so that they connect the labels to things or activities. For instance, they might label the door, sink, teacher's desk, and so on. It would be beneficial to students if these objects also carried a label in their home language. For example, table can be labeled with *table* in English, *mesa* in Spanish, *teiburu* in Japanese, and 桌子 in Chinese. Older students and parents can help with these labels.

In addition to labels for things in the classroom, we have seen teachers use labels to support children's activities. For example, when children play with blocks, they draw a sketch and label what they have built in a notebook that is at the block center before the construction is demolished. Students might also record the experiment they participated in at the science center. For almost every activity in the class, there is a notebook or chart for students to record their activities. In this way, students see real uses for literacy. See Figure 1.3 for an example by a young preschooler, Micah, who drew a sketch and labeled his train creation before it had to be cleaned up.

Teachers also take advantage of the importance of a child's name. Students' names are placed on cubbies or book tubs, for example. Children find their personal belongings here and they also use class-

FIGURE 1.3. Sketch of train with label.

mates' names in their writing. Often, preschoolers and kindergartners take great delight in copying classmates' names and reading these lists.

Labeling in a classroom is a constant—not something done at the beginning of the year and later ignored. The labels attached to objects and activities provide instruction to students in how words are connected to print. These labels, after a child's name, become the first words students can read and attach meaning to. ELLs in particular understand the connections between an object, its label, and its pronunciation.

Although the classroom's physical environment can be changed, it comes with consequences. If tables or centers are moved, young children struggle with where they are to be and what is expected of them. This is even more pronounced for ELLs who rely on classroom structure to signal expectations. It will take a few days before the new configuration becomes automatic to students. Teachers often struggle with inappropriate behavior from students as they get accustomed to the new organization.

THE SOCIAL AND EMOTIONAL ENVIRONMENT

The social and emotional environment of a classroom is one of the most critical characteristics in students' success. Unlike the physical environment, the social and emotional environment is not as apparent when first walking into a classroom. However, there are parts of the social and emotional environment that are observable. For example, observers can note whether children are expected to sit quietly all day. They can also observe to see whether student work is evident in the room. They can observe whether students understand and respect the routines established in the classroom. And, most important, they can observe and see the relationship between the teacher and the students.

In this section we consider several important parts of the social and emotional environment. They include the importance of the teacher, social interaction in the classroom, rules and routines, and differentiated instruction.

The Importance of the Teacher

Much of the research centered on teachers in urban settings, where the numbers of ELLs are the highest, reports that many don't last through their first year (Brown, 2002). Ladson-Billings (2001) noted that in Chicago there are about 1,500 teachers hired each year, and in Los Angeles about 5,000 largely because of teacher turnover. These teachers feel frustrated with their teacher education programs and the circumstances in which they find themselves as they enter their teaching career. They discover they are not prepared to deal with the challenges of urban schools and the students who attend them and, in particular, how to support the learning of ELLs.

The students who attend these schools and their parents are in a parallel situation. They find it difficult to work with their neighborhood school when teachers infrequently stay. Students find it challenging to learn when their teachers are short-timers and are not committed to the school community.

The bleak circumstances just described do not have to permeate all classrooms that find themselves rich with ELLs. We describe ways that teachers can be change agents for students and provide them with an environment that supports their learning. Teachers can come to value diversity when working with students who come to school with rich literacy traditions different from those supported in school and with language backgrounds not represented in their classrooms.

Becoming Culturally Responsive

Not unexpectedly, the first task in becoming culturally sensitive to students is to explore one's own beliefs about teaching and learning (Xu, 2000a, 2000b). Before reading further take a moment and describe how you learned in school and what you think about exemplary teaching, especially as it pertains to ELLs.

TAKE A MOMENT

Who are you as a learner?
What are the characteristics that describe an exemplary teacher of ELLs?
What literacy experiences do you value from your school experiences?
How do ELLs learn best?

Once a teacher understands who he or she is as a learner and the values attached to being an exemplary teacher of ELLs, this teacher is ready to consider the ethnic, cultural, and language profiles of students in his or her classroom. Some of these considerations might include:

- What are the social relationships expected between students and teachers? How does the teacher talk to students? How are students expected to talk to teachers? Are these expectations variable and based on learning situations? For example, can students freely talk to teachers when they are in centers or is there a protocol that requires students always to be called on to talk? Can students use their home language in school?
- What are the social relationships between students? Can they work together? What language are they expected to use?
- What is the best way to improve students' English-language proficiency?
- How much of a student's culture should be recognized if he or she is to succeed in middle-class America?
- How much homework should a teacher assign? Should teachers expect parents to support students with homework? What

should teachers expect of parents who do not speak, read, or write English?

■ How do the books a teacher chooses represent or engage his or her students?

Not all these questions have easy answers. They take time to reflect on, and they certainly change as teachers have more experience and success working with students who are learning English as they learn to read and write. What is important is that teachers think about such questions as they begin and continue to work with ELLs. These are important questions to explore with other teachers. This reflection and decision-making process are necessary for teachers to be successful in engaging their students in purposeful instruction.

In writing about culturally responsive teaching, Ladson-Billings (1994) reiterates the importance of teacher expectations of student ability—low expectations result in low achievement and high expectations result in high achievement for students, a statement that is still important today. She sees culturally responsive teaching as a way to seek excellence—where teachers, students, and families share responsibility for learning. Teachers serve as *conductors* or *coaches*; they believe that all students are capable of excellence and they assume responsibility to facilitate and coordinate learning opportunities. Ladson-Billings (1994) values teaching as an art where teachers "see themselves as part of the community. They demonstrate a connectedness with all of their students and encourage that same connectedness between the students" (p. 25). Expectations are critically important to ELLs literacy success. If teachers and their school do not really believe that ELLs can be proficient literacy learners then ELLs will mirror this belief—and the school and its teachers would have to own this result.

The belief that all students can learn with appropriate support and connections between home, school, and community is important to becoming a culturally responsive teacher. Further, culturally responsive teachers engage in strategies to support individual student learning. A few of these practices include:

■ Creating a classroom that values the voices of all—a community of learners. Seeking ways to connect families with schools. Valuing family involvement even when parents do not speak English (see Chapter 2 for many practical suggestions).

■ Treating students as individuals, and the willingness to revise instruction to meet individual student needs.

■ Appreciating student voices.

■ Facilitating knowledge and pride in various ethnic, cultural, and language backgrounds.

■ Believing that all students are capable.

Throughout this book, we share specific ways to support these ideas.

Becoming a Caring Teacher

Gordon (1999) writes that the "best urban teachers show warmth and affection to their students and give priority to the development of their relationships with students as an avenue to student growth" (p. 305). This belief stands in contrast to the organization of many teachers and schools that focus on discipline first. Although discipline is important, so that schools are safe places that support learning, it cannot be considered without focusing on building relationships with students and families. For example, in one school we visited, the rule was that no students were allowed into the building before the morning bell rang. This was a schoolwide rule to prevent student misbehavior without supervision. We witnessed students lining up outside the classroom door, hoping to gain an opportunity to chat informally with their teacher when he or she appeared. In this same school, one teacher departed from the practice (with principal support) and invited students into the room when they arrived at school. Students helped prepare the room for instruction as they chatted with their teacher. An interesting observation from this teacher was that none of his students "received citations for inappropriate behavior." He believed, "It is about the relationships. They know I will be disappointed or angry with them if they disrupt learning or engage in inappropriate behavior on the playground or in the cafeteria. We have an agreement that we are here to learn. They know I care about them and they care about me."

In *School Kids/Street Kids*, Flores-González (2002) discusses the development of students who become school kids (those who succeed in school) or street kids (those who may attend school but are not a part of it). In her book she considers the school and classroom environment as the most important factor for students. In particular, she highlights the relationships students have with teachers. Throughout her book there are quotes from students describing teachers who made them want to stay and perform in school, similar to the teacher previously described. Flores-González synthesizes these remarks and highlights the importance of elementary teachers to students developing a school-kid identity. She writes, "These close and intense relationships with teachers fostered commitment to school" (p. 33). Students chose to stay in school and become active participants in their middle and high schools' cultures by joining clubs or participating in sports because of the relationships they developed with their elementary school teachers.

The literature is filled with documentation to support the need for caring teachers. Following are a few examples:

- Students become engaged in school when they feel competent. To feel competent they must have a sense of belonging that is developed though meaningful dialogue with teachers and peers (Newmann, Wehlage, & Lamborn, 1992).
- Students' attitudes toward literacy are shaped by classroom contexts and relationships with teachers (McCarthey, 2002).
- Building rapport and relationships with children provides the power to inspire children (Maniates & Doerr, 2001).
- Teachers who make a difference are those who develop relationships with students (Ogle, 2004).

Becoming a caring teacher is certainly about relationships. However, it goes beyond just relationship building. Caring teachers are willing to work with students until they master a skill in a new language, for instance. They do not allow students to fail. They find ways to scaffold students' current learning so that they can understand the next conceptually challenging information or process. For example, a teacher may search for picture support to help an ELL with challenging vocabulary. Being a caring teacher means being responsible for student learning by providing opportunities to support and engage students. It also means acknowledging the difficult life circumstances that children may live in but not feeling sorry for them. It means respecting them as capable learners (Weiner, 1999).

Becoming a Teacher Who Builds Resiliency in Students

Benard (2004) writes, "One of the most important and consistent findings in resilience research is the power of schools, especially of teachers, to turn a child's life from risk to resilience" (p. 65). Much of the research on resiliency overlaps with work focused on culturally responsive classrooms or caring teachers. We are presenting resiliency here, as it is important for teachers to consider as they work with ELLs, many of whom find themselves living in circumstances of poverty.

Resiliency often provides the explanation as to why some children succeed in school when others do not (Waxman, Gray, & Padrón, 2004a). Resilient children find ways to cope with life circumstances and look to the future. This view moves beyond language competency and explores the life circumstances of ELLs.

Benard (1997) described characteristics of teachers who increased students' resilience. She noted that these teachers modeled three essential dimensions of resiliency: caring and establishing relationships with adults, frequently students' teachers; providing numerous opportunities for students to participate and contribute to the classroom community; and setting high expectations. She further described these teachers as ones who do not judge students but understand that they are doing the best they can. Therefore, they build on the strengths of students, are student-centered, and motivate their students.

Besides just focusing on teachers, schools and districts have found ways to create school environments that support resiliency. Waxman, Gray, and Padrón (2004b, p. 52) described how the Minneapolis Public Schools have developed resiliency policies. Their resiliency policies centered around five strategies:

1. Offer opportunities for students to develop personal relationships with teachers.
2. Increase students' sense of mastery in their lives.
3. Build student social competencies as well as academic skills.
4. Reduce the stressors that students do not need to face.
5. Generate school and community resources to support the needs of students.

When taken together, there is an enormous research base centered on teachers and their power in supporting ELLs and students of poverty in achievement. Teachers do hold the power in creating classroom communities that either support students or deter them in their academic accomplishments.

Social Interaction in the Classroom

In order to learn, students need to construct meaning (Dillon, 2000), and they do this through talking and writing. In all the discoveries about exemplary teachers, especially exemplary teachers of ELLs, one central discovery is that they provide language-rich classrooms where children have opportunities to talk about and write about their learning. In these rooms, students are often organized into pairs or small groups to provide opportunities for language in support of learning. Language-rich classrooms don't just exist. Much thought goes into creating successful ones. For example, teachers need to think through how students respond in whole-class discussions. Young children need to understand what is expected. Can they just talk when someone else finishes or must they raise their hand? Are there limits to how long they can talk? What happens at centers? Can they work with peers or must they be quiet?

It is important for teachers to find ways to actively engage students in all instruction. Teachers might simply have all students respond with a "yes" to a simple question, such as "Is Mary the name of the character in the book?" For more complex questions like "What did Mary do to show she is kind?" teachers could have students talk to a neighbor, and then a few could share with the class. Teachers can also allow children time to think before answering. For instance, all children think quietly and hold up a thumb when they have an idea. Then they could share with a partner or with the class. Archer (2007) provides a unique way for children to share with the class. As children are talking with a partner, she walks around the room and records what they say on an overhead transparency. Then, when partner discussion is concluded, she shares the overhead responses with students. For instance, she might share, "Jose said, 'Mary walked her dog, and that was kind.' Guadalupe said, 'Mary fed her dog, and that was kind.' " In this way children's voices are heard and the teacher maintains a fast pace.

Pappas, Kiefer, and Levstik (1995) describe language-rich classrooms as places where students and teachers see reading, writing, listening, and speaking as one large integrated subject with no boundaries to separate them. In order to read, students and teachers must talk about the meaning attached to the text. In order to participate in the conversation, students and the teacher must carefully listen in to learn and appropriately respond. And writing is seen as a way to engage thinking for more productive conversation. Pappas et al. (1995) see teachers as supporting the efforts of students as they learn to use language to learn.

In addition to building a language-rich classroom, teachers face other challenges when they work with ELLs. They must help students move from home to school language, and they must support students in using English as a language for conversation and learning (Cummins, 2003). This is no easy task, however, as ELLs can be quiet or can respond in single-word answers as they learn to converse in English. Moreover, students' conceptions of language, literacy, and culturally appropriate ways of doing school are influenced by the experiences they bring to school (Gutierrez, Basquedano-Lopez, & Turner, 1997, p. 369). And these experiences are often very different from those routinely engaged in at school. (See Chapter 4 for specific ideas about oral language development.)

TAKE A MOMENT

Think about the language strengths of a child as he or she enters school. What does he or she typically know about literacy? Now think about what happens when this child can no longer use his or her language to share knowledge in the classroom.

Gutierrez (2001) states, "language, the most powerful mediating tool for mediating learning, in this case the children's primary language, is excluded from the students' learning tool kit" (p. 565). She recognizes that ELLs must build a new language tool kit to accomplish literacy proficiency in English-only classrooms. This new tool kit takes time to develop as children adjust the knowledge they have in their home language to the new language expectations in school. In addition, this means moving from the more informal language of home to the more academic language of school.

The centrality of language to learning is an issue that teachers of ELLs wrestle with as they provide instruction. Many ELLs, upon entry into school, typically preschool or kindergarten, are expected to communicate only through a new language—English. With annual yearly progress expectations from the No Child Left Behind Act, these students are often expected to achieve the same literacy competencies as their peers whose first language is English. Few of these students ever have extra time in school to learn about reading and writing in English as they learn the language. They are typically allotted the same amount of time as students who come to school familiar with English to meet grade-level expectations. This is an enormous challenge for students, teachers, and parents (Nieto, 1999). Strategies to support language in the classroom are more fully detailed in Chapter 4.

Rules and Routines

The best way to keep students focused on learning is to establish consistent and predictable routines—routines that can be internalized by students so their single focus is on instruction. Sometimes, teachers complain that the day is too routine, and there is no room for spontaneity. We are not suggesting that teachers do not respond to occasional once-in-a-lifetime occurrences (like a fire truck's appearance at school), but irregularity in routines and rules leaves students guessing and insecure about what is expected of them, especially students who must employ incredible energy to understand the messages of their teacher.

In the United States, there is great variability in how schools and teachers structure routines like transitions. In other countries, especially Asian countries, routines are discrete. Each daily routine is divided by class periods, much like those in U.S. high schools. For example, in China, for every 50-minute class, students get a 10-minute break, which allows them to go to the bathroom and to get a drink. In other countries, transitions from one event to another may be less structured. So students come to U.S. classrooms with little to no experience with classroom routines to very specific experiences in how transitions and other routines occur.

While many rules and routines can be jointly constructed with students, some routines need to be established before school begins. For example, how are students dismissed to go to the bathroom or get a drink? How and when can a student interrupt the teacher during small-group work? How do students enter and leave the classroom?

It is important that students know what the typical schedule is. They know that the day begins on the carpet where they share. Then they go to centers. Following centers, their teacher shares a story, and so on. These routines become the glue that holds the school day together. When the routine is changed, children constantly wonder and question what comes next.

We have seen teachers create a few important rules for young students. For instance, they discuss how they might make the classroom a safe place. Students suggest ways to do this and teachers record the responses on a chart. Figure 1.4 shows a chart created by kindergarten students with their teacher's help. The teacher has included the names of the students, so that students can use these names to remember what was said.

Students expect teachers to maintain order and to discipline students who disrupt learning. They want teachers to:

- Uphold classroom rules.
- Privately discipline students who misbehave.
- Apply a clear set of consequences to students who misbehave.
- Involve parents or the principal when necessary (Brown, 2002).

Delpit (1995) asserts that effective classrooms are those where there are clear expectations and inappropriate behaviors are dealt with consistently and immediately.

In many early-childhood classrooms, discipline simply means teachers redirect a child from a situation in which he or she is out of control to a different one in which he or she can regain control. For example, when John is pushing over the blocks in the block area and other children complain, his teacher moves him to an easel where he can paint alone for a while. Children quickly learn that when they have pushed the expectations for an activity, they will be removed.

Be safe.
  Maria said, "No one should push."
  Carlos said, "Don't hit."
  Helen said, "Sit nice."

Be kind.
  Mike said, "Say nice things."
  Jasmin said, "Help my friends."

FIGURE 1.4. Kindergarten rule chart.

In first- and second-grade classrooms, we have seen teachers who request that the child go to a table and write in a problem-solving journal as a way of decompressing the situation. We saw one child write, "I was yelling and I am having a hard time." Another wrote, "I hit Mario and I had to go think." These teachers are using writing as a way for students to express their feelings appropriately while they settle down before reentering the classroom community. As they develop writing competency, ELLs often use drawings to convey these messages or they may write in their home language.

While teachers often struggle with this part of their curriculum, students want to know what to expect and the consequences if they misbehave. They respond to teachers who are consistent and lessen their anxiety about being a capable student in their classroom.

Differentiated Instruction

All classes have children with a wide range of ability and knowledge. Classrooms filled with students who speak other languages are even more diverse. Some children try English more frequently and become conversant more quickly than others. Others have reading, writing, or content knowledge that they bring to their classroom, while others have limited worldly experiences.

Such varied backgrounds require teachers to organize a portion of their instruction into small groups. These groups might be based on:

- Individual or group assessment where the teacher targets certain skills or strategies.
- Interest assessments where small groups of students work together on a topic or project.
- Personalities of students (e.g., not putting all shy students together).
- Varied language backgrounds so that students can support and scaffold the language of peers.
- Knowledge or vocabulary background; the teacher groups students to develop this background prior to a whole-class lesson.

Importantly, even when these groups are based on ability level, they are never constant. Teachers regroup students when appropriate. They also construct multiple groupings in their classroom so that students work with pairs, in ability groups, in heterogeneous groups, and so on.

ELLs bring additional issues with regard to grouping. If a class consists predominantly of children with a home language of Spanish, and the teacher groups them together, they will speak Spanish. Although the students are communicating, they are not moving to English communication. Thus teachers need to consider the purpose of the groupings and how they will support students in communicating in English.

We have observed that groups of young children are very aware of home language. For instance, they speak Spanish until an English-only speaking child enters the group. They often test to see if the new child knows Spanish. If not, they chat with each other in Spanish and translate for the new student. In these groupings, students have an opportunity to speak their home language but with the additional expectation that they translate to English. In mixed-home-language situations, there is often much talk about the differences in languages. Language becomes important and a topic for conversation.

Paley (1981) shares kindergarten children's talk as they worked in her classroom. In one of these conversations, the children engage in a discussion about language. Here is a snippet of this conversation that was triggered because many of the children in this room spoke other languages.

> DEANA: If you live in a different country, there's a different language there.
>
> WARREN: Wherever your mother was born.
>
> PALEY: Your mother was born in China, but you speak English.
>
> WARREN: I'm going to go to Chinese school on Saturdays when I am six.
>
> EDDIE: Someone has to teach you. My brother didn't know one word when he was born. Not even his name. (p. 117)

The strength of this conversation is that it allows students to focus on language and issues related to it. These kinds of conversations take place more easily in classrooms where multiple languages are spoken. They allow children to explore language metalinguistically, and such exploration leads to more sophisticated comparisons of language in later grades.

Another grouping of ELLs is based on providing background knowledge or vocabulary in a preteaching situation. Teachers consider the whole-group literacy instruction that is scheduled to occur. They analyze the text for unfamiliar language or content experiences and group students whose comprehension may suffer because of these issues. In this grouping they preteach important vocabulary and content necessary for understanding. Then when the whole-class lesson is shared, these students come to it as experts. They participate fully in the lesson and are successful members of the class.

Teachers of ELLs also differentiate during whole-class instruction. They tailor questions to the oral language competency of students. For instance, if the class is learning about animals, the teacher may hold up a picture of a cow. One child may be asked to point to the cow while another may be asked to complete a language form: "This is a. . . . "A third child may be asked to describe the cow. Each child successfully participated in the lesson because of his or her teacher's knowledge of each child's language strengths.

Differentiated instruction allows teachers to target instruction to the strengths and needs of individual students. It facilitates having students reach grade-level benchmark expectations.

INTERSECTIONS OF PHYSICAL
AND SOCIAL/EMOTIONAL ENVIRONMENTS

Not surprisingly, the physical and the social and emotional environments in a class often overlap. Clearly, if the physical environment does not support learning, children become off-task and have difficulty participating appropriately in the classroom. Similarly, the social and emotional environment in the classroom may support small-group work with rich conversation, for example, but if the classroom is not configured to support small-group spaces small-group work will not be very effective.

While it is important for both environments in the classroom to be in synchrony, we believe it is most important at the beginning of the day and the academic year. Bringing children into a new room and perhaps their first school experience is critical to future comfort and success. These beginning times also signal to parents how respected their child will be at school.

Beginning of the Year

To help at this important time, we offer several suggestions.

1. Have the room ready with children's names when possible. Have a sign on the door or outside the door that greets new students in multiple languages.
2. Have the classroom door open so that families feel comfortable entering and looking around before they leave their child. Be welcoming even though there are many details that most likely need attending to. If possible have another adult available who speaks the home language of the majority of parents.
3. If possible, send a letter of welcome to families (at least in English and Spanish) and invite them to the classroom before school begins so that children are comfortable in the new surroundings.
4. In some preschools and kindergartens, new students are invited to spend a day at school before they formally begin. If this is possible allow one or two children a day to stay and get familiar with the classroom. When students are too afraid to stay, encourage their parents to stay with them.
5. Ask parents to share a literacy event with you that you can share with the class. Later on, parents may bring samples of reading and writing their child does at home. Invite parents to become a part of the learning community. They may share a tradition, read a story, or help with writing.
6. Send home a booklet of important information about your class. Parents need to know what the expectations are for the year. Be explicit.
7. Make up plastic bags or some other appropriate container so that children can carry books home and back from the first day of school.

Beginning of the School Day

Once the first day of school arrives, there are many ways that teachers can transition students into the classroom. They can:

1. Greet children and parents at the classroom door. Practice saying hello in many languages and try these hellos out as you greet

parents and children. If parents follow you into the room, let them. However, stay focused on the children and their instruction.

2. Establish what happens when children enter the room. Do they go to circle? Do they go to their desks? Create a routine that does not change.

3. Have all materials ready for instruction, so there is no downtime during the day.

4. Find time to learn about students' out-of-school experiences. Some teachers allow a few children to share each day orally. Other teachers create a message that contains one or two children's experiences written together and then read. We observed one kindergarten teacher who created home journals. Each journal had a copy of the alphabet and "word wall" words, words that the teacher had on the wall and students recognized immediately. Each day children took their journal home, wrote in it, and brought it back to school. The teacher read each journal as a way to begin the day. Children listened closely to the messages of their classmates. Later, as the journals were filled with messages, she asked students to reread them and to discover what was most important about their lives outside school.

FINAL THOUGHTS

In this chapter we explored the underpinnings of successful classrooms, especially for students who come to school with a language other than English. We highlighted the many environments that exist within a classroom and how they can work together or in opposition. Without this foundation, we believe that the literacy strategies shared in later chapters will not be very successful. A well-managed, culturally sensitive classroom is essential to the learning of all students and in particular ELLs.

CHAPTER 2

Working with Families

> Reading does not consist of merely decoding the written word or language; rather it is preceded by and intertwined with knowledge of the world. Language and reality are dynamically interconnected. . . . My parents introduced me to reading the word at a certain moment in this rich experience of understanding my immediate world. Deciphering the word flowed naturally from reading my particular world. It was not something superimposed on it.
>
> —FREIRE (1987, pp. 29, 32)

Paulo Freire, a Brazilian educator and philosopher, in talking about his own experience of learning to read and write, poignantly reminded educators around the world that the process of children's becoming literate in a language began with interactions with their own environment and with parental guidance. As a rich body of research has documented (e.g., Adams, 1990; Clark, 1976; Neuman, 2005; Purcell-Gates, 1996; Taylor, 1983), parents have a critical impact on their children's cognitive, language, and literacy development. Parents are children's first teachers, which holds true for children who speak English as a native language as well as those whose native language is not English (Delgado-Gaitan, 1994; Goldenberg, 1987; Li, 2004). Furthermore, other studies (Delgado-Gaitan, 2001; Paratore, 2001; Valdés, 1996) have identified the contributions that family members (e.g., grandparents, aunts and uncles, cousins, and siblings) other than parents make in children's language and literacy development. These two key points related to family involvement with children are further discussed in the next section.

Thus this chapter focuses on working with families of ELLs, not just their parents.

In this chapter, our approach stresses an active and initiative role that *teachers* must play while working with families. This school-to-families approach is similar to a *two-way parent–school involvement model* (Faltis, 2001) where teachers reach out to parents and community; it is different from the families-to-school approach, which requires families to work with the school in order for school–family partnerships to happen. In our discussion, we begin with a need for teachers to understand the rationale for working with families. We then share different ways for teachers to learn about ELLs' culture and language. Teacher knowledge of native culture and language and efforts to build teaching on ELLs' culture and language, we believe, is a crucial step to success in working with families. Families are more likely to feel reluctant to work with teachers who know little or nothing about their children's experiences with native culture and language but also make little effort to learn about the culture and language. Another focus on working with families is how teachers can welcome families to the school and classroom. We conclude this chapter with a section on teacher–family collaboration to support literacy development in a native language and in English.

At the end of this chapter, you will be able to:

- Understand the rationale for working with families.
- Describe ways to learn about ELLs' culture and language.
- Describe ways to welcome families to the school and classroom.
- Describe different ways to inform families how to support literacy development in a native language and in English.

UNDERSTANDING THE RATIONALE FOR WORKING WITH FAMILIES

To understand the rationale for working with families of ELLs, it is important for teachers to learn about the similar and different roles that families of native English-speaking children and those of ELLs play in children's language and literacy development. In addition, teachers need to understand how cultural values and beliefs affect ways that families of ELLs perceive the role of teachers in U.S. schools and the role of families in their children's education (Goldenberg & Gillimore, 1995; Johnson, 2004; Valdés, 1996).

Families of Native English-Speaking Children

The important role that families (and in particular parents) play in native English-speaking children's language and literacy development has been well documented (e.g., Landry & Smith, 2005; Smith, Landry, & Swank, 2000; Snow, 1986). During early-childhood years, family members scaffold a learning process by modeling effective language use for children (e.g., using phrases like "please" and "thank you" while communicating with a child) and by providing feedback on children's language (e.g., saying to the child, "You mean 'I went to Jo's house yesterday' " when a child said, "I goed to Jo's house yesterday"). Family members also direct children's attention to functions and conventions of print in children's immediate environment. For example, a family member points out the big *M* on the McDonald's logo while saying, "We are going to McDonald's for lunch." In so doing, the adult encourages the child to pay attention to the beginning letter in McDonald's. When a family member reads aloud "Burger King" to a child, the adult is showing the child that print in English is read from left to right. Such guidance from family members extends from oral language to environmental print and later to print literacy. Numerous studies (e.g., McCarthey, 2000; Neuman & Celano, 2001; Snow, Burns, & Griffin, 1998) have shown that children whose family members read and discuss books with them have more successful experiences with school literacy tasks (e.g., having background knowledge of concepts about print, understanding story elements, and applying reading strategies) and also tend to be more motivated to read. Another benefit of having experiences with books and other print outside school is world knowledge gained from reading, which provides a foundation for successfully comprehending texts on various topics.

Similar to a family's guidance in children's print experiences, the family members' role in children's engagement with nonprint texts (e.g., TV shows) cannot be overlooked. Research conducted from a perspective of the New Literacy Studies (e.g., Alvermann, Moon, & Hagood, 1999; Dyson, 2003; Evans, 2005; Gee, 2003; Marsh & Millard, 2006;

New London Group, 1996; Xu, 2004; Xu, Sawyer, & Zunich, 2005) has shown that children also gain and apply literacy knowledge and skills from interactions with nonprint texts. For example, through watching their favorite TV shows (e.g., *Arthur* and *SpongeBob SquarePants*), children develop knowledge of story grammar (i.e., characters, setting, plot, and theme) (which is similar to story grammar in books) and literacy skills (e.g., making a connection to background information, and making inferences). When family members are watching TV along with their children, they can provide support for children's understanding the content of a TV show (e.g., offering an explanation for the background information related to the show) and in conventions of language used in the show (e.g., pointing out that a character is using a question).

Families of ELLs

Like families of native English-speaking children, family members of ELLs provide similar scaffolding to support children's native language and literacy development. In their study of Latino families, for example, Paratore, Melzi, and Krol-Sinclair (2003) observed that family members read books to their children and also modeled reading behaviors (e.g., reading words and looking at the illustrations in a picture book). Similar findings are presented in studies on families from various ethnic backgrounds (e.g., Johnson, 2004; Li, 2004; Xu, 1999).

In addition to recognizing a similarity in family support in language and literacy development between native English-speaking children and ELLs, teachers also need to become aware of the unique roles that families of ELLs play. It is important to remember that while all families value their children's education, not all families use the same ways to show support for the children. For example, Latino families view instilling their children with cultural values and moral standards as a more important responsibility than teaching children about school subjects. They believe that teachers are most qualified to teach their children in academic areas (Paratore et al., 2003; Perez, 2004; Rodriguez-Brown, 2003). This cultural belief and practice may mislead some to think that Latino families care less about their children than other ethnic groups. In addition Latinos, as well as other families of ELLs, may be less involved in ELLs' academic tasks due to their limited English proficiency. If family members are not literate in English, they cannot be very helpful in working with their child to complete homework. This inability to help with homework, however, does not mean that the family does not support this child's literacy learning.

It is also important to remember that family support occurs in different forms. Studies (e.g., Gonzáles & Moll, 1995; Valdés, 1996; Xu, 1999) remind us that family members engaged children in practicing and applying their native language. Such literacy practices in children's native language contribute, to some degree, to language and literacy development in English (Cummins, 1979). Many linguistic features (e.g., the concepts of a sentence and a story) from a native language and literacy strategies (e.g., linking background knowledge to a text and rereading a text to clarify and/or deepen understanding) that ELLs use can be transferred to children's learning English (Krashen, 2004).

Household studies by Moll, Amanti, Neff, and Gonzalez (1992), Gonzáles and Moll (1995), and Gonzáles, Moll, and Amanti (2005) have suggested that Latino families expose their children to rich life experiences. For example, Moll (1998) observed that family members engaged their children in selling candy they brought to the United States from Mexico. This type of experience does not seem directly related to school academic tasks, but in an indirect way, families have prepared children for academic tasks. For example, buying and selling candy involves concepts of math (e.g., money) and interpersonal communication skills (e.g., negotiation of prices). Children's understanding of these concepts helps lay a foundation for later discipline specific learning.

The notion of household literacy is very similar to the idea of everyday literacy practices from a New Literacy Studies perspective (e.g., Lankshear & Knobel, 2003; New London Group, 1996), which acknowledges a wide range of literacy practices in which students are engaged. This perspective is useful in our understanding of family support for ELLs. As discussed earlier, a family's effort to maintain the literacy skills of their native language and to provide children with an opportunity to experience different things in life also contribute to English and literacy development. To work successfully with families, an acknowledgement of family contribution at this level is needed.

The New Literacy Studies perspective further reminds us that school literacy practices can be different from those in which students are engaged outside school. This point helps us to better understand that the children's experiences with literacy practices that family members encourage may not be directly related to school literacy practices and/or have direct impact on their school achievement. In her seminal study with an African American working-class community and a Caucasian working-class community, Heath (1983) discovered that the experiences with being read bedtime stories prepared the children from the Caucasian working-class community for school success while African American children's collaborating on an oral story did not contribute much to school success. Heath's findings are consistent with the New Literacy Studies perspective that children's literacy skills and knowledge gained from their experiences with literacy practices outside school (which involve a wide range of texts) may not be reflected in their school learning (which mainly focuses on print texts).

TAKE A MOMENT

Think about the ELLs you had last year. Describe the household literacy experiences of these students. How did they contribute to their in-school literacy experiences?

Rationale for Working with Families

Only by working directly with families can teachers gain insights into the following areas:

■ *Families' cultural values and beliefs about children's education.* When teachers directly gain knowledge from families about their unique values and beliefs, they minimize a possibility of obtaining stereotypical information as possibly portrayed in media (Sleeter, 2001).

■ *ELLs' literacy practices in a native language.* Families of ELLs have knowledge of their children's literacy practices, and they are more likely to be able to explain to teachers these practices than children.

■ *ELLs' literacy practices in English.* Families of ELLs can inform teachers of their literacy practices and of children's experiences with these practices (e.g., success, enjoyment, and frustration).

■ *Similarities and differences between outside and inside school literacy practices.* Only when teachers are equipped with knowledge of the foregoing points, can teachers and families work together to make a better connection for ELLs between home learning and school learning and to make a smooth transition between a native language and English, and vice versa.

LEARNING ABOUT ELLS' CULTURE AND LANGUAGE

Developing knowledge about students' cultures and languages is another crucial component in a successful school–family partnership. This school-to-family approach reflects teachers' sincere efforts to engage families for the benefit of students. Only when equipped with knowledge of students' culture and language can teachers develop an approach of culturally responsive teaching advocated by many scholars (e.g., Au, 2002; Delpit, 1995; Grant, 2001; Ladson-Billings, 2001).

Learning about ELLs' Culture

Any language is closely connected to the culture in which this language exists (e.g., Fitzgerald & Graves, 2004; Lessow-Hurley, 2005; Moll et al., 1992). There is a unique set of ways with words in each culture. Even within the United States, the American English used by people living on the East Coast can be different from that used by those on the West Coast. This difference is partly due to the subcultures on either side of the United States. A person from the West Coast who is unfamiliar with the subculture of the East Coast may have trouble communicating smoothly with people on the East Coast. He or she may not use appropriate words or may ask questions that sound strange to the locals (e.g., "Am I able to buy a house with a big yard?").

The impact of this subculture on language use seems pale in comparison to that of the native culture each ELL brings to a classroom. In addition to the fact that culture affects the way a language is used, cultural values can also influence how families exhibit their involvement in their children's education. As discussed earlier in this chapter, Latino families may focus their responsibility of educating their children more on teaching them to become a good person rather than on helping them with school-related tasks (Paratore et al., 2003; Perez, 2004; Rodriguez-Brown, 2003). In other cultures, families may expect teachers to have additional homework for their children on a daily basis, including summer and winter breaks (Li, 2004).

Learning from People Native to the Culture

Families and community members can supply teachers with firsthand knowledge about student culture. In addition, families are a rich source of the subculture most relevant to a child's life experience. Teachers can ask families about their culture during open house or at after-school pickup time. They might suggest that families write down interesting or unique things about their culture to share with the teacher or with the class at a later time. If family members of a child speak limited English, teachers can have other bilingual students, their family members, or community members translate. If there are international students in a nearby university or college, they can be asked for help. The students often have updated information about the culture, which can be most relevant to newcomers in a classroom. We suggest that teachers keep a contact list (see Figure 2.1), they can update year after year and refer back to when needed.

Visiting a Student's Community

Another effective way to gain knowledge about the culture is to visit a student's community. These visits become more important given that most teachers do not live in the same community as their students. Visiting student communities can begin with a walk in an ELL's neighborhood to gain information about cultural practices (e.g., what food students do or do not eat, or whether people like to gather together in public places to talk). Another source of cultural practices is a community event, including church services, festivals, and the grand opening of a facility. During the event, teachers pay attention to what is on display (e.g., flowers, slogans, religious statues), what people eat and wear, and how people communicate with one another (e.g., using gesture and words vs. using mostly words). Finally, when teachers become familiar with a student's cultural practices and when the teacher's presence in the student's community has won some trust from the student's family, it is time to schedule a home visit with the family. The focus of this visit is on observing the presence of print materials, a place for study, and the communicative style between family members and their child.

Learning from People Familiar with the Culture

Although it is ideal to gain information about an ELL's native culture from a primary source, this way is not always available to every teacher. When family members and other community members speak little or no English, teachers can try to gather information from people who are

Name of English language learner	Language the child speaks	School year I have the child	Name of contact person	Phone number or e-mail address
Thi Dy	Vietnamese	2004-2005	Le Dy	123-4567
			Kevin Tran	765-4321

FIGURE 2.1. A contact list.

nonnative to that culture but familiar with it. Such people may include those who have studied the culture or who have visited or stayed in the native country for a sustained period of time. In addition, such people can share their experience of learning about the native culture. Their perspective can be helpful for a teacher's understanding of the native culture.

Learning from the Media

Teachers can gain knowledge of student culture through books, Internet resources, newspapers, and TV. But teachers must be aware of possible biases and stereotypes embedded in these secondary sources. The biases and stereotypes teachers bring to class, which can be reflected in how they teach, could have a detrimental effect on children's school learning. When teachers have a question about one particular culture, they need to make sure to check with people native to or familiar with that particular culture and compare information gained from multiple sources (i.e., primary and secondary sources).

TAKE A MOMENT

Think about the ELLs from last year's class. How did you learn about their culture? Now that you have learned some ways to gain knowledge about ELLs' culture, what plans do you have to gain this knowledge this year?

Learning about ELLs' Language

It makes sense for teachers to become familiar with ELLs' native culture in order to work effectively with families. By contrast, a relationship between teacher knowledge of a native language and effective school–community partnerships seem far fetched. We, however, strongly argue that only when teachers have some knowledge of a native language can they recognize native literacy knowledge, skills, and strategies that can be transferred to children's learning English. This knowledge allows them to take into consideration the areas that might be difficult or confusing to ELLs in lesson planning. Consequently, teachers can do a better job communicating with families about ELLs' literacy strengths and needs and about suggesting to families some ways to support their children's literacy development in a native language and in English. Teachers' sincere efforts to learn about a student's native language send a clear message to families of ELLs that teachers do care about the well-being of their children.

While all languages have phonological, syntactic, semantic, and pragmatic systems, the characteristics of each system vary, to a greater extent, from language to language. In the section that follows, we briefly list some examples of differences between a native language and English in the areas of writing system, concepts about print, phonology, semantics, syntax, and pragmatics.

Writing Systems

English, like many Western languages (e.g., Spanish, French, German, Italian), uses alphabetic letters to represent sounds. Other non-Western languages (e.g., Vietnamese, Thai, Korean) also use an alphabetic writing system. The alphabetic letters, however, look different from those used in most Western languages. For example, the word *book* is written as 책 in Korean. In a nonalphabetic language, symbols (e.g., characters) rather than alphabetic letters are used to represent sounds. For example, the word *book* is written as 書 (a traditional version) or 书 (a simplified version) in Chinese. The word *book* is 本 in Japanese, a unique language which uses both Chinese characters and a Japanese alphabetic system. For example, the word 食べなさい(*eat*) is a Japanese equivalent, in which 食 is a Chinese character, and べなさい is from the Japanese writing system. With knowledge of the writing system of a native language, teachers would understand that an ELL whose native language is an alphabetic language would probably grasp the concept of the alphabetic principle (i.e., the letter–sound relationship) in English better than another ELL whose native language is nonalphabetic. Teachers thus know why another ELL struggles with the concept and can accordingly come up with responsive assistance for that child.

Concepts about Print

Concepts about print (book orientation, print directionality, punctuation marks, and book terminology) in English are common among Western languages. Other languages, alphabetic or nonalphabetic, have their unique concepts about print particularly with regard to book orientation and print directionality. For example, readers of Hebrew, Chinese (used in Taiwan and Hong Kong), or Japanese open a book from what is called a back cover in English concepts about print. While most books written in Chinese (used in Mainland China) follow the concepts about print in English, some books do not. Print directionality of articles in Chinese newspapers varies depending on space availability. For example, a limited space only allows for an article to be arranged in a way that it is read vertically from left to right or from right to left. ELLs of some native languages may also experience difficulty with punctuation marks in English. For example, a Spanish ELL may tend to put a question mark at the beginning and end of an English interrogative sentence as he or she does in Spanish. A Chinese ELL may put a tiny circle ○ (a period symbol in Chinese) instead of a solid dot at the end of a sentence. Knowing the differences in concepts about print between a native language and English can help teachers identify sources of ELLs' confusion about English concepts about print and focus teaching on clarifying such confusion.

Phonology

The characteristics of phonology (the sound system) in each language vary greatly. First of all, not every sound in one language exists in another language, and ELLs' unfamiliarity with new sounds in English is often a source of struggle and difficulty. For example, Spanish-speaking ELLs often cannot distinguish between /sh/ and /ch/, saying *chair* for *share*, and vice versa. The sound /th/, a common sound in English which does not exist in many Asian languages, poses a challenge for ELLs who speak an Asian language.

Another area of the English phonology difficult for ELLs to master is phonemic awareness. Words in all languages cannot be broken down or analyzed at the phoneme level like English words (except for the words *I* and *a*). Chinese, Japanese, and Vietnamese, for example, are syllabic languages with a syllable as a smallest unit as opposed to a phoneme as a smallest unit in English. Thus any concepts of phonemic awareness and activities focusing on these concepts pose difficulty for ELLs who speak Chinese, Japanese, or Vietnamese. Even for ELLs who speak a native language that can be analyzed at the phoneme level, some phonemic awareness concepts can be hard to understand. For example, it will take a Korean-speaking ELL longer to understand the concept of beginning, middle, and end sound in the word *book*. Although Korean words are composed of phonemes, letters representing phonemes are not put together horizontally as in English—for the word *book*, it is 책 in Korean.

Another source of difficulty for ELLs is the letter–sound relationship in English. Not every letter in an English word has its corresponding sound. A simple example is the word *book,* whose *oo* letters only produce one sound, /ŭ/. This is not the case for many languages. Both consonant digraphs (*sh, ch, th, wh, ph,* and *gh*) and vowel digraphs (e.g., *oo, ou, oa,* and *aw*), and silent letters (e.g., *e* in *cake, gh* in *light,* and *g* in *sign*) in English can be hard for ELLs to master. Teachers need to find out if the concept of digraphs and silent letters exists in an ELL's native language in order to help ELLs master these sounds in English.

Semantics

In English semantics (the meaning system), vocabulary is a major source of difficulty due to the characteristics of multiple meanings. A closer look at the dictionary entry for the common word *run* would reveal at least 20 definitions for it as a verb and at least a dozen definitions for it as a noun. Not all languages have words with multiple meanings. In addition, the concept of homographs and homophones can be very unfamiliar to ELLs. This is true for English idiomatic expressions (e.g., *raining cats and dogs, pain in the neck, easy as pie,* and *a piece of cake*). While idiomatic expressions are not a unique characteristic of the English language, it is the relationship between the expression and its figurative meaning that does not make sense to ELLs. For example, why does the expression *easy as pie* have something to do with describing the ease of doing something? Making a pie, after all, is not an easy task to many of us. Some ELLs may feel that the idiomatic expressions in their native language make better sense. For example, the equivalent for *easy as pie* is *easy as peeling a banana* in Thai, and *easy as turning your hand* in Chinese. Multiple meanings of a word, homophones and homographs, and idiomatic expressions are the key areas in semantics in which differences between a native language and English exist. When teachers have noted these differences, responsive teaching becomes possible.

Syntax

Syntax (the structural system) in English is at the word level and the sentence level. At the word level, syntax includes word structure—base words and affixes (prefixes and suffixes). In English, many words have a prefix and/or suffix, a syntactic characteristic that is not common in every language, in particular, a non-Western language. For example, the plural suffixes (-s, and -es) do not exist in Chinese, Japanese, and Vietnamese, among other languages. Instead, plurals are reflected in the number or quantity. The phrase *two books* in English is *two piece* (a quantity word, like *piece* in a *piece of cake, school* in *a school of fish*) *of book* in Chinese. Even with Spanish, the use of affixes is not as extensive as in English.

At the sentence level, English has a set of rules regarding different types of sentences—a simple, compound, and complex sentence, a statement, a question, and a command. A statement in English, for example, must have a subject and a predicate (a verb and an object) in this order (e.g., "I go to school every day"). A statement in other languages, such as Korean and Japanese, has a subject, an object, and a verb (e.g., "I to school go every day"). Verb tense is hard for ELLs of many native languages whose verbs do not change in response to time changes. For example, in Chinese and Khmer, all the tenses are reflected in a time phrase. The sentence *I went to school yesterday* in English is *I go to school yesterday* in Chinese and Khmer. The verb *go* is not changed for any tense; the future tense of this sentence in Chinese and Khmer is *I go to school tomorrow.* In a similar way, a verb in Japanese does not change based on a tense. Instead, a word indicating a tense is added after a verb. し た is added to a verb to indicate a past tense, and ている is added to a verb for a present progressive tense.

In addition, articles (*the, a,* and *an*), which do not exist in some native languages, and many Asian languages in particular (e.g., Chinese, Korean, Japanese, and Vietnamese), are hard for many ELLs to understand and grasp. The difference in usage between *the* and *a* is even harder. Another source of difficulty is adding an auxiliary verb (e.g., *do, does, will,* and *would*) to a sentence when it is changed from a statement to an interrogative (e.g., "Maria likes reading." "Does Maria like reading?"). Third-person singular present verb tense, which is unique in English, is another problematic area for ELLs.

Pragmatics

Pragmatics is the social and cultural ways with a language, which is the most difficult area for ELLs, who must be immersed in the language in order to learn various (often subtle) ways with English. For example, in English, a question, "Could you please pass me the book?", which appears to an ELL as a yes–no question, actually serves as a formal request. If the child responds to this question with a "yes" or "no," the communication between this child and the requester is unsuccessful.

Another area of pragmatics that is extremely hard for ELLs to grasp is multiple meanings of a word, such as *okay* or *good*, which children must learn through experiences communicating with others. Take the word *okay* as an example. Not all native languages have a word that has so many meanings, which can only be derived from the context in which the word appears. When a person responds to "How is the food?" with "It is okay," he or she is saying that the food is just average, neither too delicious nor too bad tasting. When a person answers the question "Are you doing okay with this homework?" with "I am okay," he or she is saying that "I am able to complete the homework on my own." In addition, the meanings of *okay* in the foregoing two examples can become further complicated by *how* the person responds to the question (e.g., facial expression, tone, pitch).

Teachers can learn about ELLs' native languages through various sources. Family members, if they are able to communicate in English, should be the first reliable source. A second good source of information includes community members, older students who are familiar with the language, international students in a nearby university or college, and people who have a good command of a native language. Before talking with these people, teachers can prepare a list of questions so that the obtained information will be relevant. Figure 2.2 is a sample list of questions. Another source of information about various native languages comes from the Internet. Figure 2.3 lists a website with an overview of many native languages and several websites of translation tools. While using one translation tool, teachers need to make sure to cross-check the accuracy of the translation against that from another tool.

After developing some level of knowledge about a native language, teachers, while visiting the community and home, need to pay closer attention to a native language used by people in the community, and by family members and children. For example, how is a native language

1. Does your language use symbols (e.g., letters) like English? (writing system)
2. Does your language have a same set of punctuation marks as English does? (concepts about print)
3. Do you read lines of words in a book from left to right and top to bottom? (concepts about print)
4. Can you break down every word in your language into smallest units as in English (e.g., there are three small sounds, /k/, /a/, /t/ in the word *cat*)? (phonology)
5. Do many words in your language have more than one meanings? (semantics)
6. Do you need to add additional words when you change a statement into a question? (syntax)
7. Do you use different sentences while talking to different people (like one is your child and the other is your boss)? (pragmatics)

FIGURE 2.2. A sample list of questions about a native language.

Transparent Language: *www.transparent.com/*

This site offers an overview about many languages. At the home page, select a native language you are interested in learning under "Choose Your Language," and then click "Read the Language Overview."

The Internet Picture Dictionary: *www.pdictionary.com/*

This site has pictures on various topics for English, French, Italian, German, and Spanish.

Babel Fish Translation: *babelfish.altavista.com/tr*

This site allows a reader to enter a text in English and get a translation in a chosen native language. Although the translation is not perfect, teachers at least can get a look at how a native language is written.

Foreign Word. Com: *www.foreignword.com/*

This site offers word-level and text-level translation from one language to another. Multiple dictionaries can be used in translation so that one can cross-check the accuracy of the translation.

Your Dictionary. Com: *www.yourdictionary.com/languages.html*

This fantastic site has an online dictionary for more than 100 languages. In each dictionary of a native language, you can find an equivalent for an English word. Some dictionaries even allow you to listen to how a word is pronounced in the native language.

FIGURE 2.3. Internet resources for learning native languages.

written in environmental print (e.g., store names, ads, and newspapers)? How does a native language sound? For example, does it have a series of long and short sounds similar to those in English (as in Spanish)? Does it have a series of short sounds in a syllabic language (as in Chinese, Japanese, Vietnamese)? Teachers' knowledge gained from this type of experience becomes handy later on during literacy instruction. Throughout the process of learning about a native language, we suggest that each teacher keep a record of similarities and differences between English and a native language (see Figure 2.4). This record about one particular language needs to be revised and updated constantly as the teacher is learning more and more about that language.

TAKE A MOMENT

Now you have explored several examples of differences between English and various native languages. Think about your own knowledge about a native language and the languages your students speak. What are your plans for gaining knowledge of these languages?

WELCOMING FAMILIES
TO THE SCHOOL AND CLASSROOM

In addition to sincere efforts to learn about ELLs' culture and language, teachers' welcoming of families to school *and* their classrooms is another crucial step toward a successful working relationship with families. In Chapter 1, we talked about how to create a classroom environment that facilitates the comfort level of ELLs and provides them with predictable daily routines (e.g., time period for reading and time period for literacy play) and structural layout (e.g., the location for a writing center and a location for a classroom library). Here we focus on how teachers, working with their school administrators, can create an inviting and a welcoming school *and* classroom environment.

Welcoming Families to the School

Welcoming families to the school begins with creating an inviting place at the parking lot or the outside of the school building. Before the be-

Linguistic systems	Similarities between English and _____ (a native language)	Differences between English and _____ (a native language)
Writing system		
Concepts about print		
Phonology		
Semantics		
Syntax		
Pragmatics		
Other		

FIGURE 2.4. Similarities and differences between English and a native language.

ginning of a school year, many families of newcomers and some families of returning ELLs visit the school for questions and/or for registering their children. If school staff put some signs in the parking lot or outside the school building in both English and a native language that let families know how to get to the office (which is not always visible to an outsider), families would feel more at ease visiting the school. It would also be helpful to have labels in multiple native languages posted along the English sign that that identifies the office. The volunteers who speak a native language (e.g., family members and people from the community) can be invited to serve as guides in the parking lot or at the entrance of the school.

Once families are in the school office (with a welcome greeting posted on the wall in English and in multiple native languages), it is best if they can be greeted in their native language. Greeting them in their native language helps lower anxiety level, creates a sense of familiarity for families, and sends a message that the school is making a sincere effort to welcome and work with them. The office needs to be a place where families can obtain answers to questions regarding their children's schooling, and where they also can learn more about school routines and activities and get information. Although it is best to translate every piece of written information provided in the office into a native language, this practice is not always feasible given limited budgets and available human resources. But it is quite possible to put a label in a native language for each type of information (e.g., school newsletter and parent education classes). Use the translation tools provided in Figure 2.3. Be sure to use more than one translation tool or translation dictionary to cross-check the accuracy of the translation.

Welcoming families to the school continues even after they have left the school office. For many families, an open house one month or so after the beginning of the school year is the first occasion for them to visit their children's classroom and the entire school. Although most teachers always let families know they are welcome to visit the classroom, it is quite a different experience for ELLs' families to visit the school and the classroom informally. We suggest that the school enlist help from volunteers who would provide a tour of the school and the classroom and information about the routine. The school routine (e.g., daily schedule and eating lunch) is not always similar to that in an ELL's native country. Becoming familiar with the new school routine presents a challenge for older ELLs who may have adapted to the school routine in their native country and who now must adjust to the U.S. school routines. To a great extent, the school tour would also help families feel welcome at school and lower their anxiety level. (Many of us probably still remember how anxious we were the first day we sent our children to a preschool or a kindergarten class. We were worried whether they knew how to follow the classroom rules, how to go to the bathroom, and how to get along with other children, among other things. Just imagine the worries that families of ELLs would have for their children who know little or no English!)

In addition to supporting families before and at the beginning of the school year, a school's effort to make families feel they are a part of the school community needs to continue throughout the school year. This support should be evident at both the school level and the classroom level. (We discuss the support at the classroom level in the following section.) At the school level, a space on campus can be designated for families and volunteers to gather before, during, and after school to share ideas about supporting their children's education and to have their questions about schooling answered. The space can be as simple as a corner of a multipurpose room, a gym, a cafeteria, or a small room in the school building. Included in this environment can be information written in English, and possibly in a native language, about school activities and activities that families can do with their children at home. Families would appreciate a bulletin board or a question box where they can let the school and teachers know their concerns and questions. We have found that this special space (which belongs to families) at the school level plays an important role in making families feel a part of the school community. Other ways to support families at the school level can be offering parenting classes and adult English-language classes (with support from Title I and Head Start funds) or providing information about these classes (if no school funds are available) at nearby churches and/or nonprofit organizations.

Welcoming Families to the Classroom

At the classroom level, welcoming families begins with the environment. First, teachers want families to feel that the classroom is a familiar place to them. Teachers can display pictures, photos, cultural artifacts (which families can loan or donate to teachers), and labels in a native language. Families' familiarity with the classroom can be further enhanced by informing them of the daily classroom routine. After talking with families from various countries, we have discovered that not all schools in other countries have a daily routine common to that in U.S. schools. In some countries, for example, there is a recess after every 50- or 60-minute class throughout the day and different subjects are taught by different teachers. In primary grades in the United States, one teacher usually teaches all subjects. This type of difference might raise families' anxiety level for their children and discomfort level for themselves to step into a classroom. In the very beginning of the school year (rather than during an open house), teachers can send home a copy of daily routine (preferably written in English and in a native language) so that families know when it is a good time to come to observe their children and to volunteer in the classroom.

Inviting families to volunteer in the classroom is a great way to welcome them; it makes them feel that they have a place in the classroom. In particular, Moll and his colleagues (Gonzáles & Moll, 1995; Moll, 1998; Moll et al., 1992) suggested that teachers utilize families' *funds of knowledge* in teaching. *Funds of knowledge* is what families have accumulated through their life and working experiences, which, once integrated into school curriculum, can enrich it, thus enhancing student learning. Volunteering opportunities for family members speaking some English or little English include:

Working with children

- Monitoring small-group activities (e.g., writing center, classroom library, and listening center) where children are engaged in independent practices.
- Listening to children read a book aloud.
- Distributing instructional materials.
- Sharing cultural artifacts and information about a native culture or language.
- Sharing knowledge about a concept or content (e.g., a parent who works for a construction company may talk about a role of geometry in real life or the importance of an ability to read an expository text).
- Sharing how family members and children use reading, writing, listening, and speaking at home and in the community.

Supporting the teacher

- ▓ Organizing classroom centers (e.g., library and writing).
- ▓ Posting things on a bulletin board (e.g., children's writing samples, and book reports).

TAKE A MOMENT

Again, think about the ELLs you have this year, and consider their cultural and linguistic backgrounds. How do you plan to welcome their families to your classroom and to engage them in volunteering in your classroom?

COLLABORATING WITH FAMILIES TO SUPPORT LITERACY DEVELOPMENT IN A NATIVE LANGUAGE AND ENGLISH

Up to this point, we have discussed different ways to work with families at school and within the classroom. Now we need to extend this school–family partnership to ELLs' home and community by supporting family engagement in promoting their children's native language (L1) and English literacy development. To this end, we focus on two areas. One area is to inform families how to provide support for their children. The other area is to engage families in sharing their *funds of knowledge* that contribute to children's academic learning.

Informing Families to Support Literacy Development in a Native Language and English

Documenting Similarities and Differences in Literacy Practices in a Native Language and English

Some common practices that native English-speaking parents do (e.g., reading aloud to children and teaching children the alphabet) are not common in every culture. In some cultures, family members focus on other aspects of a language (e.g., oral language development). Given this difference in outside school literacy practices, teachers need to encourage families to list similarities and differences in the use of L1 and English. Figure 2.5 is a sample chart that teachers can have families complete and return 1 month or so. After gaining knowledge about lit-

Literacy practices in a native language (list each practice)	Similar to English literacy practices (circle "yes" or "no")		Literacy practices in English (list each practice)	Similar to literacy practices in a native language (circle "yes" or "no")	
Oral language practices					
Reciting a nursery rhyme	(Yes)	No	*Finding rhyming words in a nursery rhyme*	Yes	(No)
	Yes	No		Yes	No
	Yes	No		Yes	No
	Yes	No		Yes	No
	Yes	No		Yes	No
Reading practices					
Reading a book independently	(Yes)	No	*Parents' reading aloud a book to a child*	Yes	(No)
	Yes	No		Yes	No
	Yes	No		Yes	No
	Yes	No		Yes	No
	Yes	No		Yes	No
Writing practices					
Writing a thank-you note	(Yes)	No	*Writing a grocery shopping list*	(Yes)	No
	Yes	No		Yes	No
	Yes	No		Yes	No
	Yes	No		Yes	No
	Yes	No		Yes	No

FIGURE 2.5. Similarities and differences in literacy practices in a native language and English.

eracy practices at home, teachers would have a better idea about what to inform families about supporting their children. If an ELL's family members cannot read English, Figure 2.5 needs to be translated into the native language. Or, teachers can enlist volunteers from the community to help translate. It might be a good idea to encourage ELL families living in the same or nearby neighborhood to complete Figure 2.5 together.

Showing Families How to Promote Reading and Writing in a Native Language and in English

Family support for ELLs' literacy development in a native language and in English varies, depending on the age, grade level, English proficiency level, and an individual ELL's strengths and needs. Teachers share this variability with families and particularly inform families of specific steps involved in each type of support. Following are some examples of activities that families can do with their children. (Also see a description of Parent University in Chapter 9, about how to encourage family members to work with their children.)

READING A BOOK ALOUD

Before asking families to read a book aloud to children, teachers need to model the procedure. This modeling can be done during an open house in the beginning of the school year and during a parenting class (if there is one on campus). Teachers also can provide families with a checklist like the one in Figure 2.6 (which can be written in a native language) so that a family member who is reading aloud includes major steps. (Please note that some steps may be skipped or modified if a family member is reading aloud to a young ELL.) Encourage a family member to read books (or other materials) in a native language (if available). Reading books aloud in a native language can strengthen what an ELL knows about literacy concepts (e.g., story grammar) and strategies (e.g., predicting and making a connection between the known and the new) (Krashen, 2004). The practice of reading aloud can evolve into shared reading where an adult and a child alternate their reading. This happens especially when a pattern book or a book with a distinctive language pattern (e.g., rhyming words) is used and when a child has figured out the pattern in the text after a few times of adult reading aloud.

Steps in a read-aloud	Did I do this step? (Please circle "yes" or "no")	
Book title: Date: Genre: Language:		
1. Read the title, author(s), and illustrator.	Yes	No
2. Ask a child to predict from the front cover and back cover what the book might be about. Example questions: What is the book going to be about? Why do you think so? Have you read a book with a similar title or pictures before? What does the book title make you think about?	Yes	No
3. Read a few pages and stop to ask questions. (Do so for the whole book.) Example questions: What do we know about the book? What might happen in the next page? Why? Do you remember anything so far? What does this part of book make you feel and remember? Why? Do you know all the words I read? What part of the book is hard for you? Why?	Yes	No
4. Model for the child how to understand the book. Example sentences: This part of book makes me think of another book I read . . . This book makes me think of what happened to me before . . . When I do not understand this sentence, I go back to read a sentence before it or reread this sentence. When I do not know this word, I look at the picture, the words before and/or after this word. I like this book, because . . .	Yes	No
5. Ask the child to comment on the book and retell key points from the book. Example questions: Do you like the book? Why?	Yes	No

(continued)

FIGURE 2.6. A read-aloud checklist.

Which part do you like best? Why? Do you remember what happens in the book? Can you tell me about it?		
6. Ask the child if he or she has any questions about the book. Example questions: Do you have any questions about the book? Is there a part of the book hard to understand? If yes, why?	Yes	No
7. Ask the child about the strategies used during listening to the book read aloud to him or her. Example questions: What do you do when you don't get what I am reading? Does your way work? Why? Why not? What other ways can you use to help you understand the book?	Yes	No
8. Ask the child if he or she wants to read a book similar to this one or a different one. Example questions: What book do you want me to read next? Do you want to read another book by the same author, or another book about the same topic?	Yes	No

FIGURE 2.6. (*continued*)

KEEPING A READING LOG

Besides reading books aloud to ELLs, family members need to encourage children to read along with any family member and/or community member (e.g., a neighbor) and to read independently. Teachers can help families keep track of child's reading at home by providing them a reading log (see Figure 2.7). The detailed information in a reading log like Figure 2.7 (which can be written in a native language) can furnish families with evidence of a child's progress in reading and their interests. A family member or an ELL student can complete the log in English or in a native language.

MAKING TV WATCHING A LITERACY EXPERIENCE

Like their English-speaking counterparts, ELLs are exposed to media entertainment. Many ELLs watch children's TV shows in English or in a native language. It seems that TV watching has become part of children's daily experiences with print and nonprint texts. Teachers can help families make their children's TV watching a meaningful literacy experience by sharing the following list of do's for families during an open house.

- Using the caption feature of a TV so that children can read words spoken in a show.
- Watching TV with children to learn about their interests, background knowledge about various topics, and language levels.
- Asking children what they know about a TV show before watching it and what this show is going to be about.
- Sharing with children your thoughts about the show and a favorite part after the show and inviting children to do the same.
- Asking children how they understand the show and what areas of the show do not make sense to them.
- Asking children what new things they have learned from the show (e.g., new words, ideas, and concepts).

ENGAGING CHILDREN IN TALKING

In primary grades, ELLs continue to develop their oral language both in their native language and in English. The oral language acquisition in

Date:

Title of the text (e.g., book, newspaper article):

Language (e.g., English, a native language):

Type of book (e.g., a story, information, how-to directions):

Number of pages read:

Content (e.g., counting, alphabet, weather, a story about three pigs):

Difficulty level (circle one):　　Easy　　Not easy, not hard　　Hard

Reason for difficulty level (answer one question):

Why is it EASY?

Why is it NOT EASY, NOT HARD?

Why is it HARD?

FIGURE 2.7. A reading log.

English is definitely not complete (for details see Chapter 4). Daily support for children's oral language development at home can be done through families engaging children in talking about:

- What happens at school; what is learned at school.
- What happens in the community; what is observed in the community.
- Texts children have read, TV shows children have read, other experiences they have had (e.g., a trip to grandparents' house).
- What needs to be resolved (e.g., a conflict between siblings or between friends.).

ENGAGING CHILDREN IN WRITING

Learning to write in a native language or in English is not an easy task (for details, see Chapter 5). ELLs need as much practice as they can get both inside and outside school to develop and sharpen their writing skills. Families can provide children with various meaningful and natural opportunities to write in different genres. Provide families with a writing log (see Figure 2.8) (which can be written and/or completed in a native language) to document ELLs' writing experience. Like a reading log, a writing log helps families keep track of their children's progress in writing and their interests in writing. The following is a sample list of what ELLs can write at home.

- Writing a note (e.g., a thank-you note, an apology note, or a reminder) to people (e.g., a family member, sibling, friend, teacher, or neighbor).
- Writing a direction (e.g., how to get to a store) or an instruction (e.g., how to defeat a bad guy on a GameBoy).
- Rewriting a text to make it more interesting.
- Writing a caption for a picture (e.g., in a newspaper or on a billboard).
- Writing a grocery shopping list with words and pictures of items.

COLLECTING ASSESSMENT DATA

Families, and in particular parents, besides being their children's initial teachers, also have a rich set of data about their children's learning,

Name: _____

Date: _____

Type of writing (e.g., a grocery shopping list or a thank-you note):

Pictures only (circle "yes" or "no")	Yes	No
Words only (circle "yes" or "no")	Yes	No
Pictures and words (circle "yes" or "no")	Yes	No

Number of words:

Number of sentences:

Number of paragraphs:

Why did your child want to write this? (e.g., to thank his uncle who bought him a birthday present)

What did your child find easy about writing this?

What did your child find hard about writing this?

FIGURE 2.8. A writing log.

which is seldom available to teachers. A reading log like Figure 2.7 and a writing log like Figure 2.8 are full of useful data about a child's literacy experiences outside school. These types of data are especially useful to teachers of newcomers and to ELLs who are not ready to produce language and/or who are shy or quiet. Teachers can collect the data periodically throughout the school year (e.g., once a month or bimonthly) and cross-check the data from families against those teachers have gathered from classroom-based assessment about ELLs' learning at school.

Engaging Families in Sharing Their Funds of Knowledge

Much has been written about involving parents or families in supporting children's education (e.g., assisting children with homework and pretesting children before a school test), but a growing body of work has taken a school-to-community approach which values the funds of knowledge families can contribute to school, thus enriching the school curriculum (Gonzáles & Moll, 1995; Gonzáles et al., 2005). In this section, we share several examples of school activities or projects that utilize ELL families' funds of knowledge.

Cultural and Expert Journals

A teacher can start a journal in which families record interesting things about their culture. The teacher, whether his or her culture is mainstream or not, can begin the first entry in the cultural journal. At the open house in the beginning of the school year, the teacher lets each family know that they will write interesting things about their native culture in a journal sent home. Included in this journal can be photos of places, people, and artifacts, in addition to words. Each family gets to keep the journal for a week before returning it to school. Families of native English-speaking children in a class should also participate in writing. Every time the journal is sent back to class, the teacher reads the journal entry to the class. If the journal entry is written in a native language, the teacher can have it translated by those who are proficient in the language and English or by using several translation tools listed in Figure 2.3.

The procedure for an expert journal is similar, except that families

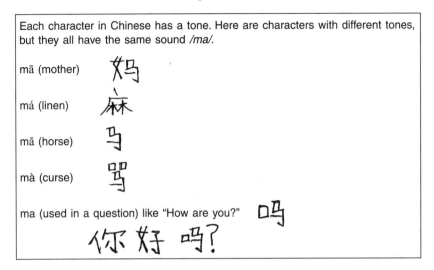

Each character in Chinese has a tone. Here are characters with different tones, but they all have the same sound /ma/.

mā (mother)

má (linen)

mǎ (horse)

mà (curse)

ma (used in a question) like "How are you?"

你好吗?

FIGURE 2.9. A sample page from a Chinese book.

write about special knowledge and skills they have (e.g., folk medicine, making origami, cooking, and teaching). By the end of the fall semester, both the cultural and expert journals are completed. The content in the cultural and expert journals broadens children's knowledge about the world and specific subject areas, and this type of enhanced knowledge lays a better foundation for successful understanding and writing about various topics. In addition, the teacher gains more information about children's cultural knowledge.

An (Alphabet) Book about a Native Language

In *Eating the Alphabet: Fruits and Vegetables from A to Z*, Lois Ehlert (1989) has pictures of fruits and vegetables for each letter of the English alphabet. Adapting this book structure, the teacher can ask each child (ELL or non-ELL) to work with his or her family to create a book about the alphabet of a native language or the consonants and vowels in a native language (if the language is a nonalphabetic; see Figure 2.9 for a sample page in a Chinese book). Families and the child can collect pictures of things or draw pictures of things that represent one particular letter or sound. This book project not only helps the child become aware of the unique characteristics of his or her native language but also allows the class and the teacher to learn about other languages.

A Class Idiom Book

Similar to writing an alphabet book about a native language, creating an idiomatic book appropriate for older children is an excellent child–family project. Books on English idioms (e.g., *In a Pickle and Other Funny Idioms* [Terban, 1983]) may serve as a model. In Terban's book, each idiom is accompanied by a picture explaining a literal meaning of the idiom. The teacher may ask each child to find an equivalent in a native language to an English idiom (e.g., *easy as pie*) and explain its literal and figurative meanings by using drawings. The teacher compiles pages from children into a class book. Writing a class idiom book helps ELLs develop a sense of pride of their own native culture and language and stimulates ELLs', non-ELLs', and the teacher's interests in other cultures and languages.

Collecting Environmental Print Items

Environmental print, due to its functional and context-embedded nature, has been considered one of most meaningful sources of print for early readers (e.g., Christie, Vukelich, & Enz, 2006; Goodman, 1986; Kuby & Aldridge, 2004; Prior & Gerard, 2004). As Xu and Rutledge (2003) stated, the environmental print that children collected in their home and community and brought to class becomes meaningful instructional material relevant to and connected to their life. The benefit of using environmental print also holds true for ELLs (Meier, 2004). The teacher can designate a day every other week for children to bring their environmental print items (e.g., cereal boxes and candy wrappers). These items, for example, can be used for show-and-tell (what a child knows about the words, the beginning letter or sound in a word). The logos and words on the items can be used for word sorts or word study related to phonics concepts (e.g., *-at* family, long- /ā/ spelling patterns). The teacher needs to inform families about which type of environmental print items to collect and where to collect these items and also about how families can use environmental print at home to support L1 and English literacy development. (For details about using environmental print, see Xu & Rutledge, 2003.)

> ### TAKE A MOMENT
>
> We have shared some ways to invite families to support students' literacy learning outside school and also to contribute to their funds of knowledge with literacy activities (e.g., creating an alphabet book in a native language). Think about the ELLs you have this year. Think of additional ways to involve families in supporting their children's literacy learning.

FINAL THOUGHTS

In this chapter, we discussed the importance of working with families by using a school-to-community approach. We have also shared different ways to learn about ELLs' culture and language, which, as we stress, is an initial and a crucial step to a successful school–community partnership. To conclude this chapter, we have presented ideas for teachers to inform families on how to support literacy development in a native language and in English and how to collaborate with families in sharing their funds of knowledge. We hope that while teaching ELLs, teachers can always consider families as valued and supportive partners.

CHAPTER 3

Assessment

To assess a language-minority child's language, literacy, and content knowledge, we need to understand the linguistic and psychological structures he or she has in both the minority and majority language and how they interact. We also need to understand how and to what degree the linguistic and psychological structures differ for fluent bilingual and fluent monolingual speakers. Interactions can take place at many levels—from the specific constructs of languages (e.g., phonemes, words) to abstract linguistic structures to metacognitive processes.
—GARCÍA, MCKOON, AND AUGUST (2006, p. 593)

After reviewing numerous studies on literacy assessment for ELLs, García et al. (2006) remind us that assessing ELLs is not as easy as it appears to be. In particular, in assessing ELLs, teachers must consider students' experiences with both English and their native language, and interactions among various aspects of language learning—ranging from understanding the basics of English (e.g., the alphabetic principle) to applying strategies (e.g., self-monitoring during reading). Given the complexity of assessing ELLs, it makes better sense to have a series of assessments tailored to ELLs' literacy experiences and needs in both English and a native language. The reality of high-stakes testing mandated by the No Child Left Behind (NCLB) legislation, however, does not always allow for modifications in assessing ELLs. Like their native English-speaking peers, ELLs must participate in statewide standardized assessment, and their performance on the assessment is included as part of adequate yearly progress (AYP) for their respective schools (Abedi, 2004). Although we understand the reasons for standardized testing for ELLs, we advocate classroom-based assessment (CBA) as a complementary tool to provide teachers with authentic, additional data on their ELLs' literacy performance.

In this chapter, we first discuss the important role that CBA plays in identifying ELLs' strengths and needs and in guiding instruction. Next, we focus on specific details of how to use CBA, ranging from selecting an assessment focus to identifying assessment materials to analyzing assessment results. In addition, we share ways to invite families and ELLs to become part of the assessment process. At the conclusion of this chapter, we share tips on managing CBA from effective teachers of ELLs.

At the end of this chapter, you will be able to:

- Develop a deeper understanding of an important role that CBA plays in identifying ELLs' strengths and needs and in guiding instruction.
- Describe how to identify an assessment focus.
- Describe how to select assessment materials.
- Describe how to analyze assessment results.
- Describe how to involve families and ELLs in the assessment process.

THE IMPORTANCE OF CBA

Standardized Assessment

Standardized assessment often includes statewide tests administered to students toward the end of a school year. It may take the form of districtwide benchmark assessments that teachers conduct several times throughout a school year. Teachers must follow a standard procedure for administering each test, and test raters/readers also have a set of guidelines for evaluating student performance. The nature of standardization allows teachers to compare the performance of their students with that of other students in the same grade level or at the same English-language proficiency level. Furthermore, test results from the same standardized test make it possible for teachers at the same grade level to plan modifications of their instruction to meet their students' specific needs. This nature of standardization, however, may also yield partial information on individual student's literacy and language performance. In addition, other features discussed in this chapter explain why a standardized test would not provide teachers with adequate information on individual student's performance.

Test Bias

The concept of test bias is not new (e.g., Au, 2000). When it comes to using standardized tests to assess ELLs, the matter of test bias gets more complicated. For example, in English, if one of the two subjects in a sentence is *I*, the word *I* always follows the other subject (e.g., "Sam and I wrote the book"). There is no grammatical rule for explaining this specific order. By contrast, in Chinese, the position of the word *I* in a sentence with two subjects depends on the role *I* plays in the content of the sentence. In the example "Sam and I wrote the book," if *Sam* is the lead author of the book, *Sam* certainly appears as a first subject of the sentence. But if *I* is the lead author, then *I* goes before *Sam* in this sentence. It is obvious that there are certain cultural and grammatical rules governing the order of two subjects of a sentence. In a standardized test, the sentence "I and Sam wrote a book," with an implied meaning that *I* was the lead author of the book, would be wrong, as it does not fit the way English is used (not that an English rule says so). This is a good example of how a standardized test can be biased on the basis of not considering ELLs' experience in their native language.

Another example of test bias is related to not considering ELLs' life experiences. In many cultures, the word *family* means more than a nuclear family (as is typical in American culture); it includes grandparents, aunts, uncles, and/or cousins. If a student's response to a comprehension question related to the word *family* suggests an extended family rather than a nuclear family, the response may be assumed to be wrong. If so, it is not clear if the test item is assessing the student's American cultural knowledge or his or her ability to comprehend the text. Likewise, it would be hard for a teacher to learn from the student's performance on this assessment whether the student lacks the English-language proficiency needed for comprehension or if the student lacks knowledge about the American culture needed to comprehend the text. Here is another example. ELLs living in rural areas may identify a picture of a pig as a *hog*; consequently, their teachers may think that students have not mastered the beginning *p* letter and sound as targeted in a test.

Proficiency Levels

A standardized test may target a certain grade level, but it may overlook the uniqueness of individual student's proficiency levels and needs. For example, ELLs whose native language is similar to English which can be analyzed at a phoneme level (e.g., Spanish, and Italian) may perform better on a test of phonemic awareness than another group of ELLs whose native language can only be analyzed at a syllable level (e.g., Chinese, Japanese, and Vietnamese). The latter group of ELLs need more instruction on phonemic awareness before they can perform satisfactorily on the test. Therefore, their poor performance on the test can mislead teachers in believing that they did not master the concept of phonemic awareness.

In addition, a standardized test requires ELLs to demonstrate their language and literacy knowledge. At times, ELLs' limited language proficiency may prevent them from demonstrating what they know. For example, beginning ELLs usually go through a silent stage (Krashen & Terrell, 1983) and may not be ready for speech or written production. Even for ELLs at the intermediate level, performance on certain tasks can be challenging. They, like beginning ELLs, need time to digest and consolidate newly learned concepts, skills, and/or knowledge. For example, an ELL may not be able to choose a multiple-choice item showing a correct sequence of events that happened in a story due to his or her limited comprehension ability. But in class, this same student may be able to retell in a correct sequence events of a story teacher has read by using pictures representing these events. Consequently, this student's choice of the wrong multiple-choice item does not represent his or her inability to sequence events (as a test reader would think based on the student's performance). Rather, the incorrectly marked item may suggest that the student lacks language proficiency that enables him or her to comprehend the story or that the student lacks comprehension ability in general.

Delayed Reporting

Another drawback of standardized tests is the delay in reporting results back to the school and teacher. Because students take these tests toward the end of a school year, teachers do not get the report on the class and an individual student's performance until summer break, long after the end of the school year. Teachers may learn about strengths and needs of their students from test results and revise their instruction for the coming school year. However, they do not get to modify or tailor their instruction for the students they were teaching; rather, these changes are for a new group of students who may reflect different strengths and needs. This situation is utterly unfair to the current year's students who should have received modified instruction during the school year based on these assessments.

Classroom-Based Assessment

Like standardized tests, the goal of CBA is to measure what students can do and where they need to improve. Unlike standardized tests, CBA is ongoing, teacher-controlled, curriculum-embedded, and tailored to ELLs' proficiency levels and individual needs (Lenski, Ehlers-Zavala, Daniel, & Sun-Irminger, 2006; O'Malley & Valdez-Pierce, 1996). When used effectively and in conjunction with standardized tests, CBA can supply teachers with valuable and authentic information on ELLs' language and literacy performance and thus help teachers make appropriate instructional decisions (Hurley & Blake, 2000; Pérez, 2004).

Ongoing, Teacher-Controlled Assessment

Because CBA is teacher controlled, it can be carried out any time throughout a school year. Teachers can vary the time and need to conduct CBA based on individual student's needs (Mora, 2006). For example, when all ELLs in the class, except for a newcomer, have mastered English concepts about print (CAP), a teacher only needs to administer a CAP assessment to this newcomer throughout a school year. Also, when an ELL starts reading a line on the page of a book for the first time, the teacher can immediately clip a blank piece of paper on a clipboard and start a running record of this student's oral reading. Furthermore, CBA allows teachers to flexibly group students for an assessment who share a similar strength or need. For example, ELLs at a similar stage of spelling development could be grouped together for assessment. It makes no sense to assess a whole class's orthographic knowledge of long-vowel sounds when students are all at various levels of spelling development, ranging from prephonemic to letter name to within word (Bear, Helman, Invernizzi, Templeton, & Johnston, 2007). Students at prephonemic-to-letter name would not be able to demonstrate knowledge of long-vowel patterns, and this assessment would yield no new information to guide instruction for these students. As discussed in Chapter 1, individual or group assessment where the teacher targets certain skills or strategies is one of the characteristics of differentiated instruction for ELLs. The assessment provides the data to efficiently group students for targeted literacy instruction.

Curriculum-Embedded Assessment

CBA reflects more curriculum-embeddedness than do standardized tests as teachers engage students in these assessments when it is appropriate to guide instruction rather than at predetermined times. Although both types of assessment are frequently based on curriculum standards, CBA is more closely aligned with what students are expected to accomplish. First, CBA can be embedded in daily teaching. For example, when a teacher asks the class to describe the shapes of clouds they have observed, before reading *The Cloud Book* (dePaola, 1975), he or she is assessing students' prior knowledge about clouds. In a similar way, a teacher might ask students for other words they know that rhyme with the words from Dr. Seuss's book *The Cat in the Hat* (Seuss, 1957) (e.g., *cat, hat, sat*) after he or she has discussed rhyming words and provided examples of rhyming words. In doing so, the teacher is assessing if students understand the concept of rhyming words and if they can apply the concept of rhyming words to words they know.

In addition, teachers can use CBA during different instructional settings, group work, individual work, and even playground and lunch time. The foregoing two examples occur in an instructional setting. Another example occurs on the playground. During this observation, teachers learn how students use a language (either English or a native language) to communicate and negotiate with others, among other things. This type of informal assessment provides valuable and authentic information to supplement results gained from a more structured assessment of students' use of language (e.g., benchmark assessment and standardized tests). In one school observation, we noticed a Vietnamese ELL, who, according to his teacher, was not able to perform any task on an English proficiency test but managed to get his playmates' attention by repeatedly using the word *hello* and waving his hands. The boy with limited English proficiency had some coping skills and knew how to use the word *hello* effectively in communicating with his playmates.

Figure 3.1 lists some examples of settings for CBA and possible target areas for CBA. As is obvious from the figure, teachers can target

Examples of settings for CBA	Possible target areas for CBA
Following a direction about a routine	Listening comprehension, sequence, understanding of the content
Reading aloud	Fluency, decoding, pronunciation
Share and tell	BICS (basic international communicative skills), CALP (cognitive academic language proficiency), sequence, vocabulary, fluency, pronunciation
Interactive writing	BICS, CALP, phonics knowledge/skill, spelling, vocabulary, comprehension of the content, concepts about print
Whole-class or group lesson instruction	Listening comprehension, concepts about print, comprehension of a story/information
Group work	BICS, CALP, understanding of directions for group work, comprehension of the academic content
Journal writing	Concepts about print, knowledge of story elements, grammatical rules, spelling, vocabulary
Working on computer (with a software) (alone)	Understanding directions, listening comprehension, decoding
Working on computer (surfing the Internet) (alone)	Concepts about print (unique to online texts), understanding directions, listening comprehension, decoding, summarizing information, navigating the sites
Working on computer (with a software program) (with a partner)	BICS, understanding directions, listening comprehension, decoding
Working on computer (surfing the Internet) (alone)	BICS, concepts about print (unique to online texts), understanding directions, listening comprehension, decoding, summarizing information, navigating the sites
Student playing during recess	BICS, comprehension of directions, vocabulary

FIGURE 3.1. Examples of settings and target areas for CBA.

multiple areas for CBA during any of the following settings: direct instruction, group work, and playing during recess.

Figure 3.2 shows a language experience chart, which illustrates how teachers can target multiple areas for CBA during one teachable moment. Ms. Gillespie, a kindergarten teacher with a class of ELLs, seized a playground problem (sand all over the playground) and turned it into a topic for the language experience approach (Stauffer, 1980). Ms. Gillespie informally assessed students' English proficiency in describing the problem. After Ms. Gillespie completed the language experience chart, she noted that most of her students produced a grammatically correct statement describing the problem. Ms. Gillespie also identified some children who needed additional instruction on sentence structure. The student who said "They put sand in tunnel two times" may have not mastered the use of article (*the*) in front of a countable noun (*tunnel*). The student who said "He throwing sand in the playground many times" needs additional instruction on sentence structure about present progressive tense (*be* + verb-*ing*). Unlike these two students, the student who said "The tunnel have sand for to make a castle" needs instruction on third-person verb tense and on expressing an idea in general.

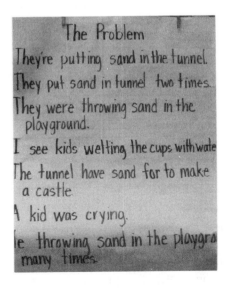

FIGURE 3.2. A language experience chart.

Although CBA has some advantages over standardized tests in helping teachers obtain more specific and detailed information on an ELL's strengths and needs, it also has its own limitations. We want to warn teachers of such limitations so that they can become aware of them and accordingly learn to address the limitations. A first limitation is the time involved in developing, administering, and analyzing CBA. The time factor may prevent some teachers from analyzing the assessment results. If so, it defeats its purpose to have CBA. In addition, with different assessment formats and foci of CBA, a teacher from one classroom may find it difficult to compare the performance of his or her students to that of students from another class. Thus, these two teachers would have less chance to collaboratively develop curriculum to address ELLs' needs.

TAKE A MOMENT

Think about the curricular standards for the ELLs in your classroom, and then think about various instructional, small-group work, individual work, and play settings where you can use CBA to assess at least one target area based on the curricular standards. Develop a chart similar to Figure 3.1 and keep it with your assessment materials so that you will have easy access to it. Also revisit the chart frequently throughout the school year to modify it to best reflect your own classroom teaching and learning activities, and your students' needs.

We have discussed the differences between standardized tests and CBA and the importance of using CBA to conduct ongoing assessment and identify students' strengths and needs. Here is a list of some forms of CBA. We encourage teachers to add more forms to complete this list.

- *Checklist*: Allowing a teacher to quickly document an ELL's proficiency level in a target area (e.g., Figure 4.4, Holistic Oral Language Assessment; Figure 8.13, Think-Aloud Checklist).
- *Structured anecdotal record (with focal areas)*: Allowing a teacher to document in detail what is observed about an ELL's proficiency level in target areas and/or literacy behaviors associated with the target areas (e.g., Figure 4.1, Observing Functions of Language; Figure 4.3, Receptive and Expressive Language Observational Assessment).

■ *Unstructured anecdotal record (targeting all areas)*: Allowing a teacher to document in detail what is observed about an ELL's proficiency in all areas related to the grade level (e.g., Fig. 3.3, Unstructured Anecdotal Record, used by Mrs. Duvnjak, a first-grade teacher).

■ *Reading log*: Allowing a teacher to assess the genre, content, and difficulty level of books an ELL has read (e.g., Figure 3.9, Reading Log with Faces).

■ *Group assessment*: Allowing a teacher to document an ELL's proficiency level of certain skills targeted in one particular basal text unit (Figure 3.4 Group Assessment, used by Mrs. Duvnjak, a first-grade teacher).

■ *Weekly assessment*: Allowing a teacher to document an ELL's proficiency level in one certain skill during one particular week (e.g., Figure 3.5 Weekly Assessment of Letter Identification, used by Ms. Gutierrez, a kindergarten teacher).

EFFECTIVE USE OF CBA

Identifying an Assessment Focus

Identifying an assessment focus seems easy, as the curricular standards and information on proficiency levels provide teachers with information as to what to assess and when to assess ELLs. But when teachers start taking a deeper look at individual students with unique experiences with languages, literacy, and life, it becomes more complicated for them to identify an assessment focus that would later yield relatively accurate and holistic information about ELLs' language and literacy proficiency. In this section, we center on three areas related to identifying an assessment focus: proficiency levels and curricular standards, areas of difficulty, and student interest and life experiences. Although we discuss each area separately, we encourage teachers, while selecting an assessment focus, to consider all three areas together and balance them in order to gain information about ELLs' strengths and needs.

Proficiency Levels and Curricular Standards

Curricular standards for English language development developed by states and the ESL Standards for Pre-K–12 Students of the Teachers of

Returned Library Books

Check-Off	Name	Anecdotal Notes:
✓	1. Alexandra	Provided elaborate explanation of story elements.
✓	2. Cecilia	
✓	3. Damir	
✓	4. Domagoj	Participated - showed leadership skills during group work.
✓	5. Erika	
✓	6. Fabian	Called home regarding playground behavior. Talked to mom 3:20 pm.
✓	7. Genoveve	
◯	8. Hailey	
✓	9. Ivo	
◯	10. John	Needed assistance with summarizing
◯	11. Ken	
✓	12. Lisa	Difficulties speaking in complete sentences during hand-off.
✓	13. Miki	
✓	14. Neda	
✓	15. Olga	1:15pm Left home - not feeling well.
◯	16. Paco	
✓	17. Reiki	
✓	18. Saito	Unfocused during phonics instruction prompted 2x. Moved her to front row.
◯	19. Tina	

DAILY RECORD SHEET   **Date:**

Check-off list. Can be used for checking off returned library books, returned folders, complete work, etc. The circle means "not complete."

FIGURE 3.3. Unstructured anecdotal record. Directions for creating a form similar to this one: List students in alphabetical order and assign each student a number. Keep this list on a clipboard and carry it with you as you teach. Jot down informational observations for each student throughout the day. File it in your grade book.

English to Speakers of Other Languages (TESOL) (available at *www.tesol. org/s_tesol/seccss.asp?CID=113&DID=1583*) provide teachers with guidance as to what to assess and when to assess students. Specifically, these standards help teachers identify an assessment focus appropriate to an ELL's proficiency level and grade level. For example, for a second-grade

Reading Unit 2, First Grade

Small Group Intervention for Pre-teaching or Re-teaching At-Risk Students

Initial consonant Riddles	Blending initial consonants	Oral Blending	Restoring Final Consonant Sounds	Dropping Final Consonants	Isolating Final Consonants
Mindy Robert	Bert	✓ Patrick ✓ Mindy ✓ Angelina Felix Taisha		✓ Frederick ✓ Jose Moises Angelina	
Blending	**Syllables Segmentation**	**Final Consonant Substitution**	**High-Frequency Words**		
Felix Nancy Taisha	Humberto Lina		Jennifer Gilbert		

(✓ means the student has met that goal.)

FIGURE 3.4. Group assessment. Directions for using a form similar to this one: Create a chart with titles of skills that you will be teaching in your reading unit for that month. Keep this chart on a clipboard. As you teach throughout the day, jot down the names of the students who seem to have difficulties with certain skills. Work with those students individually or in small groups during workshop time.

newcomer whose native language is different from English and who has had no experiences with English, an assessment of the student's knowledge of concepts about print is necessary. While the teacher uses this assessment based on the student's proficiency level, the teacher also needs to consider the student's grade level, for example, in selecting assessment materials. (We discuss more on this topic later in this chapter.) It may be inappropriate to select a similar book or other print materials used with kindergartners when assessing CAP with this newcomer because of age level.

Areas of Difficulty

Conducting CBA solely based on proficiency level and TESOL and/or state standards is not enough. Teachers must consider areas of difficulty that each ELL may have and make these areas assessment foci. In identifying the areas of difficulty, we suggest that teachers become familiar with individual ELLs' experiences with languages (English

Oct. 9-13 Letter Recognition	(A-Z)	(A-Z)	(A-Z)	(A-Z)		
	Monday	Tuesay	Wednesday	Thursday	Friday	Comments
Agustin	P					
Alberto		I				
Alvaro		I /ELL				retention
Adam	P					
Andrea	P					
Barbara		P				
Henriqua		S /P				
Humberto	P					
Jacobo		I /EO				
John	P					
Jose		S				
Malcolm	P					
Mandy				I/ELL		
Paco			I/ELL			
Rebacca	P					
Richard					I /ELL	
Sara	P					
Serena				I /EO		
Stacey					I/ELL	
Thomas			P			

FIGURE 3.5. Weekly assessment of letter identification. P, proficient; S, strategic; I, intensive; ELL, English language learner; EO, English only.

and a native language), literacy (English and a native language), and content areas. This is the point that we have stressed throughout this book.

In Table 7.1 in Chapter 7 we identify certain sounds difficult for groups of students with a particular language background. L-cluster words, for instance, are difficult for ELLs whose native language is Chinese, Japanese, Korean, or Vietnamese, while Spanish-speaking ELLs may have well mastered this L-cluster ahead of their peers. The teacher needs to continue to conduct an assessment with non-Spanish-speaking children until the concept is mastered. It is not wise to quit assessing groups of ELLs about their mastery of L-cluster words simply because a majority of Spanish-speaking ELLs have mastered it. Likewise, it becomes meaningless to assess the whole class about the mastery of L-cluster words while Spanish-speaking children have already mastered such words.

Considering ELLs' areas of difficulty also allows teachers to conduct group assessment and then use the assessment results to inform group instruction. For example, before reading the book *Too Many Tamales* (Soto, 1993), a teacher may ask the whole class to tell, based on the front and back covers and book title, what the book might be about. This very informal assessment of students' prior knowledge of the content of the book may not be enough for a group of ELLs who are not familiar with the Hispanic family tradition of making tamales at a family gathering. The teacher then needs to conduct small-group assessments on the content of the book prior to introducing the book to the whole class and then provide that group of students with the necessary background knowledge related to the book prior to the small-group lessons. Pragmatically, this means that the teacher may convene students to develop background knowledge and then reconvene another group of students into a small group when the book is read.

Student Interest and Life Experiences

Throughout this book, we have stressed the importance of considering students' interests and life experiences while providing literacy instruction for ELLs. We want to emphasize this point again in talking about identifying an assessment focus. Jiménez (2001, 2004) reminded us that to understand Latino children's literacy knowledge, teachers need to become familiar with non-school-based literacy practices in which children are engaged. Jiménez's point, we believe, applies to all children, and in particular to ELLs, regardless of their cultural and linguistic backgrounds. By considering student interest and life experiences, teachers are able to maximize an opportunity for an ELL to demonstrate his or her language and literacy knowledge.

Figure 3.6 shows the performance of a kindergartner with a late-beginning English proficiency level on a list of words developed around her popular culture interests, *Kim Possible* doll, and other dolls. The student was able to explain five of six words on the list after her teacher read each word to her. Even for the word *clothes*, which she was not

Vocabulary Test (Teacher Copy)

Step 2: Explain each word AND use it in a sentence

1. Kim
   Explanation: I don't know

   Sentence: ∅

2. doll
   Explanation: like a teddy bear

   Sentence: ∅

3. girl
   Explanation: a person, she's a girl (points to Destiny)

   Sentence: ∅

4. Barbie
   Explanation: I have lots in my room. They are pretty,

   Sentence: they got eyes, earrings and lipstick.

5. clothes
   Explanation: points to her shirt

   Sentence: ∅

6. pretty
   Explanation: beautiful

   Sentence: Barbie's are pretty.

FIGURE 3.6. Word list related to popular culture interests.

able to explain, she was able to use gestures to express her understanding. This same student was only able to recognize one word, *like*, from a preprimer word list (*me, get, home, not, he, tree, girl, take, book, milk, dog, all, apple, go, farm, went, friend, about,* and *some*) (Johns, 2005). An interesting observation is that the student was not able to identify the word *girl* on Johns's word list, but could express the meaning of this word when it was on the word list based on her popular culture interests. The student's performance on the word list related to the student's popular culture interests yields more valuable information for her teacher than that on Johns's word list. This example illustrates the importance of considering students' interests and life experiences when assessing ELLs. We are not suggesting that each teacher develops a word list based on each ELL's interests. Rather, we encourage teachers not to rely only on a single, traditional assessment tool to assess ELLs' literacy knowledge.

> **TAKE A MOMENT**
>
> Identify two ELLs in your class whose native languages are different. Think about an assessment focus for each student. Ask yourself how the focus for one student is similar to and/or different from that for the other, and how the focus for one student is similar to and/or different from that for other ELLs in the class.

Selecting Assessment Materials

Selecting assessment materials is often beyond a teacher's control when it comes to standardized tests. But it becomes important and feasible when teachers use CBA with ELLs. It is well known that an ELL would not perform well on a reading comprehension test on a topic unfamiliar to the student and/or a test with words not at least in the student's receptive vocabulary (Peregoy & Boyle, 2000). In Chapter 6 we discuss how to select various instructional materials for literacy instruction for ELLs. In this section, we focus on how to choose alterative materials that can be used to effectively assess ELLs' language and literacy achievement.

In selecting materials for assessment, the first thing that teachers need to consider is the purpose of the assessment. Teachers may ask, "Will the use of this type of material help me to get what I want to know from this assessment?" If a teacher wants to assess students' understanding of story elements (e.g., character and plot), the materials used for assessment should clearly reflect these elements. For example, the book *Corduroy* (Freeman, 1968), a wonderful children's classic, would not be a good book to use for assessing students' knowledge of story elements. The main reason is the complexity of sentence structure evident throughout the book. If this book is used, the assessment result would be confounded by the factor of sentence structure; the purpose of assessing story elements cannot be achieved completely. In a similar way, if a teacher uses a cloze strategy (a teacher selects a passage and leaves every fifth word out, for instance, and the student is expected to use an appropriate word in the blank that maintains meaning) to assess students' ability to use four linguistic cueing systems of English (graphophonic, syntactic, semantic, and pragmatic), the teacher needs to find a cloze passage on content that is relatively familiar to students. If the content is unfamiliar to students, it would be difficult for the teacher to know whether a student's poor performance is due to the lack of content knowledge or to the lack of ability or knowledge of the four cueing systems.

A second area that teachers need to think about is the students' proficiency level. If the assessment material is beyond a student's proficiency level, all that a teacher gains from the assessment is what the student cannot do, not a balance of what the student can do and what the student cannot do. This point becomes especially important when it comes to assessing beginning ELLs.

For example, after the teacher has read a storybook to the class, the teacher asks students to retell story events in order. In so doing, the teacher excludes beginning ELLs, who are not ready to produce language, from participating in this activity which allows them to demonstrate what they have comprehended about the story. To address this issue, the teacher can take another copy of the storybook apart and laminate each page. When it is time for the class to retell events, beginning ELLs can use the pages with pictures to show what they know about the sequence of the story events. Providing beginning ELLs with a piece of paper for them to draw the events is another approach.

Thanks to the Internet, teachers have access to a large number of images and clipart pictures online. The traditional print resources like environmental print are equally useful. We suggest that teachers include these resources in the assessment of beginning ELLs and caution them not to include resources that are beyond students' linguistic proficiency and scope of knowledge.

Figure 3.7 shows a way to use pictures (from Inspiration Software or from *office.microsoft.com/en-us/clipart/default.aspx*) to assess beginning ELLs' understanding of a concept. In the semantic map, a teacher first includes two pictures (with a label) related to the concept *weather* and then asks an ELL to do the same. By looking at what the student has done with the semantic map, the teacher understands that the student has some knowledge of the concept. If the student had been asked to use words to complete the map, which is beyond the student's current proficiency level, the teacher may not have gathered as much information from the map about students' understanding of the concept.

Even for ELLs at the intermediate level, materials other than worksheets can be helpful for gathering authentic assessment data. For example, a teacher asks students to circle words in collected environ-

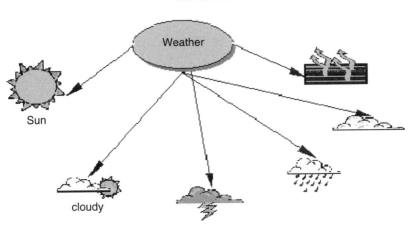

FIGURE 3.7. A semantic map on weather.

mental print that meet certain criteria (e.g., rhyming with a target word, beginning with a target sound, and containing a target vowel sound or a particular spelling pattern). Figure 3.8 shows environmental print words that have different spelling patterns of the long-*e* sound. Instead of asking students, who may have limited vocabulary, to produce words containing a long-*e* sound, allowing students to find words from their

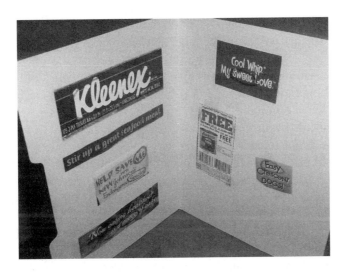

FIGURE 3.8. Different long-*e* sound patterns in environmental print words.

environmental print that fit the criterion demonstrates their knowledge. (These words are in students' receptive vocabulary.) In so doing, the teacher can develop a good knowledge of how much students know before asking them to actually produce long-*e* words with different spelling patterns.

TAKE A MOMENT

Think about the assessment materials you used last year. Which ones were effective and resulted in instructional change? Make a list of assessment materials that you think you might try this academic year, and think about how you might use the information you glean from these assessments.

Analyzing Assessment Results

When analyzing assessment results, it is never sufficient for teachers to just count and document the number of errors. The number of errors only informs a teacher of what an ELL cannot do. To plan instruction based on assessment results, a teacher needs to find out *why* the student has made such errors. Information about the *why* is valuable for the teacher in offering differentiated instruction for that particular student. For example, some Spanish-speaking children tend to put a short-*e* sound in front of a word starting with an *s* sound. The word *school*, for example, becomes *eschool*. After learning about the Spanish orthography, the teacher would understand that in Spanish the *es* combination acts like an English blend in the beginning of a word. Equipped with this information, the teacher is able to find out the source of the Spanish-speaking ELLs' errors and plan instruction targeted at teaching children to note a difference between Spanish words beginning with *es* and English words beginning with *s*.

In addition to understanding why an ELL has made one particular type of error, a teacher also needs to explore the quality of errors. High-quality errors are more reflective of the student's growing knowledge in one area than low-quality errors are. If a Spanish-speaking child read the word *house* as *casa*, the child demonstrated an understanding of the meaning of the word *house*. Maybe it is hard for the child to pronounce an English word beginning with the /h/ sound, which is silent in Spanish. By contrast, another Spanish-speaking child read the word *house* as /ōs/, which is a nonsense word in English. The former child obviously has a better knowledge about the word *house* than the latter one.

Goodman (1996) suggested that teachers learn from an analysis of a student's oral reading miscues about how the student used one or more linguistic cueing systems while making errors. Her suggestion, we believe, can apply effectively with analyzing ELLs' oral reading. In Table 3.1, we list three ELLs' readings of the word *happy* in the sentence "I am happy." It is obvious that ELL 3 understood the meaning of the sentence and demonstrated a good command of sentence structure. ELL 2, while being able to produce a grammatically correct sentence, overlooked the meaning of the sentence. ELL 1 only paid attention to the visual feature of *happy* and produced *hop* whose meaning was not related to *happy* at all. With the word *hop*, the sentence became grammatically incorrect.

The process of identifying the reason(s) an ELL has made certain errors and analyzing the quality of the errors provides a teacher with valuable information specifically related to the student. Equipped with this information, the teacher can plan instruction targeted at the student's unique needs.

TAKE A MOMENT

Select a few ELLs from your class. Look at their performance on one particular assessment. Identify the possible reason(s) for each student's errors on the assessment, and analyze the quality of the errors. Then compare your analysis for each student to see if there is a similarity and/or difference among the reasons for and quality of errors.

Involving Families and ELLs in the Assessment Process

In the United States, children go to school for approximately 180 days or so each year, which is less than half a year. If children do not practice

TABLE 3.1. Students' Oral Reading

Students	Students' oral reading of *I am happy*.
ELL 1	"I am hop."
ELL 2	"I am hopping."
ELL 3	"I am glad."

and apply what they have learned at school when they are not at school, it is hard for them to retain the learned knowledge and to consolidate their skills and strategies. This also holds true for ELLs who are learning a new language and are constantly playing a catchup game with their native English-speaking peers in the process of language and literacy development. In Chapter 2, we discussed how teachers can engage families in supporting their children's language and literacy learning. Working with families, we feel, becomes more important when it comes to CBA (Valdez-Pierce, 2003). Information about ELLs gained from twice-a-year teacher–parent conferences would not be adequate. We suggest that teachers develop some informal assessment forms for families to complete. Some examples are Figures 2.5, 2.7, and 2.8. The forms can be written in a native language and collected at designated dates throughout a school year (not just at the beginning or end of a school year).

Similar to the role that families play in the assessment process, the role that ELLs themselves play should not be overlooked. Research (e.g., Duke & Pearson, 2002) on readers who are native English speakers has shown that good readers are constantly engaged in a process of applying strategies, evaluating what they have read, analyzing the text being read, and modifying the way they read, among other things. By not involving ELLs in the assessment process, teachers might lose a great deal of useful data on the process of ELLs' language and literacy learning. For example, after you have taught a wide range of reading comprehension strategies, how would you know that an ELL is using these strategies? Information from a checklist such as Figure 8.13, along with a one-on-one conference with each ELL, would supply teachers with valuable information on how ELLs use language and literacy for meaningful purposes in nonschool social settings.

Including ELLs as part of the assessment process is not limited only to those at the intermediate and advanced proficiency levels. Beginning ELLs can provide teachers with some information about their learning process. Teachers just need to find appropriate assessment tools. For example, in Figure 3.9, after the teacher has modeled how to log in books under different columns, an ELL can write down a book title under a column of a very happy face (indicating the book is very easy), a happy face (indicating the book is just right), or an unhappy face (indicating the book is too hard). By looking at this log, the teacher can learn about the pattern of book choice for reading in terms of book genre, difficulty

Date	Too easy	Just right	Too hard
11/10/06	Do You Want to Be My Friend?		
11/13			Spot's First Walk
11/15/06		Ten Black Dots	
11/16/06		Ten Black Dots	
11/17/06			Brown Bear, Brown Bear, What Do You See?
11/21/06			Mouse Paint

FIGURE 3.9. Reading log with faces.

level, and student interest. Upon gathering this information, the teacher can plan instruction accordingly.

> **TAKE A MOMENT**
>
> Think about how you might involve families and ELLs in the assessment process. Write about an action plan, and try one or two things from the plan during this school year. Then reflect on new ways to learn about your students' literacy learning that you have discovered by engaging families and ELLs.

FINAL THOUGHTS

In this chapter, we discussed the importance of using CBA to gain valuable information about ELLs' language and literacy learning experiences and outcomes. Specifically, we shared different components associated with using CBA: identifying an assessment focus, selecting assessment materials, analyzing assessment data, and involving families and ELLs in the assessment process. By now you have probably realized that CBA involves a more complex process than standardized tests, and that teachers have to put more energy and time into it to make it a successful and effective type of assessment.

To conclude this chapter, we would like to share some tips from teachers of ELLs whose work has been featured in this chapter. The first tip from Ms. Gutierrez, Ms. Gillespie, and Mrs. Duvnjak is that each day, a teacher needs to pull out, during small-group activities, at least five students for individual assessment. By the end of a week, every student has been assessed on a target area. Another tip is about trying to document each student's performance in a target area on one piece of paper (as shown in Figures 3.3, 3.4, and 3.5). In doing so, a teacher gains a good sense of how every student's performance rates in relation to his or her peers, who needs to be grouped with whom for further assessment or for group instruction, and who needs long-term, intensive intervention. The last tip is about involving students. The three teachers often ask their students if they know what needs to be improved, and they remember to check if there has been an improvement in a target area. We hope that these teachers' tips will help with implementing CBA in your classroom.

CHAPTER 4

Oral Language Development and Instruction

Language is not simply the instrument by which we communicate thought. The language we speak will shape the thoughts and feelings themselves.
—PATERSON (1981, p. 8)

Oral language provides the foundation for literacy development (Genesee, Lindholm-Leary, Saunders, & Christian, 2005). That being said, what does it mean for a child whose first language is not English when he or she arrives in a school where the language of instruction is English. Do teachers wait for a certain critical mass of oral proficiency in English before starting more formal literacy instruction or do they just begin instruction and allow oral proficiency to develop simultaneously with reading and writing? This is an important question for teachers to consider as they work with ELLs.

When children first learn their home language, they begin as infants to produce all the phonemes necessary to be a speaker of that language. Between ages 1 and 3, children acquire about 1,000 to 3,000 words and start to form simple, often one-word, sentences. From ages 3 to 5, they start to play with language and become aware of rhymes and phonological aspects of language such as words that begin with the same sound. From 5 to about 8 they learn more sophisticated vocabulary and complex structures of the home language (Geva & Petrulis-Wright, 1999). With this development in mind, what must a child do to now add a new language to this rich language base in his or her home language upon entry to school?

That is the focus of this chapter. It begins with an exploration of the important elements of a language, then shifts to what is entailed in learning a new language. Finally, we consider strategies to support oral language learning in classrooms.

At the end of this chapter, you will be able to:

■ Describe the formal and informal elements of language.
■ Describe and observe children using language for a variety of purposes.
■ Describe the important dimensions of learning a new language.
■ Describe the stages of learning a new language.
■ Describe strategies that directly support oral language development.
■ Describe the importance of phonological awareness and describe strategies to support its development.

FORMAL AND INFORMAL ELEMENTS OF LANGUAGE

What exactly is expected for a person to learn to speak a language fluently? For most children and adults there is little focused attention on speaking. The ability to converse develops within a family that initiates and responds to a child's early attempts to communicate. Following these initial attempts, more sophisticated control of oral language develops from single words to complex sentences.

While this process often develops without much awareness, language does have important elements, some more formal than others (Richgels, 2005). Richgels (2005) describes these essential elements of language.

Formal Elements

Phonology

Phonology is the sounds in language. It includes prosody—the rhythm of a language as it is spoken to phonemes—the smallest sound elements within a word. Phonology is focused on pronunciation.

Morphology

Morphology focuses on the units within words that carry meaning. A word such as *heart* has a single morpheme while a word such as *talked* has two (*talk* + *ed* signaling past tense).

Semantics

Semantics focus on meaning, but beyond a single word. It centers on the ways words are placed together and their shared meaning—for example: *Mary chased the bat. Mary struck out when she was at bat.* The meaning of *bat* changed in each sentence, but it required the whole sentence to recognize the difference in meanings.

Syntax

Syntax is centered on language forms within a sentence. This can involve active and passive sentence structures. It also includes sentence structure such as simple, complex, or compound for instance.

Lexicon

The lexicon of a language is its vocabulary.

Informal Elements

Paralinguistics

Paralinguistics involve learning about signs, gestures, and facial expressions that parallel language production. This is the important nonverbal part of language.

Functions of Language

The functions of language were described by Halliday (1975). These functions include:

- Instrumental—Expression of needs and wants ("I want an apple.")
- Regulatory—Regulation of others' behavior ("Stop that!")

- Interactional—Interaction with others ("Want to paint?")
- Personal—Expression of opinions or feelings ("I like you.")
- Imaginative—Imagination ("I am a Power Ranger.")
- Heuristic—Inquiry ("Why?")
- Representational—Information ("Look at that snail.")

Halliday's work moves beyond a simple look at the formal elements of language. The functions reveal the purposes of language—the reasons children use language. Children new at a language often use the first two functions of language before others. In many early-childhood classrooms, teachers use these structures to describe students' use of language, especially as they are developing competency in English. Figure 4.1 shares such an observation tool for this purpose.

Conversation or Discourse

Children need to understand how to engage in conversations with peers and with teachers. Often children struggle with conversations. They need to learn how to begin a conversation, how to respond, how to take turns, and so on. The ability for children to engage in conversations is the foundation for many classroom activities such as cooperative work, book clubs, and so on.

They also learn that conversation structures in school may be very different than those at home. At home they are welcome just to talk whenever they have something to say, while at school their conversations may be limited to when they are called on. They learn about conversational language as well as the academic discourse of school. Within academic language they learn how to ask and respond to questions, for example.

In addition, they learn to observe the language of school and to participate in conversations with the language capabilities they have. Pérez and Torres-Guzmán (1992) wrote about young children as they became aware of different languages. When children are as young as 3, they may ask how to say a word in English or Spanish. They shared an example where a young child asked how to say *brown* in Spanish. The child knew the word in English but had forgotten the word in Spanish. They also talked about code switching, where children use both languages in conversation. In code switching children use some aspects of either language. For instance, children who have Spanish as their home

Name: _____ **Date:** _____

Setting: _____

(Write down samples of speech to document each function of language observed.)

Expression of needs and wants ("Give me the paper.")

Regulation of others' behavior ("Stop!")

Interaction with others ("Let's play.")

Expressions of opinions or feelings ("I like . . . ")

Imagination ("I am a fireman.")

Inquiry ("What is that?")

Information ("That is a map.")

FIGURE 4.1. Observing functions of language.

language might say "está raining" or "es a baby." Padilla and Liebman (1975) noted that when children code switch, they maintain correct word order as demonstrated in the foregoing two examples. They would not say, "A es baby."

Understanding and Forming Stories

In U.S. classrooms, much of the early literacy curriculum is based on listening and responding to stories, telling stories, and writing stories. Children may come to school with very different ideas on how stories are represented (Heath, 1983). Heath's work describes how children in different socioeconomic circumstances come to school with varying ideas about stories. Not surprisingly, children from middle-class settings understood stories in similar ways to their teachers, frequently resulting in school success.

In addition to different understandings about story, there is also a developmental progression in a child's understanding of a story (Applebee, 1978). Applebee learned about this progression by asking students to retell a story they just heard. At first, young students retold stories in a random way or in *heaps*, as Applebee labeled them. From these random retellings, students retold a story in a sequential way by identifying the major elements. Students then moved to a summary where they left out some facts but included the most important ideas or events. The next levels of sophistication moved beyond the literal parts of a story to inferential understandings. Students began to analyze characters or plot, and finally they formed generalizations about a story or reported the themes they observed. For instance, they might say that this story was about forming relationships or survival.

LEARNING A NEW LANGUAGE

Children who enter schools in the United States who are literate in their home language—not English—are often expected to become proficient in speaking and comprehending English as they learn to read and write in English. Often teachers wonder how they can help students develop competency in English and how long this process might take. They are aware of the importance to literacy development of ELLs acquiring English-language proficiency.

Although teachers and schools want ELLs to learn English as fast as possible, it takes time. Current estimates are that it takes 3 to 5 years to achieve advanced proficiency in oral language (Genesee et al., 2005). Progress from initial learning to middle levels is fast, but progress from middle levels to advanced levels takes longer. August (2002) noted that acquiring academic English can take from 4 to 7 years. Not surprisingly, if ELLs use English more inside and outside the classroom, they improve and accelerate their English learning. Furthermore, ELLs who engage in conversation with teachers and peers make stronger gains (Chesterfield, Chesterfield, Hayes-Latimer, & Chavez, 1983).

Moreover, Strong (1984) observed that as ELLs develop oral proficiency in English, they have more opportunities to interact with other students and develop friendships with students who have other home languages. These friendships provide opportunities for additional practice in speaking and listening to English. Further, as ELLs engage in English conversations, their English-speaking competency becomes more complex, with a richer repertoire of language skills and use of academic English (Rodriguez-Brown, 1987).

While it takes time and conversation-rich environments to learn a new language, learning the new language is very much like learning a first language (Samway & McKeon, 1999). To learn a new language, there must be opportunities to communicate about real things and events. Children need places inside and outside the classroom to practice their new language where errors are accepted and recognized as part of the process of acquiring English.

TAKE A MOMENT

Picture a classroom where many of the ELLs speak Spanish as a home language. When the teacher groups students she wonders if she should place all of her ELLs in one group or disperse them throughout classroom groupings. What are the strengths and issues surrounding each of these placements?

Three Dimensions of Language Proficiency

There are three observable dimensions of language that develop concurrently: conversational fluency, discrete language skills, and academic language. They differ in several ways: (1) time to reach proficiency; (2)

experience and instruction to support their growth; (3) contexts where they are shared; and (4) components of language on which they rely (Cummins, 2003).

Conversational Fluency

Most children come to school with conversational fluency in place. This is the language of informal conversation that is supported by facial expressions, gestures, and so on. It occurs in school and out of school in places like the playground. ELLs typically develop this dimension within 1 to 3 years. Cummins (2003) has referred to this language competency as Basic Interpersonal Communicative Skills (BICS).

Discrete Language Skills

This dimension occurs as the result of direct instruction. It involves phonological, literacy, and grammar knowledge. For young students these skills are centered on letters, letter sounds, and decoding ability. ELLs learn these skills as they acquire English through development of vocabulary and conversational proficiency.

Academic Language Proficiency

Academic language is the more formal language of school. It involves the knowledge of less frequent vocabulary words, for example. Students who use academic language exhibit the ability to talk about summaries of text, write in active or passive voice, and discuss abstract concepts such as power or bravery. Academic language takes a considerable time for ELLs to develop, ranging from 5 to 7 years. Cummins (2003) has also labeled academic language as Cognitive Academic Language Proficiency (CALP).

Stages of Learning a New Language

Students tend to go through specific stages in learning English, but there is great variability in this process. First off, students come to school with varying competencies in using and understanding English (Cummins, 2003). Teachers will want to know the home language of students and how proficient they may be in speaking and understanding English as well. This knowledge helps in providing appropriate instruction. New York State has developed a home language questionnaire in several languages (e.g., Spanish, Chinese, Haitian-Creole, and Russian), which can be used to gain some knowledge about a student's proficiency from parents. These questionnaires can be downloaded from *www.emsc.nysed.gov/biling/hlq.htm.*

Second, students who are less inhibited in practicing the new language tend to make greater gains than those who are more reticent. Finally, teachers make a difference in the ease with which students come to learn English. In classrooms where there is space for conversations, both social and academic, students tend to become more adept in English (Bartolomé, 1998; Gutiérrez, 1995).

Although time to converse is important, teachers also adapt their own language patterns. They speak slower, use shorter sentences, paraphase and share a message in several ways, and explain word meanings. They also use gestures, pictures, and objects to make the meaning of their message clear. They avoid idioms as they are difficult for ELLs to understand. Teachers become aware of the language expectations of a lesson as well as its content expectations (Echevarria, Vogt, & Short, 2004).

In addition to proficiency with English, willingness to converse, and classroom discourse support, the age of a student plays a role in the development of English. Collier (1987) examined achievement test scores of ELLs. He found that students who were 8 to 11 years old when they entered U.S. schools took about 4 years to reach the 50th percentile on achievement tests. They achieved this performance level faster than younger or older students. Collier reasoned that they had learned to read and write in their home language and their task was solely to learn English. Younger students had to learn the new language and to read and write, and this required about 5 to 8 years before they reached the 50th percentile. The students who were at greatest risk for success in U.S. schools were those who were 12 or older. Few of them ever moved beyond the 40th percentile on achievement tests.

Children pass through several stages as they acquire a new language. Following are the identified stages of learning a new language (Echevarria et al., 2004; Krashen & Terrell, 1983):

■ *Stage 1: Silent/receptive stage or preproduction.* In this stage, students are becoming comfortable in the new setting. They begin to understand the comments of the teacher and other students. Students may use nonverbal communication like the shake of their head or pointing to a word or picture. Students do not respond verbally.

■ *Stage 2: Early production.* Students understand the main idea but not every word in the message. They may respond with one- to three-word groupings. Students begin to produce words that are frequently used in the classroom. They may mispronounce words.

■ *Stage 3: Speech emergence.* Students initiate simple sentences. They can use a more expansive vocabulary and pronunciation improves.

■ *Stage 4: Immediate fluency.* Students begin to use longer, more complex sentences. They may make errors as they use these more complex structures. They move from a translation stance to one where they think in the new language.

■ *Stage 5: Advanced fluency.* Students begin to converse as native speakers of English. They use academic discourse.

While students are at each stage, there are specific strategies to support ELL development that parallel the stages. In Figure 4.2 we pair the stage of language development with strategies that teachers may use to facilitate development to more complex use and understanding of English.

Parallel to understanding a student's stage of English acquisition and instruction is assessment. Figures 4.3 and 4.4 illustrate two structures to record observations of students' oral language proficiency. Figure 4.3 contains a checklist that a teacher can use during various periods of the year to document a student's growth. It includes both receptive and expressive language expectations. These observations can me made in the classroom or on the playground, among other locations. Figure 4.4 highlights a more holistic way to assess a student's oral language proficiency. This rubric provides a global placement of a student.

There are other ways to assess student oral proficiency that are grounded in specific classroom activities. For example, teachers can assess language production through observation of students engaged in:

■ Role playing
■ Giving directions
■ Participating in dramatic play
■ Sharing
■ Telling a story
■ Playing games

Stage	Instructional strategy
1. Silent/ receptive stage	1. Use of total physical response (Asher, 1977). Teacher or students act out an action that the student is to do (e.g., "Sit down," "Close the door"). 2. Use real objects (realia) or illustrations to facilitate comprehension. 3. Teachers ask students to: "Show me the dog." "In this story Matt is sad. Point to Matt."
2. Early production	1. Begin a sentence either as a command or a part of text—student completes it by filling in a word. 2. Ask yes or no questions. 3. Students share using an object such as a favorite toy. 4. Teachers might say: "In this story the witch is wicked. What is another word for wicked? She is not very nice. She was mean. Would you like to have a sister who is wicked or nice? Wicked? Nice?"
3. Speech emergence	1. Expand question format to *how* and *why* questions. 2. Provide opportunities for the student to practice English (e.g., partner or small-group work). 3. Provide language models that students use in responding—"The main idea is . . . "; "The meaning of *entertain* is . . . "; or "I predict this story is about. . . . " 4. Teachers provide time for daily sharing. This sharing moves beyond talking about an object. It might include talking about what happened outside of school. 5. Teachers might say: "In this story, Mike is sad because he can't find his dog. He thinks he is lost and he is not sure that he will find him. I would be very sad if I lost my dog. Do any of you have a dog? How would you feel if your dog was lost?"
4. Immediate fluency	1. Provide opportunities for the student to compare language (e.g., structures and idioms). 2. Provide opportunities for students to work in small groups. 3. Help students understand additional words for those they overuse such as nice. 4. Teachers might say: "We just read about Matilda. We learned that she loves to read but her parents don't. Can you think of another story we read where learning to read was important? How were the characters similar? What was different?" Or: "In our story, it said that she thought it might rain cats and *(continued)*

FIGURE 4.2. Stages of language development and instructional strategies.

Stage	Instructional strategy
	dogs. Do you think cats and dogs are going to fall from the sky? What might the author have meant? Is there an expression like this in your language?"
5. Advanced fluency	1. Focus on more abstract vocabulary. 2. Provide opportunities for students to work in small groups. 3. Teachers might say: "We read about the similarities and differences between frogs and toads. We are going to create a chart that lists these similarities and differences."

FIGURE 4.2. (*continued*)

By observing in a variety of settings, teachers get a deeper understanding of a child's use of English. If a teacher only observed while a child told a story, he or she would only get a partial view of a child's language knowledge, one that might negate other language strengths.

PRACTICES TO SUPPORT
ORAL LANGUAGE DEVELOPMENT

Several strategies have already been mentioned in this chapter. One of these involves the speech production of the teacher. The teacher thinks about his or her oral output and enunciates clearly. Rather than speeding up, the teacher slows down, uses shorter sentences, paraphrases, and so on. Another strategy is using illustrations, objects, or actions to support meaning getting where appropriate.

In conjunction with the above-mentioned strategies is the faith that a teacher has that a child can respond. It may take an ELL longer to respond or converse as he or she is thinking of the word or phrase in English, but providing this wait time allows such a student to contribute positively to the discussion. Moving on to another child diminishes the opportunities for this child to participate. Frequently the teacher may need to scaffold a response for a child, where he or she might respond with a yes or no. Eventually, this child will be able to provide longer, more complex responses with less teacher support.

Teachers can use a multitude of strategies to support understanding of their instruction in English as students become familiar with English. We list several of these possible supportive strategies.

Name: _____	Date: _____	
Receptive language—listening	YES	DETAILS
Understands language in social settings.		
Understands language in academic settings.		
Follows single-step directions.		
Follows multiple-step directions.		
Sorts by size, color, shape, etc., following directions of teacher.		
Understands temporal and spatial concepts like *first*, *last*, *in*, etc.		
Understands book language like *Once upon a time*, *the end*, *page*, etc.		
Other		
Expressive language—speaking	YES	DETAILS
Communicates personal needs.		
Responds to conversation of peers and teacher.		
Initiates conversation between peers or teacher.		
Names objects.		
Repeats phrases.		
Participates in academic conversation (whole class or small group).		
Retells a story.		
Uses subject–verb agreement.		
Uses correct word order.		
Asks questions.		
Other		

FIGURE 4.3. Receptive and expressive language observational assessment.

Name: _____	Date: _____
5	• Speaks in social and academic conversations. • Uses varied vocabulary including abstract words. • Speaks fluently. • Masters grammatical structures and word order.
4	• Engages in multiple turns in a conversation. • Varies sentence structure. • Expands vocabulary. • Participates in classroom academic conversations.
3	• Initiates conversations. • Retells a story. • Speaks hesitantly. • Has a limited vocabulary.
2	• Uses language for social needs. • Uses single words for responding. • Understands simple directions.
1	• Understands little or no English.Repeats words or phrases. • Uses single names for objects.

FIGURE 4.4. Holistic oral language assessment.

Small Groupings of Students

ELLs frequently find it difficult to converse with the whole class. Teachers find ways to informally group students so that they have multiple opportunities to engage in conversation. Teachers might ask students to discuss a prediction with a neighbor. They can include strategies like Think–Pair–Share, where students talk about a character, event, and so on with a partner before they share out loud with the class.

Students might also be arranged in small groups for projects. In these small groups, informal conversation is encouraged so that students get time to practice.

Sharing Time

Sharing is a common experience in preschool and kindergarten classrooms. If teachers ask children to bring personal objects tied to an instructional theme, students may find it easier to talk about them. They will be able to "borrow" some of the repeated language centered on the theme. For example, if the theme is focused on community helpers, a child might bring in a Rescue Hero® like Billy Blazes. He or she could talk about the figure and relate it to information he or she has about firemen.

Dramatic Play

Dramatic play, especially in centers, provides comfortable opportunities for young children to practice oral language. In pretending to be a waitress, for instance, the "performer" can ask other students what they want from a menu. In other centers the child may pretend to be a fireman or a policeman. In housekeeping, the child may role-play being a mother, father, or baby. Each of these centers should have props available to help students converse in English.

Puppet Play

When young children are reticent about speaking in small groups or to the whole class, using a puppet can often lessen their anxiety. For example, the puppet might be the one learning English. The teacher or another child can help the puppet learn to converse in English. The puppet might be the expert in translating the word in one language to another.

Storybook Reading

Although reading stories is a common occurrence in early-childhood classrooms, teachers need to consider the stories they choose to read to ELLs. For instance, many stories contain references to American culture or assume background knowledge that ELLs may not have. For example, many nursery rhymes and fairytales may not be familiar to ELLs. This does not mean that they should not be shared in the classroom. Rather, teachers may need to be more explicit in sharing each story. Perhaps taking time for conversation before reading to clarify potential points of confusion will be sufficient. In other cases, just paging through the book and chatting about the illustrations will clarify confusing parts or characters.

Teachers also need to explicitly identify literary terminology. They might say, "In the beginning of this book, we read . . . " or "I remember that in the middle of this story, Ann . . . " or "At the end they solved the problem by . . . " They may make a chart of the characters, labeling each one, or they could create a chart with the critical elements of the plot. Teachers explicitly share the important terminology related to books, stories, and informational text as well as discussing the meaning gathered through reading.

Teachers support students in gaining meaning by making connections to personal events or to other texts. For example, a character may feel sad because he or she couldn't find a friend in school. This situation provides an opportunity for students to talk about similar experiences and to gain a fuller understanding of this book and others related in theme.

One other consideration for teachers is the text they choose to read aloud. They should scan their selections and make sure that they represent children from many cultural backgrounds. For young children, teachers may start with simple, predictable text or text that has multiple languages within. Children will become comfortable with repeated patterns in text and may even repeat them when they hear them a second or third time. They will also listen when they hear their home language within a book. If teachers are not able to read a child's home language, they can enlist the help of parents or older brothers and sisters. Samples of these texts are shared in Figure 4.5.

Directed Listening–Thinking Activity

This active strategy is directed by the teacher and is geared to the comprehension strategy of prediction (Stauffer, 1975). Importantly, the teacher is reading the text to students as they listen. Following are the steps of this process:

1. Share the title of the book and the cover illustration. Students respond to the question, "What might this story be about?" Teachers might record the predictions on the chalkboard or on chart paper. Predictions should relate to the story guided by information from the title or cover illustration.

2. The teacher reads to an appropriate stopping place. At this point, the teacher can return to the predictions to determine which are supported by text and which should be discarded or revised. It is impor-

---

Repetitive structures
Asch, F. (1981). *Just like daddy*. New York: Simon & Schuster.
Carle, E. (1973). *Have you seen my cat?* New York: Philomel.
Martin, B. (1983). *Brown bear, brown bear, what do you see?* New York: Holt, Rinehart & Winston.

Rhyme
dePaola, T. (1985). *Hey diddle diddle and other Mother Goose rhymes*. New York: Putnam.
Messenger, J. (1986). *Twinkle, twinkle, little star*. New York: Macmillan.

Books with other languages included
Ancona, G. (1994). *The piñata maker: El piñatero*. San Diego: Harcourt Brace.
Emberly, R. (1990a). *My house: A book written in two languages*. Boston: Little, Brown. (Other books are available with Spanish and English.)
Haskins, J. (1992). *Count your way through Africa*. Minneapolis: Carolrhoda. (This book is repeated in numerous languages like Chinese, German, Japanese, Spanish, and so on.)
Levine, E. (1989). *I hate English*. New York: Scholastic.
Raschka, C. (1998). *Yo! Yes!* New York: Orchard Books.

FIGURE 4.5. Books for young children.

tant that students do not see this as a right or wrong event. Authors can write the story in a variety of ways; rather, the students are determining whether their predictions match the author's writing. Teachers may ask students to think about what might happen next. This process may result in new predictions.

3. Teachers may repeat this process at subsequent stopping points. For young children one stopping point is usually sufficient.

4. After reading, the teacher once again draws students' attention to the predictions. They determine which predictions were supported in text. Teachers may guide students back into text to find the places where their predictions were verified.

CD-ROM Storybooks and Other Electronic Support Products

CD-ROM storybooks are books (CD versions) that are placed into a computer. A child who interacts with such a book has a variety of choices. He or she can listen to the story in English or in Spanish (a few other languages like French or German may be available). The child can point to words and the computer will read them. He or she can click on numerous places on the screen and butterflies may fly, doors may open, and so on. Shamir and Korat (2006) provide guidelines to help teachers select CD-ROM books. They suggest that teachers consider the content of the book, a child's ability to control the reading, and other features to find appropriate CD-ROM books.

Teachers can also use other books or activities that are supported electronically. Some of these products involve students responding by pointing to a letter that the book or game pronounces. Other products expect students to follow a story in a similar way to the CD-ROM text. These materials provide additional support for young students during independent time in a classroom. They allow ELLs to hear words and see them written in text multiple times for instance.

Wordless Books

Because wordless books have few or no words, they provide an illustrated text that children can narrate. Children could tell the story in their home language and later with support create this same story in

English (Xu, 2003). These books are especially important for families that rely on their home language for communication. Parents and their child can interact with these stories in their home language without trying to decipher English words.

Language Experience Approach

When teachers use the Language Experience Approach (Carrasquillo & Rodriquez, 2002), they record the words of students and form a text that will be read by the children on repeated occasions. For very young students, the teacher might record only a few sentences and then use the students' names so that they can find the part they offered. For instance, the teacher would write "Mary said, 'The spider is scary.' " For older students, the text might be longer with names omitted.

The process for creating a language experience chart is as follows:

1. The teacher shares an object that stirs discussion among students. (We use a hermit crab here for our example.)
2. When conversation slows down, the teacher puts away the object.
3. The teacher then encourages students to offer comments about the object that the teacher records. (We recommend using an overhead as the teacher can see students as or she records the message. Also, the overhead makes it easy to produce a copy for students' individual reading.)
4. The teacher points to words as they are recorded and models speech-to-print match. The teacher models left-to-right writing, punctuation, and so on. There is an issue that teachers need to consider as they record a student's words. If a child uses ungrammatical English like "me and my mom," should the teacher record it as is or change it? If the teacher corrects it and writes "My mom and I," the child may read it as "me and my mom." We recommend writing it the way the child has offered it, knowing that with modeling the child will learn the correct form. Teachers may find this difficult to do and may make the corrections. If this happens, the teachers must provide guided practice so that the child reads the text as written.
5. The teacher, with student support, reads the text.

6. The teacher and students reread the text.

7. The text is returned to each day until students have mastered it.

Figure 4.6 shows a language experience text for young students and a similar version for older students.

Media Center

In the media center, the teacher may have CDs or tapes to which children can listen. Through listening children will become familiar with stories and also the sounds of English. If the center has a computer, children can listen to a book that may be familiar, perhaps one adapted from a favorite television show. Following listening, they could visit the website that highlights the show. A media center can offer children multiple opportunities for linguistic input.

Centers

Centers provide relevant materials that support conversation (Morrow, 2005). In a science center children can talk about what they see under a magnifying glass, what a turtle does, or what objects float or sink. In a social studies center they can explore a globe and flags. In an art center they can paint or manipulate clay. In a math center, they can weigh objects or balance them. These centers provide concrete experiences that support language production.

For young students

The Hermit Crab

Ricardo said, "He has a shell."

Marta said, "He moved on the rock."

Tyler said, "He is inside his shell."

For older students

Hubert the Hermit Crab

The hermit crab is sitting on the rock. He doesn't want to move.

We put him in a little bit of water and he moved fast. We could see his legs.

When we took him out, he went to sleep.

FIGURE 4.6. Language experience text.

TAKE A MOMENT

Think about the strategies and recommendations for oral language support just discussed. What other strategies or recommendations might be added to this list?

METALANGUAGE

Metalanguage is a concept where language becomes a focus or object of study (Watson, 2001). As children develop fluency in oral communication in any language, they become aware of elements of language such as letters, words, sentences, and so on. The awareness of these elements becomes important as children begin to investigate the text. For instance, in learning to decode, children become aware of the sounds represented by letters, which they combine in a left-to-right movement to form words. They learn that in text, words are separated by spaces, and so on. For children who are new to English, learning about English words can be very different from learning words in their home language. To represent one word in English may take several words in another language, or a word may be represented by characters rather than letters.

Papandropoulou and Sinclair (1974) explored how young children think about language, particularly what they think about words. Figure 4.7 presents a partial transcript of Paulo trying to explain what a word is. The format is borrowed from Papandropoulou and Sinclair.

In this example, it is easy to discover that for Paulo a word is anything he can do. When asked about *the*, he paused for a full 5 seconds. Then he decided it was a word because he can say *the* things. Similarly, he saw *from the house* as one word because he can go in the house.

Paulo follows the pattern discovered by Papandropoulou and Sinclair. He decided that a word is a word if there is an object or action attached to it. He also matched time to a short and a long word. Sleeping is long and being at the computers is a short word. When asked what a word is, he resorted to saying, "Halloween."

This example demonstrates that learning the language centered on language, such as what a word or sentence is, is a complicated process. Children come to school typically not aware of this aspect of language

TEACHER: Is *table* a word?

PAULO: Yes, sometimes I sit at a table.

TEACHER: Is *the* a word?

PAULO: (*5-second pause*) Yes, when I say "the things" my dad will say "the things" too.

TEACHER: Is *give* a word?

PAULO: Yes, sometimes I give stuff.

TEACHER: Is *from the house* a word?

PAULO: Yes, you can go in the house.

TEACHER: Tell me a long word.

PAULO: *When I go to sleep.* I sleep a long time.

TEACHER: Tell me a short word.

PAULO: *Computers.* I am only there a short time.

TEACHER: Tell me what is a word.

PAULO: *Halloween* is a word.

FIGURE 4.7. Paulo's "What Is a Word?"

knowledge. It takes explicit instruction on the part of the teacher to help students acquire this knowledge. The foregoing example also provides a view into how students who are learning English may be confused as they participate in learning activities in the classroom. For instance, when the teacher talks about letters or words, they may not have an exact understanding of what these are.

PHONOLOGICAL AWARENESS

Phonological awareness is the umbrella term used to orally distinguish units of speech, like words and syllables. Phonemic awareness falls under this umbrella and it refers to the ability to identify phonemes in words and to manipulate them (e.g., take the *s* off of *seat* and what word remains). Importantly, this is an oral understanding of parts of words like syllables and phonemes. There are several expectations for children under the phonological awareness umbrella (Adams, 1990; Armbruster, Lehr, & Osborn, 2001). They include:

1. Identify rhymes and produce rhymes (e.g., "What rhymes with *bear*?").
2. Identify number of syllables in a word (e.g., "There are two syllables in *okay*.").
3. Identify onsets and rimes (e.g., "The first part of *tin* is *t* and the last part is *in*.").
4. Blend or split syllables (e.g., "Put *br* and *ead* together. The word is. . . . " or "What words are in the word *inside*?").
5. Identify the number of phonemes (e.g., "How many phonemes are in *dog*?").
6. Manipulate phonemes.
   a. Phoneme isolation ("What is the first sound in *house*?").
   b. Phoneme identity ("What sound is the same in *fat, fun,* and *fig*?").
   c. Phoneme categorization ("Which word does not belong from the list?")
   d. Phoneme blending ("Combine phonemes to create a word: *m-a-n*.").
   e. Phoneme segmentation ("Divide this word into its phonemes.").
   f. Phoneme deletion ("Take the *t* off of *train* and you have. . . . ").
   g. Phoneme addition ("Add *s* to *peak* and what word do you have?").
   h. Phoneme substitution ("Change the *m* in *man* to a *t* and you have. . . . ").

Similar to the previous discussion about metalanguage, phonological awareness is not something that is implicitly understood by most children. Explicit instruction is often needed for children to acquire this foundational literacy knowledge. Phonemes are abstractions and are complicated. For example, in the word *dog* there are three phonemes, in *chip* there are three as well, and in *chain* there are three. So even if a person could spell the word, the number of letters does not match the number of phonemes necessarily.

Moreover, phonemes are different in various languages. For instance, Spanish and English share the following consonant sounds (*b, d, f, g, k, l, m, n, p, t, w, y*) (Goldstein, 2000). Students whose home language is Spanish may not have difficulty with the aforementioned phonemes; however, they may have problems learning phonemes not represented in their home language. Helman (2004) shared possible pronunciation errors that Spanish-speaking youngsters may have. They may pronounce the *d* in *den* as *then*, *j* in *joke* as *choke*, or the *v* in *van* as *ban*. To further complicate matters, in Spanish there are phonological differences among Spanish-speaking groups (Pérez & Torres-Guzmán, 1992). Pérez and Torres-Guzmán report that Puerto Rican students may pronounce an *l* at the end of a word as an *r* (*amol* for *amor*).

In some languages like Chinese and Japanese phonemes do not exist. The smallest unit in these languages is a syllable. To further complicate things, Korean can be analyzed at the phoneme level, so not all Asian languages are the same. And although Korean can be analyzed at the phoneme level, not all words can be analyzed by considering the sounds at the beginning, middle, and end as in English. Given the ways that a Korean word is written, often the reference is to say the upper-left sound, upper-right sound, and bottom sound. Learning about a child's home language helps teachers understand when a child has difficulty with a concept like phonemes in English.

Teachers of young children do not need to spend a significant amount of time teaching phonological activities (about 20 hours in an academic year), but they do need to teach children about the sounds of language. Teachers need to recognize that phonological awareness is critical to students' later reading development (Adams, 1990; Armbruster et al., 2001). Similarly, they need to understand that phonics and phonological awareness are not the same thing. Phonological awareness is about understanding the sounds of a language. Phonics is about understanding the connection between letters and sounds or the representation of sounds through writing.

Teaching Phonological Awareness

Rhyming

Have children listen to rhymes and model which words rhyme. Students might add to the list of words that rhyme. For example, if in the rhyme, they discover that *hat* and *mat* rhyme, they could add *fat* or *bat*.

Counting Syllables

During read-aloud, the teacher could have students clap the syllables in words. Later students might move a tile for each syllable they hear in a word. So they would move two tiles for a word like *happy*.

Onset–Rime

Teachers would provide several words that where students identify the onset and then the rime—for example, *t-ap*, *r-ide*, or *m-ug*.

Phoneme Manipulation

Using the previous list, teachers guide students through phoneme isolation to phoneme substitution. They might also use tiles, where students move a tile for each phoneme they hear in a word. Thus if the teacher says "run," the students would move three tiles and pronounce each phoneme: *r-u-n*. Letters would not be on the tiles; the teacher is checking for awareness of the number of phonemes.

We have found that teachers engage students in phonological awareness activities at the beginning of a whole-group reading lesson. They might do a few phonological awareness activities just before reading a story. Later, they might return to the text to highlight rhyming words. Often, their core reading program provides daily phonological awareness activities.

For children who require more systematic instruction, systematic phonological awareness programs are available. *Road to the Code* (Blachman, Ball, Black, & Tangel, 2000) is one text that has a research base to support its effectiveness. There are 44 lessons in this text that build a child's phonological knowledge. Most of the activities require a student to move tiles to represent phonemes. There is careful structuring of the activities and explicit teacher modeling throughout. In our observations, we have seen ELLs benefit from active engagement with a difficult concept like phonemes.

FINAL THOUGHTS

The issue of oral language development and the timing of literacy instruction is one that permeates conversations among teachers and researchers. However, there are a variety of answers. The National Research Council reported (Snow et al., 1998) that reading in English should be delayed until students have a small amount of oral English proficiency. The International Reading Association (2001) concurred and added in its resolution targeting second-language literacy instruction that whenever possible ELLs should receive literacy instruction in their home language first or simultaneously with learning of oral English and reading and writing. They write, "Literacy learning in a second language can be successful, it is riskier than starting with a child's home language—especially for those children affected by poverty, low levels of parental education, or poor schooling" (n.p.).

Fitzgerald (1995a) questions a one-way relationship (oral language then reading instruction) as she does not see correlational studies as providing sufficient support for either position—English orality must precede English reading instruction or vice versa. She further explains that the research base is mixed regarding orality and reading instruction. In her work with Noblit (Fitzgerald & Noblit, 1999) she affirms that orality and literacy can develop together. Other researchers (Elley, 1998; Gersten, 1996) suggest that as ELLs are involved in reading instruction, especially comprehension work, their oral language development is increased.

In support of Fitzgerald, the executive summary for *Developing Literacy in Second-Language Learners* (August & Shanahan, 2006b) noted that even though learning to read and write in a child's home language has benefits, this support is not necessary for ELLs to become successful readers of English. They indicate that more current studies are showing support for instruction in only English (*www.cal.org/natl-lit-panel/reports/Executive_Summary.pdf*).

Pragmatically, most teachers engage students in learning to read and write as they develop their oral language proficiency. Fortunately, the research indicates a bidirectional support for oral language and reading and writing proficiency. As students increase their oral language proficiency they simultaneously increase reading and writing proficiency. Conversely, as they increase their reading and writing proficiency, there is a similar increase in oral language proficiency.

CHAPTER 5

Encouraging All Students to Become Writers

> Writing is not merely a tool for transmitting knowledge; it is also a source of knowledge; it is not only a problem space but also a resource for dealing with language and thought.
>
> —TOLCHINSKY (2006, p. 84)

Young children become talkers at around 19 months of age (Hart & Risley, 1999). Writing development follows oral language development and typically occurs when a child is 3 (Shanahan, 2006). Shanahan (2006) writes that written language takes longer than oral language to develop fully, but it "has the potential to be affected by oral language and reading, and likewise can influence the development of those systems" (p. 171). Similar to talking, young children want to write (Graves, 2004)—they just need opportunities to do so.

What exactly is writing? The response to this question varies and often depends on who is being asked and when. Thus, for example, a young child might respond that he or she is writing:

- A story
- A name
- Letters
- Numbers

Other responses for children and adults might include:

- A journal
- The alphabet
- A narrative
- A recipe

- A letter
- A form
- A report
- A novel

- A list
- An email message
- A text message
- A web page

From this small list of possible forms of writing, it is clear how expansive writing is and how, through a gradual process, students come to learn about these choices.

As well as learning potential forms of writing, children learn the many purposes of writing, which include to represent, to learn, to inform, to describe, to convince, to entertain, to problem solve, to remember, to reflect, and so on.

Clearly, learning to write is not just about learning the alphabet and sound–symbol relationships and putting them on paper. It results in a cognitive change for the child—for the acquisition of writing transforms a child's view of language. When children write, they have a fixed representation of oral language. They can explore it, as it doesn't vanish like a spoken word. They learn about representing words and ideas through marks. They learn about the way words are represented in their language. They learn how to compose sentences and longer text structures.

Tolchinsky (2003) writes about first understandings of print and what they might be. She says that often we believe that babies only gaze at the faces of people near them. She argues that there is no reason that they wouldn't observe animals, advertisements, clocks, and so on. Thus from infancy print becomes a part of a young child's world. Moreover, Tolchinsky expands our views of the ways young children might come to writing. We tend to think that young children are first exposed to print as their parents read picture books to them or when they are given a crayon and paper on which to record marks. However, Tolchinsky says that in today's world, children might first explore writing electronically on a computer, and a mouse may be their first writing implement. In this scenario, writing on paper would follow the understanding of writing on a computer.

In this chapter, we explore how children come to understand writing. In this discussion we share important benchmarks and writing examples from children. We end the chapter with activities that support the writing development of young ELL children.

At the end of this chapter, you will be able to:

- Describe the process of learning about writing.
- Describe and identify various writing milestones.
- Describe the importance of learning about concept of word in print.
- Describe multiple strategies to support writers.

LEARNING TO WRITE

Making Marks

At about 18 months, children begin writing by making marks (Gibson & Levin, 1980). Tolchinsky (2006) describes this writing as similar to a young child's babbling. In babbling a sound is important, and in this first writing the mark is important. Interestingly if a child is given a pencil or pen that does not leave a mark, he or she discards it. The visible representation is necessary for the child to continue with the implement. Early writing is also a noisy endeavor as it is often accompanied by talk and drawing (Bissex, 1980). Children rely on talk as they write and they often use drawing to support and extend their written message (Dyson, 1988).

Drawing and Writing

Levin and Bus (2003) studied the early drawing and writing of young children. They discovered that until about 3, young children's writing and drawing are similar. However, at about age 3, children make larger scribbles for drawing and smaller, tighter scribbles for writing. Brenneman, Massey, Machado, and Gelman (1996) noted that even more than size separates drawing from writing. In drawing, young children use large, circular scribbling strokes. For writing, they take their hand off the page and stop and start their writing. Importantly, while the child is conveying a message through this early writing and drawing, an outsider without information from the child would not be able to read it.

For the youngest children, and in particular ELLs, often the way into writing is through drawing. In Figure 5.1 Hieberto used his knowledge of basketball to compose his text, thus creating a multimedia text. He drew a part of a basketball game with his favorite players, Sheldon Williams from

FIGURE 5.1. Hieberto's basketball drawing.

Duke University's Blue Devils (which he drew in blue) and Ray Allen from the Seattle SuperSonics (which he drew in green). As he drew he talked about the players and basketball. His mother recorded the names of the players for him, so that he was able to see their names become print. Similar to earlier scribbling, Hieberto is relying on others to fill in important details of his story-drawing. For instance, there is no basketball or net present to help someone understand this is a basketball story.

Dyson (2001) describes this story-drawing process as one in which children use the more representative media first—drawing, talk, or gestures—to convey a message. As their writing proficiency matures, they rely less on drawing in particular as the primary way to convey meaning. She reminds us that children *symbol weave* as they write messages where many different forms of meaning occur simultaneously (e.g., as seen in Figure 5.1, where Hieberto drew, talked, and dictated his message). In addition, children often rely on popular media as sources for their text. While Hieberto chose basketball, other children may choose cartoons, television shows, or movies to form their texts.

Making Meaning

At first, when children write, they are focused on meaning. For instance, they may make a long squiggle to represent a horse and a short one to represent a frog. The line's length is related to the size of the animal (Ferreiro & Teberosky, 1985).

Teachers also recognize the focus on meaning when they take dictation from a young child. Often the child talks about what should be recorded at a rapid speed, so rapid that the teacher cannot record it. What is interesting is that the child does not seem to take notice of the teacher's recording of his or her language. Later as the child makes stronger connections between oral language and writing, he or she will wait for the teacher to finish recording a phrase before producing new commentary.

In addition, the focus on meaning is evident is in a scribble drawn by a child that represents a whole story. The child's writing is interwoven with drawing and speech as a message is recorded. The story is a scribble that has features of writing and drawing within it. Figure 5.2 presents an example of such writing. When just looking at the figure, it appears to be one undecipherable scribble. However, this scribble represents a full retelling of a ride on a roller coaster. Carlos, while sitting next to his teacher, told her and wrote about his ride on a roller coaster and how it went up and down. If Carlos's teacher hadn't been next to him, this scribble would have been just that, an undecipherable scrib-

FIGURE 5.2. Carlos's roller coaster story.

ble. These texts are often unrecognized as they take the child to interpret them while they are created.

What Is and Isn't Writing

Children first focus on three aspects of writing: (1) differing lengths of writing strings; (2) spaces between words; and (3) graphic variations in size and shape. We talk about lengths of writing strings and graphic variation in this section. Later in this chapter, we thoroughly discuss the recognition of concept of word in print or the spaces between words.

At first, children believe that many letters represent something that is bigger. This demonstrates similar thinking to the idea that a long scribble represents something big. So when they write, children produce long random letter strings to represent a large thing abstractly (e.g., many letters for elephant and a few for mouse). Following this logic, children show confusion when comparing the names of an adult who has a short name and a child who has a long name. Such situations often create changes in a child's thinking beyond such a physical representation of meaning.

Ferreiro and Teberosky (1985) noted that the number and kinds of letters were important for a child to determine whether a word in print is a word. Children from 4 to 7 expected words to have at least three letters. Thus, following their reasoning *to* is not a word but *cat* is. Also, they worried about whether a word was readable when it had too many letters.

Children also considered the kinds of letters that formed a word. They did not believe that a word with a single repeated letter was a word (e.g., *MMMMMM*); they wanted to see variety in letters. Tolchincky (2003) also reported that 5-year-old children expect a combination of consonants and vowels in words before they are able to map sounds to symbols. They are sensitive to possible and impossible combinations of letters. She shared that when young Spanish children are requested to look through a series of letters to determine whether they are real words, they elected combinations of letters that could be possible combinations in Spanish—they considered the letters and the configuration of letters to make their determinations.

As children continue in their writing understanding, they begin to experiment with several principles documented by Clay (1975). In the recurring principle, children learn that a limited amount of letters appear again and again in words. Often children write by using the letters from their name over and over again, believing that each variation is a new word, thus demonstrating the generativity principle. For instance, Joey wrote OEYOE, OEYOEYOE, and EYOEO. He continued with variations of his name to represent a multitude of words for an entire journal page.

Harste, Woodward, and Burke (1984) observed that young children's scribbling for writing also represents their home language. In their study, young children's scribbling of Arabic, Hebrew, and English resembled each language. Children included distinguishing marks of their language, thus showing their careful attention to written language from a very young age.

Name Writing

Typically the earliest conventional written word by most children is their name (Bloodgood, 1999; Ferreiro & Teberosky, 1985). Liberman (1985) noted that young children often use the letters within their name to represent other words (as in the previous example of Joey's writing). Thus one's name becomes the genesis for the representation of multiple words.

Learning to write one's name is no easy task. Children need sufficient motor control to shape the letters within their name. As this motor control develops, children often represent the letters in their name with letter-like forms that gradually more closely represent the conventional configuration of the designated letter. They must remember the configuration of each letter in their name and its order within their name and realize that there is no flexibility in this order of letters. Finally, they must recognize that letters are separate units with spaces between them (McGee & Richgels, 1996). Figure 5.3 shows several snapshots of Gerard's name-writing development throughout preschool. The first snapshot shows a scribble that begins with a form similar to a G. He then moves to a more expansive scribble that shows some spacing between letters. His third representation more closely resembles letters. His fourth example is just the letter G. At this time, he refused to make the other letters as he said he did not know how. By the end of his preschool experience he was able to conventionally represent the letters in his name with spaces between each of them.

We have found two very special books that tie in to students' names, although they move beyond just writing a name. The first book,

FIGURE 5.3. Gerard's name writing.

The Name Jar (Choi, 2001), shares the story of a young Korean girl and her entry to U.S. school. Her name is difficult to pronounce in the United States and she considers taking on an American name. Children in her classroom help her with this project and they collect names in a jar. The book ends with her retaining her Korean name. The second book, *My Name Is Yoon* (Recorvits, 2003) is about another little Korean girl. In this book, she writes her name in Korean and English. Throughout the book she shares her frustrations and successes in learning to read and write in English. We believe that these books enrich the name writing experience and allow children to consider the importance of a name and how names are written in other languages.

TAKE A MOMENT

Think about all the elements involved in coming to understand writing. Now brainstorm several ways that parents and teachers of young children can support this important development. Think about learning to write your name in one language and later learning to write it in English. What challenges does a child face? Keep this list and use it later in this chapter where several ways to support student writing are shared. Use your list to expand on what has been presented.

WRITING DEVELOPMENT

Thanks to the work of Charles Read (1975), educators came to understand that there was a typical development in writing knowledge as shown through children's invented spellings of words. Read accomplished two major results through his work: (1) educators learned about the interesting developmental errors of children, and (2) his work opened the door for very young children to be engaged in writing activities from their first entrance into school. Once the expectation moved from conventional spelling that resulted in handwriting practice and copying to providing opportunities for meaning making in writing with best-guess spelling, preschool curricula changed to accommodate this new view of writing. Soon writing centers with a variety of writing implements appeared in preschool, kindergarten, and primary classrooms.

Richgels (2001) notes that Read's work allowed children to write and through this writing they practiced phonemic awareness. He sees writing and phonemic awareness linked as young children write letter by letter and often can be heard orally sounding each letter before they commit it to paper. These observations led Read to discover that children brought much unconscious knowledge to the task of writing. For instance, when asking a child why he or she used an *a* to represent the long sound of *a* in the word *cane*, the child could not articulate the reason. As Read noted this behavior in several children, he realized that the children were using the letter name to represent long-vowel sounds. It took more development before they realized that in most words representing long vowels takes multiple letters, as in *cane, plain,* or *may.*

Closely following the work of Read, Henderson (1990) at the University of Virginia launched several studies that targeted children's stages of word development as demonstrated in their invented spelling. His early work has been extended through the work of many doctoral studies, and this body of work centered on invented spelling and corresponding instruction has come to be known as the Virginia Studies. We share the stages of writing development as documented by this work. Although there are a variety of names used for these stages or, more currently, phases of development, we use the following terms to describe this development: *prephonemic, semiphonemic, letter name, within word pattern, syllable juncture,* and *derivational constancy* (Bear & Barone, 1998). We believe this work provides a window into students' writing development in English, especially as ELLs become proficient in writing.

Prephonemic Writing

Prephonemic is the earliest writing that children do. It may look like scribbling as shown in several examples in this chapter or it can consist of random letters or numerals. The important aspect of this writing is that children are not yet representing phonemes in words, and as a result, their work cannot be read without their assistance.

In our experience, when we have asked children to read this writing, they may respond with a different reading each time. If there is a drawing, they rely on the drawing for their reading, with variations in what they believe they represented. They might say, "It is basketball," or "They are playing basketball." Or, they may respond, "I know how to write, but I don't know how to read. You read it," leaving an adult puzzled as to what to do.

Semiphonemic Writing

When children are identified as writing semiphonemically, they are representing some phonemes, typically the first and last. This writing is much more difficult than prephonemic writing. In prephonemic writing, children just fill the space with their marks. However, once a child understands that letters and sounds are related, they struggle to record the correct letter on their paper for the sound they want to represent. This process takes considerable energy; teachers and parents often describe the intense sounding out that young children do as they search for the right letter, and the resulting production is less. Children will sometimes combine both of these phases of development in that they start to represent words by phonemes and then scribble or use random symbols to fill the page. Figure 5.4 shows how Niki began using phonemes in her writing (MI ANML) and then she used random letters to complete her thought about an animal that lives in the forest. In Figure 5.5 Tai wrote about seeing a rainbow: "I see a rainbow." Importantly, she has represented the most salient phonemes, with rainbow getting three phonemes for the beginning, middle, and end of the word. As children start to use phonemes their writing is easier to read by others and does not need as much support from the writer. Their reading of their writing is also similar from reading to reading.

Tolchinsky (2003) describes semiphonemic writing in several languages. She notes that children use the letters, consonants, or vowels

FIGURE 5.4. Niki's writing.

that are most frequent in their home language. Thus English-speaking children use consonants most frequently, as seen in Figures 4.4 and 4.5. However, although Hebrew children also rely on consonants, Spanish children most often use vowels. A few reasons for this behavior are that vowels are more stable in sound in Spanish and there are only five (in English there are at least 14 vowel sounds).

Letter-Name Writing

Letter-name writing is considered a pivotal point in a young child's writing development. Here children represent each phoneme within a word,

FIGURE 5.5. Tai's rainbow writing.

and at this time spaces also appear between words (see the next section for a more detailed discussion) (Bear, Invernizzi, Templeton, & Johnston, 2003). Not surprisingly, children make interesting errors during this time. They use a one-to-one correspondence strategy so each phoneme gets one letter. This is why long-vowel words are represented with a single letter—CAK for *cake*—and words with digraphs are also represented by one letter—CIP for *chip*. Children hear the two sounds but they rely on their one letter for each sound strategy resulting in simplified spellings. Read (1975) also discovered that children used the previous short vowel to represent the vowel they were attempting, so when writing *pin*, they would write *pen*. There is a complicated description of why children are doing these substitutions that has to do with the great vowel shift. A simple way to get at what children are doing is to say "bade" out loud, then say "bed." You should notice that your tongue is in a similar place in your mouth. Children unconsciously use this information and they use the long-vowel letter to represent the short-vowel sound.

In Figure 5.6, Jerry demonstrates his letter-name strategy as he writes: "Es mi amigo." Although he has not represented each phoneme, he has represented most phonemes in his writing. While his teacher provided a translation, his writing is easy to read.

In Figure 5.7 Angela was asked to write words in a developmental spelling inventory (Bear et al., 2003; Bear & Barone, 1989). Her teacher wanted to discover the strategies she used to represent words. Her teacher asked her to write single-syllable words (*bed*, *ship*, *drive*, *bump*, and *when*). Angela wrote *bed* as *bat*. She knew the beginning phoneme, used the *a* substitution for *e*, and then put a random phoneme at the end. For *ship*, she used the *s* to represent the digraph *sh*, and then once again used the *a* for the vowel, and she correctly used the *p* at the end. For *drive*, she relied on sound, a *g* for *d*, and did not represent the *r*. (Adults rarely enunciate the *dr*; rather they make a sound more like *g*.) She then used an *i* for long *i* and a *v* for the final phoneme. *Bump* can be explained in a similar fashion to *bed*, and when writing *when*, Angela was tired and relied on a semiphonemic strategy.

Within-Word Pattern

Children who are described as using a within-word pattern represent all the phonemes in single-syllable words. They may confuse how to represent a long-vowel pattern (*maek* for *make*), but they know that using just a

FIGURE 5.6. Jerry's letter-name writing.

single *a* for a long-*a* word does not work. They have experienced the confusion of representing words with a single letter and then trying to read words like *can* and *cane* where can is used for both. In Figure 5.8, Sam wrote about how he likes cookies. His spelling of *like* is typical of within-word-pattern writers in that he knows the *i* will not be sufficient to represent the long-*i* pattern, so he writes *ie* for the long-*i* pattern.

Syllable Juncture and Derivational Constancy Writing

We have collapsed these categories as they are infrequently observed in the primary grades. Children who are considered syllable juncture writers represent most single-syllable words correctly. They struggle with adding affixes to words. Their dilemmas center around dropping letters or doubling letters as in *hopping* or *hoping*. They also ponder whether *cattle* is spelled with an *el* or *le*.

Children who are derivational writers can write most words correctly. They are exploring the meaning aspects of English. They learn that sound may change but spelling holds constant, as in *revise* and *revision* (Templeton, 1983). They explore the roots of words so that they see the connection between roots and meaning, as in words with *mal* or

FIGURE 5.7. Angela's spelling.

bene. Finally, they take on the schwa sound and learn that it can be represented by any vowel and finding related words will help with spelling, as in *inspire* and *inspiration.*

Research endeavors focused on writing development in other languages report similar development. Chi (1988) studied Chinese children in Taiwan to note their writing development. She found that even in a logographic system children's development paralleled what has been described for alphabetic languages. Children began with scribbling by using pictures. They then moved to using strokes that were unrecognizable to strokes that were interpretable. Then they represented characters that were readable and moved to making characters that were homonyms (same pronunciation but different meaning) to conventional formation of characters.

CONCEPT OF WORD IN PRINT

Concept of word is the understanding that words, when written, are marked with spaces between them (Morris, 1980, 1993). This concept

FIGURE 5.8. Sam's within-word-pattern writing.

occurs even in nonalphabetic languages, as each word/character (e.g., Chinese, Korean, Japanese) has a square shape, and the size is consistent across words/characters. Each English word, however, has its unique size and length, depending on the letter shape and number of letters in a word.

Frequently teachers and parents are unaware of how sophisticated this concept is and fail to notice its development. Children move from hearing words in a speech stream with no discernible breaks within words to awareness that in writing there are breaks between words. Often this understanding requires children to use marks to separate words before they are comfortable with spaces. Teachers and parents will notice dots and dashes between words that mark their boundaries. In Figure 5.9, Kennady wrote about a bird that visits her. She has used small circles to mark the separation between each word.

Figure 5.10 is a sample of a child's full understanding of concept of word in print. Carlos wrote about children being in a boat. He no longer needs dots or dashes to separate words. Carlos was in a bilingual first-grade class and he learned to write in both Spanish and English. His concept of word in print developed concurrently in both languages.

Concept of word is easily assessed by observing students' writing. The foregoing samples provide a window into this understanding.

Children who are prephonemic writers clearly do not understand how words are represented in print. They are learning about letter configurations and letter–sound correspondences. Children who are semiphonemic writers have a partial understanding of concept of word in print. They can track words until there are multisyllabic words in text. For example, if they are pointing to the words in a simple, memorized poem like "One, Two, Buckle My Shoe," they will have no trouble reading and pointing to *one, two*. However, when they come to *buckle*, they will say *buck* and then *le* while pointing to *my*. They might correct by pointing to *shoe* and saying *my* and *shoe* or they might go back to the beginning to try to figure out why their finger pointing doesn't match up to each word. Once children are letter-name writers, they have concept of word. They may demonstrate this concept early on by using dots or dashes between words, but quite quickly they feel comfortable just leaving spaces between words. And they can read and point to words, quickly correcting when they are off because of a multisyllabic word.

Concept of word in print is critical to reading and writing proficiency. When teachers ask children to compare words or find the first word in a sentence, a child who does not have concept of word is un-

FIGURE 5.9. Kennady's writing.

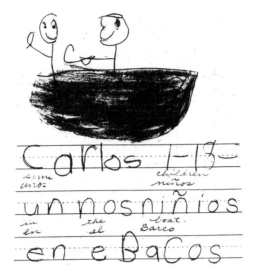

FIGURE 5.10. Carlos's writing.

able to do this. Children who have concept of word are able to track print and are developing into beginning readers and writers, where they can read or write one whole word at a time, rather than relying on each letter (Bear & Barone, 1998).

TAKE A MOMENT

Think about the writing development that we have shared. What can teachers learn by closely observing student writing?

LOOKING CLOSELY AT ELL WRITERS

Much of the information shared in this chapter comes from research done with children writing in English who have English as a home language. We share this information because it provides a window to the expected development of ELLs in English as well. Fitzgerald (2001) summarized the current research on ELLs' writing development. The first question she pursued was, "Is the development of ELLs' writing similar to first-language development?" In her exploration of studies, she found that most documented similar trajectories. There was one study that provided interesting information about spelling development in Spanish–English. Davis, Carlisle, and Beeman (1999) found that Spanish students learning English had extensive growth in English spelling in first and second grade. Later in third grade, they made greater advances in Spanish spelling.

Fitzgerald also pursued a second question: "Is there a transfer of knowledge from first-language writing to second-language writing?" She indicated that when reviewing studies focused on transfer, the results supported transfer of skills from one language to another. Figure 5.10 shows this transfer, where Carlos transferred his understanding of concept of word from English to Spanish.

In a third question focused on phonemic awareness and spelling, Fitzgerald did find differences for ELLs. Similar to children whose home language is English, phonological processing was related to writing and spelling for ELLs (Arab-Moghadam & Sénéchal, 2001). However, Fitzgerald reported contradictory findings in other research where Cantonese, Mandarin, Gujarati, Urdu, and Punjabi speakers had less developed phonemic awareness but performed better in spelling (Wade-Woolley & Siegel, 1997). Further complicating this research is a third study (Jackson, Holm, & Dodd, 1998) that reported that bilingual Cantonese children performed equivalently to English preschoolers in phonological awareness and spelling. Although once these children moved to first grade, monolingual children outperformed them in spelling less familiar words and in complicated phonemic tasks.

Edelsky (1982) discovered that children kept separations between their home language and English when writing. For instance, when writing in Spanish, children used accents and tildes, but not when writing in English. She also discovered that children wrote more complex text in their home language, while English lagged behind. It required further oral language development before similar complexity showed up in English writing.

The importance of the research on ELLs' writing is that writing should be encouraged for ELLs even before they have rich oral vocabularies in their new language—English (Hudelson, 1989; Urzua, 1987). Writing provides opportunities for ELLs to learn about writing, to practice phonemic awareness in English, to develop reading skills and knowledge, and to reflect on learning. Through writing, children, including ELLs, have the opportunity to explore words as they remain fixed and allow for scrutiny. They develop understanding of marks and letters and how they represent words and ideas. They make comparisons between oral language and its written representations, thus sharpening their knowledge of both. Most important for young children, the main source of learning about letter–sound correspondences, word separation, grammar, and idea representation is through writing.

SUPPORTING YOUNG WRITERS

Before looking at specific activities to encourage ELL writers, we offer several overall suggestions shared by Samway (2006) to create supportive classroom environments. She recommends:

1. ELLs need to write from the very first days of school. They need to write often for a variety of purposes.
2. ELLs need instruction as well as opportunities to write.
3. ELLs need time to talk, think, and read to become successful writers.
4. ELLs will model the kinds of writing their teachers find important. If the focus is correct spelling and grammar on first drafts, this is the kind of writing that will be produced—correct but limited in content.
5. Writing in a home language values the home language as children learn to write in English.

As explained in the first chapter, we believe that the classroom environment and teacher beliefs are the most important ingredients to successful writing for all students, and in particular for ELLs.

We now share several activities to support student writers. They vary from teacher-directed to independent student activities. Many of the activities begin with a great amount of teacher scaffolding, but as students become familiar with the activity, teacher support lessens.

Personal Readers

Personal readers are collections of dictated stories or simple rhymes that children learn to read independently (Bear, Caserta-Henry, & Venner, 2004). They work well with young children as there is limited text that they can read or write. The process of creating a text to place into a personal reader is begun by having the teacher offer for discussion something that is interesting. For ELLs it could be as simple as a fruit or vegetable. One of the strengths of this activity for ELLs is the close connection of an object with discussion and writing. Once discussion slows down, the teacher sits with one student and records what he or she says about the fruit or vegetable. This text is then placed into a folder that the child returns to each day to read. Texts are accumulated within the folder for student rereading.

Personal readers support reading, writing, and word knowledge. Children watch as the teacher records their words. The teacher models how words are recorded in print. Children become aware of spaces between words, punctuation, and grammar, among other concepts. If teachers are metacognitive in the recording process and explain to children why they capitalize a word or why they end a group of words with a period, for instance, they build children's understanding of such elements. This activity is very teacher supported and requires one-on-one time with a student. Teachers have used aides and parents to work with students on the dictation part of this activity, freeing them to work with small groups of students.

Digital Language Experience Activity

Labbo, Love, Prior, Hubbard, and Ryan (2006) offer a version of a typical language experience dictation. She recommends taking digital photos of students as they engage in various classroom activities. Then the teacher shares the photos with students and engages them in discussion. Following the discussion, she imports the photos to presentation software like PowerPoint and records student comments, as students observe, right on the slides. Students see their talk being recorded. The PowerPoint can then be shown and/or individual copies can be made for student reading or to serve as a source for student writing.

This variation of language experience is particularly powerful for ELLs as it allows them to engage in dialogue centered on classroom activities. For young children this might involve a discussion of various centers in the room. For first and second graders this activity could center on social studies, math, or science learning. These added dimensions of visualizing, talking, and writing strengthen the content of what is being taught through multiple exposures to it.

Interactive Writing

Interactive writing is another form of language experience where the teacher and students share the pen during writing (Button, Johnson, & Furgerson, 1996; Pinnell & McCarrier, 1994). Similar to the ideas to stimulate language experience activities shared previously, the teacher again finds something that stimulates discussion. Frequently, teachers combine interactive writing with a morning message. When this is done, students frequently contribute things that have happened to them at home or away from school since the close of school the previous day. We have seen teachers listen to many students and then zero in on one message. Once the message has been decided, various children contribute to the writing. For instance, children who are aware of initial consonants might be called on to record initial consonants. Other students might offer a whole word. Teachers are careful to call on students who can be successful with the element they are asked to write. This is another teacher-structured activity that supports students in conventionally recording a message.

Structured Writing

One form of structured writing uses sentence formats that support young writers, especially ELLs. For instance, if teachers are engaged in a theme about transportation, children can create books where each page asks for a different form of transportation. Figure 5.11 shares the frames that were written on each page of a small book. The burden of writing is reduced through such structures and all children are successful as the illustration and simple text allow them to read their writing.

Another form of structured writing is the creation of a paper with three to six blocks. As young children create a story or informational text, they draw and briefly write about each part in each block. Then, when they create a story or report, they can use the block structure to guide their writing. Figure 5.12 shares Lizbeth's first-draft idea creation in blocks and then her final-draft writing. Lizbeth is a first grader who came to school with Spanish as her home language. Her story is focused on the linear event of breaking her arm. Her final draft demonstrates how she was able to compose a complete text.

Wordless books also serve as a frame for writing. ELLs can use the

Cover Transportation	1. I _____ to school.	2. I _____ to the store.
3. I _____ to Australia.	4. We took a _____ to the farm.	5. I love to ride in a _____.

FIGURE 5.11. Writing frames for book on transportation.

picture support to write their own text. By using wordless books, students move into writing longer text that contains characters and plot.

Wall-Text Support

As teachers engage students in reading or writing activities, they create charts to which students can refer later. For instance, we observed one teacher create a comparison chart of two stories children had heard. The children began with a comparison of two main characters; later they added comparisons of the setting and plot. In other classrooms, we have seen KWL charts and vocabulary charts. In one kindergarten class, the teacher had students compare the names of family members in English and Spanish (see Figure 5.13). She used this chart for a short time while they read and wrote about family. This text support helps ELLs in conversations centered on reading and writing activities as they have written support to facilitate their discussion. The charts also serve as models for writing.

In another classroom, we saw a teacher work on an attribute chart with preschool children. They were studying animals and as they talked the teacher recorded important information that they could use for further discussion (see Figure 5.14).

In many classrooms, we have noted the use of word walls (walls that are organized by the alphabet and teachers add words under each letter). Teachers and students add to the word wall when necessary, and they engage in activities with the word wall such as finding words that begin with certain letters or words that show action. Similar to other wall-text support, ELLs can use the word wall when writing or reading.

Importantly, this wall-text support does not result in beautiful bulletin boards. Rather, this text support is spontaneous and stays on the wall as long as it is used. Charts are continuously replaced with new

My hand

I was running and I was having fun. Next I broke my hand. Then I was at the hospital. Also I was hungry so I ate. Then I went to sleep. Next my arm was fixed. It had a white cast. Then I went to my home.

by Lizbeth

FIGURE 5.12. Lizbeth's writing.

My Family	
English	Spanish
aunt	tía
uncle	tío
mom	mamá
dad	papá
brother	hermano
sister	hermana
baby	bebé
grandmother	abuela
grandfather	abuelo
cousin	primo/prima

FIGURE 5.13. Family name chart.

ones. Word wall words are retired and new ones added. There is constant transition in the text support available to students. Often this text support is accompanied by illustrations that provide additional support for ELLs.

Writing Centers and Journals

ELLs need multiple and consistent opportunities to write. Young students come to know writing through more contextual settings like play centers where writing is expected (e.g., a pretend store where they write bills or inventory). Writing centers also allow routine exposure to writing. The center might have paper, pencils, and erasers. Children typically rotate through this center, or teachers allow children free access to the center. We have seen young children place a paper on a clipboard and walk around the room copying any words they see. Other children sit at the center and compose stories or reports.

Animal	Farm	Zoo	4 legs	2 legs
Pig	Yes		Yes	
Chicken	Yes			Yes

FIGURE 5.14. Attribute chart.

In addition to the traditional supplies available at a writing center, we have seen a computer or two. Children use programs like KidPix Deluxe software and compose on the computer. Young children especially like the stamping component of this program, as they can include visuals with their writing (Barone, Mallette, & Xu, 2005). They also love printing their work so they can share it with others.

Young children also enjoy journal writing, and teachers often include it as part of their day. In one kindergarten we saw children enter the room, find their journals, and begin writing. Their teacher used this time to mingle with the children and chat about what they were writing. We often heard her compliment children on new attempts at writing. For example, she told one child that she noticed how he was now using letters for words and how she loved reading his work.

Teachers have choices in how they structure journal writing. They can allow open topic choices or they can guide the topics. In most classrooms we see a combination of guided and free writing. Importantly, journal writing is first-draft writing (it is not expected to be revised or edited) and allows children to practice writing. In many early-childhood classrooms, students have opportunities to practice phonemic awareness, spacing between words, sharing meaning, and so on. It is often a social time as children help one another with their messages. For instance, one child might ask another child for help with a letter or for information about what he or she is writing. Dyson (1997, 2003) has written extensively about the social aspects of young children's writing and how they influence each other's texts.

Writing Workshop

Another broad structure that supports ELLs' writing is a recurring writing workshop. The workshop generally is from one half hour to an hour each day. Children brainstorm ideas, write drafts, revise, edit, and share. Within this time children learn to write a variety of texts for a wide variety of audiences (Barone & Taylor, 2006). To see a short video of what such a writing workshop looks like in primary classrooms with much diversity, visit *www.coe.wayne.edu/wholeschooling/ws/video/writingwkshop 1-2mlage.html.*

Often the most difficult part of this process for ELLs is getting started on writing. Teachers might get the children started by talking about writing possibilities. The children might then list or draw some of the things or events they want to write about. Getting started can also follow instruction, particularly thematic instruction. Through thematic organization of the curriculum, children might revisit a topic several times during the writing workshop. On one day they might write some facts about animals. On another day they might try a story about bear. And perhaps on another day they might write a list of all the things that a bear eats. Children may also need to draw before writing, particularly the youngest writers. Following drawing, they often recount what was in the illustration.

Teachers also utilize journals or writers' logs to get children started. Children flip through their journal or log and find what they have most often written about. They then choose this topic or event for writing. And one more way for children to start writing is through an imitation of a recently read or heard book, a watched cartoon or movie, or a video game. Often children rewrite a fairytale with new names for the central characters and perhaps new animals. For example, the three pigs become geese and the wolf is a fox. Or, they may write a version of a cartoon that they watched before coming to school.

Once children begin to write and feel comfortable with the routine of writing workshop, they are more willing to write. Teachers sometimes find that ELLs struggle with an English word when they only know it in their home language. We have found that just having the child write the word in his or her home language, the best that he or she can, and then returning to it later allows the child to hold meaning rather than focusing on a single word and losing the message.

We have also observed that at first an ELL may be reluctant to write, especially if he or she comes into the class after the beginning of the academic year. The child may just draw during this time and the teacher may need to take a dictation if the child is willing to talk about the illustration. With support and the expected writing workshop routine, even a reluctant child will try. We have noted that other children are often the ones who move this child from drawing to drawing and writing.

The writing workshop allows students to move from rough drafts to revision focused on meaning to final editing. Each part of the process supports writers in refining and improving their writing. The final step, editing, allows ELLs to refine their understanding of English conventions such as grammar, punctuation, and spelling.

Writing to Learn

Another important aspect of writing is writing to learn (Armbruster, 2000). Similar to journal writing, this is first-draft writing where meaning takes precedence over correctness. Teachers might have children write about a topic they will explore before the exploration. In this way, the teacher has a sense of what the students know about the topic.

Teachers also use writing to learn throughout lessons and as a follow-up to units or themes. For example, in math the teacher may ask students to show how they solved a problem and then write about the solution. Very young children may draw nine objects to show 9. First graders may show how they solved the equation 2 + 3. They would then describe their solution process.

In science young children can write one fact each day that they learned about a particular topic. For instance in a second grade classroom, the teacher asked students to write one fact in their study of earthquakes as part of a weather events unit. Maria wrote: "Some earthquakes happen in Reno because we have so many hills and earth plates bump into each other" (spelling corrected). These writings were used each day as a path to learning about weather. Students read what they wrote to each other. Following this sharing the teacher created a chart with important facts about earthquakes. Later when they learned about tornadoes, they compared facts across these weather events. The teacher also used these facts as a way to learn about what her students remembered and understood about weather events. She was also able to correct any misunderstandings quickly.

Writing to learn is important as it provides a means for children to share what they have learned. Through this writing, they get a sense of where they are confused. Sometimes teachers find it difficult to fit in time for this writing, but when time is found teachers learn about what students know and where further instruction is needed. It also provides a forum for quiet children or children still hesitant to speak in English to share what they are learning.

FINAL THOUGHTS

Throughout this chapter we have described how children learn about writing, the development of writing in alphabetic and nonalphabetic languages, and strategies to support writing. We believe that writing is more important than ever in student lives. Electronic communication favors writing, and it is a form in which students will engage frequently. Even young students, particularly those in families that use computers for communication, may learn about this form before others, such as paper and pencil. Often ELLs have had many experiences using the Internet to converse with family members in distant countries.

Finding time for writing is a challenge even in the classrooms of our youngest students. However, creative teachers find ways to embed writing in almost all classroom activities from writing in centers to writing workshop time. They also find ways for children to explore multiple genres in writing. They recognize, for instance, that young girls are often most interested in narratives, especially narratives about friends, whereas boys' narratives are often modeled after cartoon shows and have elements of violence (Dyson, 2003). They also are mindful of filling their classrooms with informational genres and charts to support student learning and writing.

When thinking of young ELLs the focus often goes to oral language, vocabulary, and reading. All these are certainly important and are discussed more thoroughly in other chapters. However, writing is often a very successful way of supporting ELLs as they learn about the structures of English through writing. Writing often serves as the medium for oral language and other learning.

CHAPTER 6

Instructional Materials
Supportive of Student Learning

> Text difficulty and accessibility reflect either the ease or
> difficulty English-language learners may have in com-
> prehending a text and how interesting and accessible the
> material will be for them. Of course, the more interest-
> ing and accessible the material is, the better the chance
> that students will pursue it, understand it, and learn
> from it, and enjoy it.
> —FITZGERALD AND GRAVES (2004, p. 332)

Fitzgerald and Graves (2004) identified a factor that makes English
language learners' experiences in becoming literate in English easy or
difficult: texts they are reading. Every day, teachers use instructional
materials to teach, and ELLs read texts chosen by their teacher or by
themselves. The quality and accessibility of instructional materials are
crucial for ELLs to achieve success in classrooms as well as for teachers
to engage ELLs and enhance their learning. How to select materials for
instruction and for ELLs to practice English language and literacy is as
important as the instructional strategies teachers employ during teaching. If a teacher introduces a book related to ELLs' native culture and
their background knowledge, students are more likely to feel interested
and confident in reading or listening to the book. However, it is not
enough for a teacher just to consider the content familiarity in selecting
instructional materials. If this same book has difficult vocabulary and
complex sentence structure, ELLs experience frustration in a similar
way as when they are reading a book with unfamiliar content but with

familiar vocabulary and simple sentence structure. Content familiarity, vocabulary, and sentence structure are just three text factors, among others, that affect ELLs' reading experience. These text factors are interwoven with one another, making text selections complicated and challenging for teachers.

In this chapter, we explain why text factors make a reading selection easier or harder and present how various types of instructional materials support different needs of ELLs. First, we discuss the characteristics of written language, which make becoming literate (in a native language as well as in a nonnative language) not as easy as becoming fluent in oral language. Next, we explain various factors that make a reading selection easy or difficult for ELLs. Specifically, we focus on the factors related to the structure and content of the text and the intersection of both structure and content of the text (Barone, Mallette, & Xu, 2005; Fitzgerald & Graves, 2004; Lipson & Wixson, 2003). The factors related to the structure of a text are sentence structure and length, text structure and length, and coherence. The factors associated with the content of the text are vocabulary, familiarity, and interestingness. The intersection of text structure and content is the quality of writing, predictability, and cognitive load a text puts on an ELL. Finally, we present various types of instructional materials for promoting ELLs' oral and written language.

At the end of this chapter, you will be able to:

- ■ Understand the characteristics of written language and the differences between oral and written language.
- ■ Describe the structure and content factors of a text and intersection of structure and content factors of the text.
- ■ Understand the effect of structure and content factors on the difficulty level of texts for ELLs.
- ■ Become familiar with various types of instructional materials for promoting ELLs' oral and written language development.

THE CHARACTERISTICS OF WRITTEN LANGUAGE

Every child who was born healthy and has been growing up in a language-rich environment learns to talk and communicate in oral language with others. Developing an ability to read and comprehend a written text, however, is not that easy. A child has to learn, through formal instruction, most skills and strategies necessary to enable him or her to read. We, however, do acknowledge that young children have developed some knowledge about written language (e.g., print convention and functions) before schooling (Goodman, 1986; Sulzby, 1985). The difference between the process of becoming proficient in oral language and that of becoming literate could be due to the length of time children have been exposed to written language, which has some effect on their degree of familiarity with it. A key reason for the difficulty in developing literacy is the differences between oral and written language (i.e., informal vs. formal and context-embedded vs. context-reduced). To understand this reason would help teachers of ELLs have a better sense of why it usually takes ELLs longer to become literate and the numerous challenges ELLs experience.

TAKE A MOMENT

Think about a book you have read. Then think about a movie or TV show adapted from the book. Or, you can first think about a movie or TV show and then a book adapted from the movie or TV show (e.g., the *Arthur* TV series by Marc Brown, who developed the TV series before the book series). When you were watching the movie/TV show, what differences did you notice in how the story was told in the movie/TV show and how the story was presented in the book?

Informal versus Formal

Oral language tends to be informal in sentence structure and in diction (word choice). In daily communication, it is acceptable for a person to say a sentence with fragments. For example, Person A tells Person B, "I went to the bookstore yesterday. You know, my favorite bookstore, Barnes & Noble." By contrast, when what Person A said is written down as a sentence, it reads: "Yesterday, I went to Barnes & Noble, which is my favorite bookstore," or, "Yesterday, I went to my favorite bookstore, Barnes & Noble." Most sentences in written language include a complete thought, free of fragments and grammatically correct.

Another difference between oral and written language is word choice. Colloquial words (e.g., idiomatic expressions, slang, and informal words) are often used in daily communication. Take the word *okay*, for example. The word can have a dozen meanings, and we all feel comfortable with using this same word to express different meanings.

> The food is okay.
> It is okay to read a book before writing a journal.
> The 3:00 P.M. appointment is okay with me.

In written language, different words would replace the word *okay* in each of the foregoing three sentences. The word *average* or *mediocre* means the same as *okay* in *The food is okay*. The phrase *Go ahead* or *You can* would replace *It is okay to* in *It is okay to read a book before writing a journal*. The phrase *fits my schedule* has the same meaning as *is okay with me* in *The 3:00 P.M. appointment is okay with me*.

Context Embedded versus Context Reduced

In face-to-face communication, the context provides rich clues to the language exchange between/among people. For example, when José says, with a sincere smile, to Brian, "John looks really good in those new overalls," José means exactly what he is saying. But if Jose is uttering the same sentence with his eyes rolling and/or with an unusual (sarcastic) tone, he is actually ridiculing John. The facial expressions, tone, and pitch give clues to what the sentence actually means. By contrast, when this sentence becomes part of a written text, it is up to a reader to figure out its true meaning by piecing together what he or she has read in the previous text related to John, Brian, and José. There is obviously no way for the reader to ask the author to clarify the meaning in text, such as the way one speaker can question another in a conversation.

The context-reduced nature of written language puts demands on readers who must rely on their background knowledge of the topic and the clues the text provides to make sense of the text. If a reader has limited or no knowledge of the topic, he or she has to rely heavily on the contextual clues to construct meanings. Take a look at the sentences in the opening of *Geoffrey Groundhog Predicts the Weather* (Koscielniak, 1995): "One morning, after a long winter's nap, Geoffrey Groundhog popped out of his burrow to look for his shadow. It was February 2, Groundhog Day" (p. 5). If an ELL comes from a tropical country, he or she would have no direct experience with the winter season, and his or her background knowledge about winter and animal hibernation is most likely from secondary sources (e.g., books, TV shows, and radio shows). This knowledge can be limited. Or, it is possible that he or she has not yet developed this type of background knowledge. Given these situations, this reader has to rely heavily on the contextual clues to make sense of the text, including inferring information not written in the text. (For details on the effect of prior knowledge on ELLs' comprehension, refer to Chapter 8.)

Challenges for ELLs

The differences in oral and written language present several challenges to ELLs. First, according to Cummins (1979, 1986, 1989), for ELLs, oral language is related to Basic Personal Communicative Language (BICS), which is often used in contextualized daily communication. By contrast, written language is related to Cognitive Academic Language Proficiency (CALP), which is often used in decontextualized academic tasks. It usually takes ELLs 5–7 years to fully develop academic language. Unlike their native English-speaking peers, who have developed some knowledge of the English language during their early years, ELLs are pressured to develop both BICS and CALP at school because school tasks require ELLs to be proficient in both areas. If a teacher focuses on ELLs' oral language development in teaching, overlooking their needs in English literacy, ELLs experience difficulty in completing literacy tasks. This holds true for ELLs who have had experiences with written language but limited opportunities to practice oral English.

Second, the context-reduced nature of written language makes literacy tasks more demanding. Cummins (1996) categorized second-language learning tasks into four groups. As illustrated in the examples in Figure 6.1, when the context for a task is reduced, a learner has limited context clues to rely on to help him or her complete the task. Literacy tasks most often fall into the context-reduced and cognitive demanding category. One of the goals in teaching ELLs is for teachers to contextualize literacy tasks so that they become less demanding for ELLs. We discuss details about this in the section "Types of Instructional Materials for Oral and Written Language Development."

In addition, the difference in written language between English and a native language (as briefly discussed in Chapter 2) would cause confusion to ELLs. This difference is greater for some ELLs whose native

Categories	Examples of tasks
Context embedded, cognitive undemanding	• Carrying on a conversation about a topic familiar to both speakers • Copying down words from a whiteboard
Context embedded, cognitive demanding	• Carrying on an conversation about a topic related to one particular subject area (e.g., science, social studies, or math) • Describing an object during show-and-tell
Context reduced, cognitive undemanding	• Asking or answering questions about a read book • Listening to a book on tape
Context reduced, cognitive demanding	• Listening to a talk on a topic related to a subject area (e.g., science, social studies, or math) • Giving a talk on a topic related to a subject area (e.g., science, social studies, or math) • Writing a story • Reading a narrative text or an expository text

FIGURE 6.1. Examples of Cummins's four categories of tasks.

language (e.g., some Asian languages and African languages) is very different from English than for other ELLs whose native language is similar to English in some way (e.g., Spanish). While teaching a group of ELLs from diverse linguistic backgrounds, teachers need to keep in mind this variability in language differences.

STRUCTURAL FACTORS OF TEXT

Sentence Structure and Length

Many languages have a set of sentence types similar to the English language—a simple, compound, and complex sentence; a statement; a question; and a command. As discussed in Chapter 2, a sentence structure in English can be totally different from that of a native language. In many Asian languages, for example, there is no verb tense; that is, a verb does not change when a sentence states something that happened in the past, in the present, or in the future. Given that, ELLs may treat verbs reflective of a tense (and in particular a past tense of an irregular verb) as a new word (e.g., *went, gone,* and *going*) or as a new phrase (e.g., *will go, is going to read,* and *has/have gone*). In selecting a text (and in particular for ELLs at the beginning level), teachers need to make sure that there are similar sentence structures present in the text. In so doing, teachers can focus on one or two sentence structures in teaching and can devote more time to helping ELLs comprehend the text.

Sentence length can also make a text more challenging for ELLs. Even with a simple sentence, when a writer puts a great deal of information in that sentence, ELLs have to process a main idea and other relevant information. Consider this sentence from *Ladybug's Birthday* (Metzger, 1998): "The flighty fireflies explored Ladybug's house, flying here and there" (p. 11). The sentence states the action of fireflies (*fireflies explored Ladybug's house*), describes the fireflies (*flighty*), and explains the action (*flying here and there*). In selecting texts, teachers need to be aware of ELLs' English proficiency levels and, in particular, their knowledge of and experience with sentences of different lengths.

Text Structure and Length

Another difference between oral and written language is that written language has its own structure. Each text genre has its unique way to present information. Here we focus on three text genres that primary-grade students often read and write: narrative text (storybooks), expository text (informational books), and poetry. Although we are cognizant that teachers may have a good knowledge of text structure and length and their impact on literacy development, we think it is important to discuss the subject with them within the context of teaching ELLs and, in particular, within the context of how text structure and length can pose challenges to ELLs and to teachers of ELLs.

Narrative Text Structure

As early as 1947, Gates related a reader's understanding of a story structure to comprehension. Scholars in the reading community further expanded his concept of *sense of story* (e.g., Mandler & Johnson, 1977; Rumelhart, 1975; Stein & Glenn, 1979). Sense of story is a reader's understanding of a structure or a set of rules (similar to grammatical rules) governing how a story develops and what needs to be included in a story. According to story grammar or narrative text structure, each story has a character (or characters); a setting (or multiple settings); a plot, which includes a problem or problems, problem solution attempts, and problem solutions; and a theme or themes (something that authors want readers to learn from a story). Although all stories written in English follow the general text structure, variations of how each story is presented to readers exist. For example, the text from the first three pages of *Charlie Needs a Cloak* (dePaola, 1973) explicitly introduces the character (Charlie), the setting (on the farm), and a problem (Charlie had everything except a good cloak). By contrast, the excerpt from *Swimmy* (Lionni, 1963), a long one, only presents characters and the setting, and readers need to infer part of the story problem (see Figure 6.2).

Expository Text Structure

Similar to stories, most informational books follow an expository text structure, which governs how information is presented. Some authors present information in a book by telling a story. The structure of these books is similar to a story structure (e.g., *Mouse Paint* [Walsh, 1989]). There are five common patterns of expository text structure: description, sequence, comparison and contrast, cause and effect, and problem and solution (Meyer & Freedle, 1984). An expository text with a *de-*

Text	Story grammar		
	Character(s)	Setting	Problem
Swimmy A happy school of little fish lived in a corner of the sea somewhere. They were all red. Only one of them was as black as a mussel shell. He swam faster than his brothers and sisters. His name was Swimmy. (n.p.)	Swimmy and his brothers and sisters (a happy school of little fish)	Somewhere in the sea	
One bad day a tuna fish, swift, fierce and very hungry, came darting through the waves. In one gulp he swallowed all the little red fish. Only Swimmy escaped. (n.p.)	A tuna fish		All little red fish were in danger (inferred)

FIGURE 6.2. An example of story grammar.

scription structure provides details on a topic through specific examples and depiction of characteristics. In a *sequence* text, concepts or items are listed in a numerical order. In a text with *comparison and contrast* structure, two or more topics (e.g., things and concepts) are compared and contrasted. A *cause-and-effect* text explains cause(s) and effect(s) of an event, a phenomenon, or something similar. In a *problem-and-solution* text, one or more problems are presented and followed by one or more solutions.

Figure 6.3 lists an example of each text structure pattern. Many informational books do not have only one expository text structure;

Text structure pattern	Example
Description	*GRRR! A Book about Big Cats* (Berger, M. & Berger, G., 2002) Lions, tigers, leopards, cheetahs, and jaguars are big cats. They're a lot like small cats. But big cats are much bigger. And big cats do not purr. They roar! GRRR! (p. 5)
Sequence	*How A Book is Made* (Aliki, 1986) A book starts with an idea. The AUTHOR thinks of a story. She writes it down. It is harder than she expected. Sometimes she can't find the right words. She has to look things up. At last she is satisfied. She sends off her MANUSCRIPT to her EDITOR at Goodbooks Publishing Company. (pp. 6–7)
Compare and contrast	*Sounds All Around* (Pfeffer, 1999) Shake a can of marbles . . . rattle, rattle, rattle. Shake a can of cheese puffs . . . pluff, pluff, pluff. Shake a can of pencils . . . clank, clank, clank. Your sounds fill the air. (p. 6)
Cause and effect	*Shadows* (Otto, 2001) The light shines on your hand. But it cannot shine *through* your hand. (p. 16) You make shadows on the wall when your hand blocks the light. (p. 17)
Problem and solution	*The Best Book of Weather* (Adams, 2001) Many countries are trying to reduce the amount of smog in their cities by cutting car exhaust fumes and lowering smoke emissions from factories. (p. 22)

FIGURE 6.3. Examples of different types of expository text structure.

rather, several structure patterns are used to present information. Consider the following two-sentence excerpt from *The Best Book of Weather* (Adams, 2001): "The climate is hottest at the Equator and coldest at the North and South Poles. This is because more of the Sun's rays reach Earth at the Equator than at the poles" (p. 10). The first sentence has a compare-and-contrast pattern, and the second sentence is explaining the difference in the climate between the equator and the North and South Poles (*cause and effect*).

In addition to text structures different than stories, expository texts also have unique features that help present complex information. Figure 6.4 lists these features and their respective functions. Some informational books have more listed features than others, depending on the topic and reading level of the book. For example, *Sounds All Around* (Pfeffer, 1999), a book about sounds in our life and in nature, has different text structure patterns but only one feature listed in Figure 6.4— one- or two-word label for a picture that explains a concept. By contrast, *The Magic School Bus: Inside a Beehive* (Cole, 1996) has features of sidebar texts and diagrams.

Poetic Text Structure

Similar to stories and informational books, poetry has its own structures. There are rhymed verse, free verse, narratives, and haiku, cinquain, and diamante (Tompkins, 2003; Tiedt, 1970). A rhymed verse, a common form of poetry, has rhyming words and a pattern.

In *Baa Baa Black Sheep* (Trapani, 2001), the *-op* and *-oon* rhyming is used, and the rhyming pattern appears in the first–second and third–fourth lines:

> Baa, baa, black sheep, have you any slop?
> I've just finished my last drop.
> I'll waste away if I don't eat soon.
> One nibble out to hold me till noon.*
> > *Permission was secured for this
> > quote from CharlesBridge Publishing.

By contrast, a free verse does not follow a rhyming scheme, and the poet focuses on expressing ideas and feelings (e.g., shape poems and I wish poems). In a narrative poem, a poet is telling a story in a way similar to an author of a story. One example of this type of poem is Rowena

Features	Functions
Heading and subheading Table of contents	Tell a specific topic and subtopic.
Appendices Sidebar text Footnotes Endnotes Captions for pictures Lists	Provide additional information.
Diagrams Figures Graphs Maps	Provide additional information through visual representation.
Index	Provides a location in the book for a specific set of information.
Glossary	Explains terminology.
Bibliography/references	Presents a set of sources from which authors have drawn information.
Further readings	Provides a list of additional sources for readers.
Credits/acknowledgment	Expresses an appreciation for others' work from which authors have drawn information.
Quizzes or activities	Engage readers in exploring the topic presented in the book.
Websites CD-ROMs	Provide Internet resources.

FIGURE 6.4. Expository text features and functions.

Bennett's *The Gingerbread Man* (cited in de Regniers, Moore, White, & Carr, 1988), which tells a traditional story of the Gingerbread Man. Haiku, cinquain, and diamante are poems that have specific syllable patterns. A three-line haiku poem, for example, has only 17 syllables in a 5–7–5 syllable pattern (Tompkins, 2003).

Challenges for ELLs

Text structure within different genres presents several challenges to ELLs. First, a text structure guides readers in predicting the forthcoming content in a text and in comprehending the text. For example, while reading a narrative text, readers with knowledge of narrative text structure anticipate reading about characters, plot, and setting. After having read an introduction of characters, they become curious about the plot (e.g., what happens to the characters in one particular setting). To make use of the knowledge of text structure in reading a particular genre, readers must become familiar with its structure (Peregoy & Boyle, 2000). It will take much practice reading this type of text genre in order to grasp its structure. This applies to ELLs as well. In addition to learning about text structures of various genres, ELLs are also developing their literacy skills in English. So they shoulder double burdens.

As clearly illustrated in Figures 6.2 and 6.3, there is a great variability in text structure for each text genre. Furthermore, when one text genre is mixed with another, the text structure reflects both genres and also possibly a hybrid text structure (e.g., Joanna Cole's *Magic School Bus* series with a narrative text structure). This variability makes it difficult for ELLs to develop a good body of knowledge about the text structure of each genre. Again, it would take a considerable amount of exposure to various types of text for ELLs to gain full understanding of text structure of various genres.

The text length can also make ELLs' reading experience less successful. This is especially true for students at the beginning and intermediate proficiency levels. If a text is too long, they have to process too much information simultaneously. If, in addition to that, ELLs are not familiar with the structure of the text genre, they are facing a greater challenge—that is, they lose the contextual support knowledge that text structure can provide.

Coherence

A coherent text is one with presented ideas closely tied together. As Binkley (1988) stated, a text with a coherent structure serves as a "roadmap to understanding" (p. 104) which makes ideas flow naturally (Goldman & Rakestraw, 2000) and which helps ELLs to anticipate the following portions of the text. In discussing stories for young children and those experiencing reading difficulties, Lipson and Wixson (2003) point out that it is not a good practice for authors to use unnatural language and/or to leave out important information in order to control text difficulty. To echo their view, we think it is necessary to limit the use of decodable texts with ELLs only to the time when phonics concepts and skills are taught. The texts should not be used for teaching comprehension. After all, the goal of reading these texts is practicing a phonics pattern like the *-an* word family—*Ian ran. Dan ran. Stan ran*—not necessarily gaining new ideas or reading pleasure.

TAKE A MOMENT

Now that you have learned about the structure factors of a text and their respective effect on ELLs' learning to be literate, select one text from each genre that your ELLs experienced difficulty with during the last school year. Think about what structure factor(s) of the text affected your ELLs' comprehension.

CONTENT FACTORS OF A TEXT

Vocabulary

We agree with many scholars in the field that vocabulary can be a determining factor causing major comprehension difficulty for ELLs (Fitzgerald & Graves, 2004; Garcia, 1991; Gersten & Baker, 2000). There are three reasons for this. First, vocabulary used in written texts, and especially in texts within subject areas, is different from the words expressed in oral language that is used for daily communication (Corson, 1997; Cummins, 2003). Words used in oral language are often high-frequency words, single- or two-syllable words, and from the Anglo-Saxon lexicon. These types of words are relatively easy for ELLs to master via reading and listening to books read aloud. By contrast, words used in written texts for academic purposes are low-frequency words, multi-syllabic words, and words derived from Greek or Latin roots. To master these types of words, ELLs need ample exposure to various text genres on a wide range of topics.

Another reason that vocabulary can make a text more difficult is that ELLs who are at the beginning and intermediate levels cannot automatically go through the subprocesses of reading a text (e.g., decoding, making connections, and predicting) and comprehending it as skilled readers do (see Chapter 8 for details on subprocesses) (Fitzgerald & Graves, 2004; Peregoy & Boyle, 2000). If an ELL has focused too much attention on figuring out the meaning of unfamiliar words while reading a text, he or she would have limited cognitive resources for constructing meaning from the text. Consequently, the student would have poor comprehension, which is something all teachers do not want for their students.

A final reason is that it takes years for a student to develop full knowledge of a word (Nagy & Scott, 2000). Thus ELLs, who must master words (at their grade levels) used in oral language and also those used in written language, including informational texts, have an additional burden. Similar to their native English-speaking peers, young ELLs have a limited repertoire of reading strategies and decoding strategies in particular to rely on to help them figure out unknown words (Hiebert & Raphael, 1998). In English, there are many words with multiple meanings. Take the word *run*, for example. The most familiar meaning is associated with leg movement as in *I run to school everyday*. But the meaning of *run* in *I've got to run* is a little bit different. Students might later learn other meanings of *run*, as in *The water is running, He has a runny nose, This software cannot run on this computer,* and *She is going to run some errands*. The meanings of *run* in these examples are just a small percentage of meanings for the word *run* as listed in the dictionary.

Given the three reasons that vocabulary makes a text more difficult for ELLs, teachers need to be mindful in selecting materials. We agree with Fitzgerald and Graves (2004) that a few difficult words may not pose a challenge to ELLs. But we want to stress that these few words cannot be those related to the central meaning of a sentence. Look at the underlined words in the following sentences taken from Miranda's (1997) *To Market, To Market*, a book often used with kindergartners and first graders: "Home again, home again, jiggity jig!" "Uh-oh! That pig left the pen." "To market, to market, to buy a plump goose." "To market, to market, to buy a live trout." and "To market, to market, to buy a spring lamb" (n.p.). The picture on each page where a sentence appears does not support the meaning of the word. Therefore, ELLs cannot figure out the meaning of each word through the picture. Furthermore, the meaning of the words *pen* and *spring* are less familiar to students. The word *live* is a homograph that is pronounced differently from the word *live*, as in *I live in a city*, and has a different meaning. There are more examples from this book that have unfamiliar words. Thus this book is clearly not suitable for ELLs at the beginning and intermediate levels of language development.

Familiarity

Besides the vocabulary factor, the unfamiliarity with the content of a text can also increase the difficulty level of a text. Consider the following excerpt from *Yu-Gi-Oh! Reshef of Destruction* (Prima Games, 2004).

The Defense Trick

> There's a simple way to get past cards that have a strong DEF but a weak ATK. The computer is normally very aggressive against cards that are brought into play face-down in the Defense Position, because it assumes the card isn't attacking because it's too weak or of the wrong alignment to challenge the cards in play. If a card with a strong DEF is holding you back, bring out any monster and immediately set it to defend. When the computer takes its turn, it tries attacking the new card, which leaves the strong defender in a weak Attack Position, making it easy to destroy on the next run. This little feint can be a real LP saver. (p. 17)

As skillful readers, we are able to decode every single word in this excerpt but may not be able to comprehend the content. This is largely due to our limited background knowledge about *Yu-Gi-Oh!* Unfamiliarity with the content of a text can affect comprehension of skillful readers, let alone ELLs who are developing English-language skills and becoming readers.

For selecting texts with familiar content for ELLs, Barone et al. (2005) suggest that teachers consider the following areas:

■ *Bilingual texts.* Seeing their native language in a text brings a sense of comfort to ELLs. In addition, the text written in a native language provides some contextual support for ELLs in their process of making sense of the text. (See Figure 6.8 for some sample texts.)

■ *Texts on native cultures.* When a text is about a native culture familiar to ELLs, they have some background knowledge related to the text, thus enabling them to be more successful in comprehending the text. (See Figure 6.8 for some sample texts.)

■ *Texts on life experiences.* Similar to a text on a native culture, a text about a life experience shared by ELLs provides a better chance for ELLs to make a connection between the text and their life experience. This chance would increase their engagement with the text and better support their comprehension. Some examples of life experiences are daily routines (e.g., morning routine at home and routine at school), playing, friendship, family, food, and traveling. (See Figure 6.7 for some sample texts.)

■ *Texts related to TV shows or movies.* When a text is related to a TV show or a movie and when ELLs have seen the show or a movie, they have a better chance to comprehend the text. This is largely due to their familiarity with the plot, which would free up some of their cognitive resources for other subprocesses involved in reading and comprehending a text. Some examples of other subprocesses are decoding, chunking, figuring out text structure, and using cognitive and metacognitive strategies. (See Figure 6.6 for some sample texts.)

■ *Texts on the same concept/theme.* A set of texts on the same concept or theme allow ELLs to explore a concept or a theme in depth. While reading a new book in the text set, ELLs can build on what they have already learned about a concept or a theme from reading other books in the set and gain new information from this new text. This spiral process not only makes activating prior knowledge and making meaningful connections easier for ELLs but also makes reading texts less challenging and more effective. (See Figure 6.11 for some sample texts.)

■ *Texts written by the same author.* When ELLs have read several texts (often a book series) written by the same author, they become familiar with the plot, author's craft, and/or text structure. This familiarity lessens the burden on ELLs who would devote less time to figuring out author writing style, text structure, and plot/other relevant information. (See Figure 6.8 for some sample texts.)

Interestingness

Interestingness of a text is one of the main reasons readers want to read the text. This is true for ELLs as well. Teachers of ELLs need to keep in mind that not all texts they find interesting are appealing to ELLs as well. While selecting interesting texts for ELLs, teachers need to withhold their own emotional experience with texts. Instead, they need to think about elements that make certain texts interesting to ELLs. When ELLs are reading texts interesting to them, active engagement can occur. If a text cannot hold an ELL's interest, the child probably will pay less attention to the language and the content, thus making the reading experience less effective.

Fitzgerald and Graves (2004) offered some ideas on locating interesting materials for ELLs. They encourage teachers to first learn about ELLs' interests. We support their suggestion. Not all boys in first or second grade enjoy the humor in Dav Pilkey's *Captain Underpants* series; some boys consider Junie B. Jones in Barbara Park's *Junie B. Jones* series an interesting character to explore. Likewise, books based on the PBS's *Dora the Explorer* TV show may appeal more to Spanish-speaking children than to ELLs who speak other native languages. Fitzgerald and Graves have also suggested that books written by authors whose ethnicity is the same as ELLs' are appealing. Some authors whose ethnic background is similar to that of ELLs are Alma Flor Ada, Yangsook Choi, Carmen Lomas Garza, Pat Mora, Allen Say, and Gary Soto.

We also think that texts with a focus on issues and/or routines that ELLs deal with in their daily life have the potential to increase the interestingness level, because the ELLs can have a personal connection to these texts. Here are some examples of such texts.

- Levine's (1989) *I Hate English!* describes a Chinese ELL's experience of learning English in New York, which is very similar to the experience of many ELLs.
- Ada's (1995) *My Mother Plants Strawberries* shares a girl's longing for her mother who works long hours in a strawberry field in order to support her family.
- Bang's (1999) *When Sophie Gets Angry—Really, Really, Angry . . .* describes a young girl's process of learning to deal with her anger in different ways.

Finally, we have found wordless texts (e.g., *Do You Want to Be My Friend?* [Carle, 1971]) appealing to ELLs, who might feel less intimidated by reading because there are no English words on each page. (See Figure 6.7 for more examples.) In addition, wordless texts provide ELLs with an opportunity to focus on constructing meaning based on illustrations. They are free to make up a story, in their home language or in English, out of a wordless text in a way that makes sense to them. This freedom increases their active engagement with the text.

INTERSECTION OF STRUCTURE AND CONTENT FACTORS OF TEXT

Quality of Writing

For the quality of writing, we refer to both structure and content of the text, which affect each other. The following example from the opening sentences in Freeman's (1968) *Corduroy* shows how the structure of a text can have an effect on the presentation of content: "Corduroy is a bear who once lived in the toy department of a big store. Day after day he waited with all the other animals and dolls for somebody to come along and take him home" (n.p.). The complex structure of the sentences definitely prevents ELLs at the beginning or intermediate levels from getting ideas quickly. Although this book is considered a children's classic for primary-grade children, it is not suitable for young ELLs.

Similarly, the content of a text affects its structure. For example, in an effort to control vocabulary, authors may use words sharing a similar rime (e.g., du*ck* and tru*ck*), or only sight words or some high-frequency words familiar to ELLs. Consequently, the linguistic input in the text becomes contrived and unnatural. It is detrimental for ELLs to read texts with unauthentic and unnatural English. The text with such sentences as *Ian ran. Dan ran. Stan ran.* should be limited and used only for practice with recently taught phonic patterns. If the text is used for the purpose of teaching the *-an* rime (word family), other texts with the same rime and with a more authentic language should also be used.

Predictability of Text

If a text is predictable, it would have more potential to interest and engage ELLs. Predictability of a text can be based on structure and content of the text. A pattern book has a linguistic pattern repeated throughout the book. For example, in a pattern book, *Jump, Frog, Jump* (Kalan, 1981), the sentences "Jump, frog, jump" and "How did the frog get away?" are repeated on various pages. English-language learners, after becoming familiar with a linguistic pattern, can join with their teacher in a shared reading and later in choral reading (Barone et al., 2005). They also get multiple exposures to sight words and high-frequency words. Often pattern books have varying rhyming patterns, which makes a text predictable.

Some book series allow ELLs to predict. Because a book series often has the same set of characters and a similar setting and plot, ELLs have a better chance to anticipate what might happen in the next text. For example, Laura Numberoff's *If You . . .* series encourages students to predict what the animal character is going to ask for again after the boy has given it something. Students are able to predict after reading several books in this series and after coming to understand the plot pattern in the book. At times, illustrations provide clues that enable readers to predict. For example, in *The Hat* (Brett, 1997) and *The Mitten* (Brett, 1989), a part of the illustration on each page lets readers know which animal is going to appear on the following page.

Cognitive Load

We have discussed structure and content factors of a text and the interactions of these factors and their effect on text difficulty levels. The last factor—the one that comprises all factors—teachers of ELLs need to consider is the cognitive load a text can put on ELLs (Hiebert, Brown, Taitague, Fisher, & Adler, 2004). While selecting materials for ELLs, teachers always need to ask first how much cognitive load ELLs have to bear. To answer this question, teachers need to look at all structure, content, and interactive factors we have discussed. Teachers can use the checklist in Figure 6.5 to determine whether the text is appropriate for ELLs. If there are too many comments about a chosen text under the Concerns column, the cognitive load the text puts on ELLs would be too heavy, and the text would not provide comprehensible input for ELLs (Krashen, 1985). By contrast, if there are many checkmarks for a chosen text under the No Concerns column, the text is more likely appropriate for ELLs.

	Concerns (list each concern)	No concerns (Put a ✓ under each factor)
Book title:		
Grade: Date:		
Structure factors of a text		
Sentence structure and length		
Text structure and length		
Coherence		
Content factors of a text		
Vocabulary		
Familiarity		
Interestingness		
Intersection of structure and content factors of a text		
Quality of writing		
Predictability		
Cognitive load		
Decision on the text (circle one): Use it Not use it Use it with other texts		

FIGURE 6.5. Checklist for cognitive load.

> **TAKE A MOMENT**
>
> Now that you have read about the structure and content factors of a text, interactions among these factors, and the effect of such factors on text difficulty level, use the checklist in Figure 6.5 to evaluate some texts you used with your ELLs last school year. Try to determine a connection between these factors and the difficulty your students experienced.

TYPES OF INSTRUCTIONAL MATERIALS FOR ORAL AND WRITTEN LANGUAGE DEVELOPMENT

In this section, we focus on a presentation of various instructional materials for fostering ELLs' oral and written language development. We organize the material based on instructional purposes. There are three categories of materials: (1) texts promoting oral language development; (2) texts promoting written language development; and (3) texts integrating language and content learning. While reading this section, please keep in mind that the materials we are referring to go beyond the print-based books and also include nonprint materials, such as books on tape and TV shows. In addition, we want to point out that the texts listed in the following section are good literature for students, non-ELLs and ELLs. Although teachers of non-ELLs have used these texts, we believe that the texts would be beneficial to ELLs as well. Based on Figure 6.5, these texts tend to have less cognitive load for ELLs.

Texts Promoting Oral Language Development

In Chapter 4, we discussed ELLs' oral language development and various instructional strategies for fostering their oral language development. To align with the developmental stages of ELLs, we focus on texts used for listening and speaking development. Listening involves linguistic input for ELLs, which needs to be comprehensible to ELLs (Krashen, 1985) and reflects authentic language use (Fitzgerald & Graves, 2004; Lenters, 2004/2005). Speaking is associated with linguistic production, which progresses in a linear fashion— silent stage, early production, speech emergence, immediate fluency, and advanced fluency (Echevarria et al., 2008; Krashen & Terrell, 1983).

Listening and speaking are closely related partly because they are both considered oral language, and largely because one affects the other. For ELLs to learn to speak (or to produce linguistic units), they must have had ample experience with the English language; that is, they have heard various linguistic patterns (e.g., sentence structures) and understood the usage (e.g., the different implied meaning of the word *good* as used in *He is a good son, He is a good student*) and cultural and social features of English (e.g., *Pass the book to me* vs. *Would you please pass the book to me?*). Figure 6.6 lists some examples of texts for fostering ELLs' listening skills.

In a similar way, ELLs' ability to speak allows them to increase their opportunities to communicate with others for various social purposes. Different types of communication further provide them with additional linguistic input, which in turn enhances their ability to produce English. In addition to strategies and activities discussed in Chapter 4 to promote ELLs' oral language development, in Figure 6.7 we suggest some texts that would invite ELLs to talk and communicate with others.

TEXTS PROMOTING WRITTEN LANGUAGE DEVELOPMENT

The books listed in Figures 6.6 and 6.7 and other books (e.g., alphabet books and big books discussed in other chapters) can also be used to develop ELLs' written language. In particular, teachers can use these books for reading aloud, shared reading, guided reading, buddy or paired reading, and independent reading. Most of the books are appropriate for ELLs at the beginning and early–intermediate stages of language and literacy development. In Figure 6.8, we focus on texts that target ELLs' high level of comprehension, vocabulary development, and content learning.

In Chapter 5 we discussed various writing strategies and activities teachers can employ to scaffold ELLs' writing development. In Figure 6.9, we focus on texts that provide ELLs with an opportunity for a scaffolded, meaningful, and personal experience in learning to write.

Types of texts and purposes	Sample texts
Books with repetitive (predictable) and rhyming patterns • Allowing ELLs to become familiar with some linguistic patterns. • Reducing cognitive load for ELLs through repeated linguistic patterns. • Allowing ELLs to become familiar with rhyme and rhythm of English. • Fostering ELLs' phonemic awareness and understanding of various word families.	Bernal, R. (1993). *The ants go marching one by one.* Lincolnwood, IL: Publications International. Capucilli, A. S. (1995). *Inside a barn in the country.* New York: Scholastic. Capucilli, A. S. (2000). *Inside a zoo in the city.* New York: Scholastic. Carle, E. (1993). *Today is Monday.* New York: Scholastic. Colandro, L. (2003). *There was a cold lady who swallowed some snow!* New York: Scholastic. Grossman, B. (1996). *My little sister ate one hare.* New York: Crown. Harper, C. M. (2002). *There was a bold lady who wanted a star.* New York: Little, Brown. Martin, B. (1983). *Brown bear, brown bear, what do you see?* New York: Holt, Rinehart & Winston. Martin, B. (1991). *Polar bear, polar bear, what do you hear?* New York: Holt, Rinehart & Winston. Martin, B. (2003). *Panda bear, panda bear, what do you see?* New York: Holt, Rinehart, and Winston. Root, P. (1998). *One duck stuck.* Cambridge, MA: Candlewick Press. Taback, S. (1997). *There was an old lady who swallowed a fly.* New York: Viking Penguin. Williams, L. (1986). *The little old lady who was not afraid of anything.* New York: HarperCollins.
Poetry • Allowing ELLs to become familiar with rhyme and rhythm of English. • Allowing ELLs to become familiar with different poetic patterns.	Deady, K. W. (2004). *All year long.* Minneapolis: Carolrhoda Books. de Regniers, B. S., Moore, E., White, M. M., & Carr, J. (1988). *Sing a song of popcorn: Every child's book of poems.* New York: Scholastic. Hopkins, L. B. (1990). *Good books, good times!* New York: HarperCollins. Katz, B. (1997). *Truck talk: Rhymes on wheels.* New York: Scholastic. Koller, J. F. (1999). *A monkey too many.* San Diego: Harcourt Brace. Rogasky, B. (1994). *Winter poems.* New York: Scholastic. Sierra, J. (2000). *There's a zoo in room 22.* Orlando, FL: Harcourt Brace. *(continued)*

FIGURE 6.6. Texts for fostering ELLs' listening skills.

Types of texts and purposes	Sample texts
Storybooks for read-aloud (with a simple plot and illustrations supporting the print) • Providing ELLs with an experience with story elements. • Fostering ELLs' listening comprehension.	Aylesworth, J. (1992). *Old black fly*. New York: Holt. Carle, E. (1987). *A very hungry caterpillar*. New York: Philomel Books. Dodds, S. (1993). *Charles tiger*. New York: Houghton Mifflin. Fearnley, J. (2004). *Billy Tibbles moves out!* New York: HarperCollins. Hutchins, P. (1968). *Rosie's walk*. New York: Macmillan. Martin, B., & Archambault, J. (1989). *Chicka chicka boom boom*. New York: Simon & Schuster. Middleton, C. (2004). *Enrico starts school*. New York: Dial Books for Young Readers. Murphy, S. J. (1999). *Rabbit's pajama party*. New York: HarperCollins. Weston, T. (2003). *Hey, pancakes!* San Diego: Harcourt Brace. Wood, D., & Wood, A. (1994). *The little mouse, the red ripe strawberry, and the big hungry bear*. New York: Scholastic.
Informational books for read-aloud (with a simple concept) • Providing ELLs with an experience with basic expository text structures. • Providing ELLs with background knowledge about concepts.	Crews, D. (1986). *Ten black dots*. New York: Greenwillow Books. Ernst, L. C. (1996). *The letters are lost*. New York: Viking Penguin. Marzollo, J. (1996). *I am water*. New York: Scholastic. Marzollo, J. (1997). *I am an apple*. New York: Scholastic. Mayo, M. (2002). *Emergency*. Minneapolis, IN: Carolrhoda Books. McGrath, B. B. (1998). *The Cheerios counting book*. New York: Scholastic. Morris, A. (1995). *Shoes, shoes, shoes*. New York: Lothrop, Lee & Shepard Books. Murphy, S. J. (1997). *Every buddy counts*. New York: HarperCollins. Shannon, G. (1996). *Tomorrow's alphabet*. New York: Greenwillow Books.
TV shows and books based on the shows (familiar to ELLs) • Reducing cognitive load. • Providing contextual support for ELLs' comprehension.	Cartoon Network *SpongeBob SquarePants* *The PowerPuff Girls* PBS Kids *Arthur* *Barney and Friends* *Clifford* *Curious George* *Dragon Tales*

FIGURE 6.6. (*continued*)

Types of texts and purposes	Sample texts
	Jakers *Sesame Street* *The Berenstain Bears* Nick *Pokémon* *Rugrats* Nick Jr. Blue's Clues *Dora the Explorer* *Go, Diego, Go!* *Max & Ruby* *Miss Spider*
Books on tape • Providing a natural linguistic model for ELLs. • Scaffolding ELLs' reading of the text.	*school.booksontape.com/index3.cfm?* *www.simplyaudiobooks.com/*
Online books • Providing ELLs with contextual support via animation, and effects of sound, font, and color. • Providing ELLs with an experience with story elements. • Fostering ELLs' listening comprehension.	*pbskids.org/jakers/stories/* *www.icdlbooks.org/* *www.magickeys.com/books/* *www.starfall.com/n/level-c/index/load.htm?f*

FIGURE 6.6. (*continued*)

TEXTS WITH INTEGRATED CONTENT

We have talked about texts, respectively, for promoting ELLs' development of listening, speaking, reading, and writing skills. Another set of texts, in content areas, can also be used for developing ELLs' language and literacy skills. Houk (2005), Freeman and Freeman (2005), and the National Council of Teachers of English (2006) have argued that ELLs' language and literacy development can be best achieved through content learning. Texts on one particular topic allow ELLs to learn content through language and learn language through content. This is particularly true for young children who are naturally curious about their

Types of texts and purposes	Sample texts
Books with repetitive (predictable) and rhyming patterns • Inviting ELLs to participate in a shared reading after they have figured out a pattern. • Reducing cognitive load for ELLs through repeated linguistic patterns. • Fostering ELLs' understanding of various word families.	See Figure 6.6.
Wordless books • Allowing ELLs to practice with describing an illustration. • Allowing ELLs to practice with forming a story.	Anno, M. (2004). *Anno's Spain*. New York: Philomel Books. Anno, M. (1983). *Anno's USA*. New York: Philomel Books. Baker, J. (2004). *Home*. New York: Greenwillow Books. Carle, E. (1973). *I see a song*. New York: Simon & Schuster. Carle, E. (1997). *Do you want to my friend?* New York: HarperCollins. Day, A. (1991). *Good dog, Carl!* New York: Simon & Schuster. Hoban, T. (1987). *26 letters and 99 cents*. New York: Greenwillow Books. Hoban, T. (1990). *Exactly the opposite*. New York: Greenwillow Books. Lehman, B. (2004). *The red book*. New York: Houghton Mifflin. Liu, J. S. (2002). *Yellow umbrella*. La Jolla, CA: Kane/Miller. Rohmann, E. (1994). *Time flies*. New York: Crown. Sis, P. (2000). *Dinosaur!* New York: Greenwillow Books. Spier, P. (1982). *Rain*. New York: Doubleday. Tafuri, M. (1984). *Have you seen my duckling?* New York: Greenwillow Books. Wiesner, D. (1991). *Tuesday*. New York: Houghton Mifflin.
Books with an interesting, and/or personally relevant information/story	Alexander, J. (2005). *Dad, are you the tooth fairy?* New York: Orchard Books. Cohen, M. (1967). *Will I have a friend?* New York: Aladdin Books. *(continued)*

FIGURE 6.7. Texts for fostering ELLs' speaking skills.

• Allowing ELLs to practice academic language through discussion. • Increasing ELLs' comprehension ability.	deGroat, D. (2005). *Brand-new pencils, brand-new books*. New York: HarperCollins. DeZutter, H. (1993). *Who says a dog goes bow-wow?* New York: Doubleday. Ehlert, L. (1989). *Eating the alphabet*. Orlando, FL: Harcourt Brace. Falwell, C. (1993). *Feast for 10*. New York: Houghton Mifflin. Hutchings, A., & Hutchings, R. (1997). *The Gumming counting book*. New York: Scholastic. Hutchins, P. (1974). *The wind blew*. New York: Macmillan. Levy, J. (1995). *Abuelito goes home*. Worthington, OH: Macmillan/McGraw-Hill. Lyne, A. (1997). *A my name is . . .* Dallas: Whispering Coyote Press. Slate, J. (1996). *Miss Bindergarten gets ready for kindergarten*. New York: Dutton. Slate, J. (2000). *Miss Bindergarten stays home*. New York: Dutton. Weeks, S. (2005). *I'm a pig*. New York: Laura Geringer Books.
TV shows (familiar to ELLs) • Inviting ELLs to share the plot, favorite part(s), or character(s). • Encouraging ELLs to make text-to-self, text-to-text, and text-to-world connection.	See Figure 6.6.
Environmental print (EP) • Providing ELLs with an experience of talking about something familiar to them. • Providing ELLs with an opportunity to explore the functions and conventions of print.	• Food packages and labels (e.g., cereal boxes, candy wrappers, and price tags). • Household items (e.g., calendars and office supplies). • Signs (e.g., road/street, store, school, bus stop, and license plate). • Advertisements (e.g., grocery ads and coupons) (for more examples of EP, see Xu & Rutledge, 2003).
Community artifacts • Providing ELLs with an experience of talking about something familiar to them. • Increasing ELLs' background knowledge about the world in general and about specific concepts.	• Display at a social or cultural event (e.g., Cinco de Mayo celebration, Chinese New Year celebration, Tết [Vietnamese New Year celebration], and Muslim New Year celebration). • Ethnic food, clothing, toys, and containers. • Print materials in a native language (e.g., books and newspapers). • Nonprint materials in a native language (e.g., music CD and movie DVD/VHS tapes).

FIGURE 6.7. (*continued*)

Types of texts and purposes	Sample texts
Storybooks with a range of plot • Exposing ELLs to varied narrative text structures. • Developing ELLs' understanding of narrative text structures.	Cronin, D. (2000). *Click, clack, moo cows that type.* New York: Simon & Schuster. Cronin, D. (2002). *Giggle, giggle, quack.* New York: Simon & Schuster. Hartman, B. (2002). *The wolf who cried boy.* New York: Putnam's. Lionni, L. (1975). *A color of his own.* New York: Knopf. Scieszka, J. (1992). *The stinky cheese man and the other fairly stupid tales.* New York: Viking Penguin. Trivizas, E. (1993). *The three little wolves and the big bad pig.* New York: Macmillan. Walsh, E. S. (1994). *Pip's magic.* Orlando, FL: Harcourt Brace.
Book series Establishing familiarity with a plot, setting, and characters. Reducing cognitive load. Enhancing comprehension.	Arnold Lobel's *Frog and Toad* series Barbara Park's *Junie B. Jones* series Cynthia Rylant's *Poppleton* series Dav Pilkey's *Captain Underpants* series Joanna Cole's *Magic School Bus* series (picture books) Jonathan London's *Froggy* series Laura Numberoff's *If You . . .* Series Marc Brown's *Arthur* series Scholastic's *I Spy* series Scholastic's *Pokémon Junior* series (chapter books) Tedd Arnold's *Huggly* series
Books and TV shows about English Conventions • Allowing ELLs to learn about English grammar through reading. • Making a study of English grammar more interesting for ELLs.	PBS *Between the Lions pbskids.org/lions/index.html* PBS *Sesame Street pbskids.org/sesame/index.html* Cleary, B. P. (1999). *A mink, a fink, a skating rink: What's a noun?* Minneapolis: Carolrhoda Books. Cleary, B. P. (2001). *To root, to toot, parachute: What's a verb?* Minneapolis: Carolrhoda Books. Heller, R. (1987). *A cache of jewels and other collective nouns.* New York: Grosset & Dunlap. Heller, R. (1988). *Kites sail high: A book about verbs.* New York: Grosset & Dunlap.

(continued)

FIGURE 6.8. Texts for fostering ELLs' reading skills.

Types of texts and purposes	Sample texts
	Heller, R. (1989). *Many luscious lollipops: A book about adjectives*. New York: Grosset & Dunlap.Heller, R. (1991). *Up, up and away: A book about adverbs*. New York: Grosset & Dunlap. Heller, R. (1997). *Mine, all mine: A book about pronouns*. New York: Grosset & Dunlap. Heller, R. (1998). *Fantastic! wow! and unreal!: A book about interjections and conjunctions*. New York:Grosset & Dunlap. Leedy, L., & Street, P. (2003). *There's a frog in my throat*. New York: Holiday House. Pulver, R. (2003). *Punctuation takes a vacation*. New York: Holiday House.
Informational books • Allowing ELLs to become familiar with various expository text structures. • Allowing ELLs to learn about content through learning English.	Aliki. (1986). *How a book is made*. New York: HarperCollins. Bebega, D. (2004) *Let's read about Betsy Ross*. New York: Scholastic. Berger, M., & Berger, G. (2002). *GRRR! A book about big cats*. New York: Scholastic. DePaola, T. (1975). *The cloud book*. New York: Holiday House. Ehlert, L. (1988). *Planting a rainbow*. San Diego: Harcourt Brace & Company. Heller, R. (1983). *The reason for a flower*. New York: Putnam. Murphy, F. (2002). *Always inventing: The true story of Thomas Alva Edison*. New York: Scholastic. Murphy, S. J. (1996). *The best bug parade*. New York: HarperCollins. Otto, C. B. (2001). *Shadows*. New York: Scholastic. Rockwell, A. (1986). *Fire engines*. New York: Dutton. Simon, S. (2003). *Cool cars*. New York: SEASTAR Books.
Bilingual and multicultural books • Providing ELLs with texts of linguistic and cultural information. • Enhancing ELLs' engagement with texts.	Ada, A. F. (1995). *My mother plants strawberries*. Worthington, OH: Macmillan. Ada, A. F. (1997). *Gathering the sun: An alphabet in Spanish and English*. New York: Lothrop, Lee & Shepard Books. Brusca, M. C., & Wilson, T. (1995). *Three friends/Tres amigos*. New York: Holt.

FIGURE 6.8. (*continued*)

Types of texts and purposes	Sample texts
	Carle, E. (1996). *La mariquita malhumorada.* New York: HarperCollins.Carle, E. (1996). *The grouchy ladybug.* New York: HarperCollins. Carle, E. (2000) *Does a kangaroo have a mother, too?* New York: HarperCollins. Carle, E. (2002). *El canguro tiene Mamá?* New York: HarperCollins. Choi, Y. (2000). *My name jar.* New York: Knopf. Dooley, N. (1991). *Everybody cooks rice.* Minneapolis: Carolrhoda Books. Dooley, N. (1996). *Everybody bakes bread.* Minneapolis: Carolrhoda Books. Dooley, N. (2000). *Everybody serves soup.* Minneapolis: Carolrhoda Books. Elya, S. M. (1996). *Say hola to Spanish.* New York: Lee & Low Books. Feder, J. (1995). *Table, chair, bear: A book in many languages.* New York: Houghton Mifflin. Hoffman, M. (1991). *Amazing grace.* New York: Dial Books for Young Readers. McMillan, B. (1989). *Es la hora de . . .* New York: Lothrop, Lee & Shepard Books. McMillan, B. (1989). *Time to . . .* New York: Lothrop, Lee & Shepard Books. Mora, P. (1992). *A birthday basket for Tía.* New York: Macmillan Mora, P. (1996). *Uno, dos, tres: One, two, three.* New York: Clarion Books. Roe, E. (1991). *With my brother/Con mi hermano.* New York: Macmillan. Soto, G. (1993). *Too many tamales.* New York: Putnam. Waters, K., & Slovenz-Low, M. (1990). *Lion dancer.* New York: Scholastic. Young, E. (1989). *Lon Po Po.* New York: Philomel Books.

FIGURE 6.8. (*continued*)

surroundings (nature, people, and immediate world). When teachers make a text set related to a content area available for ELLs to explore, they also provide ELLs with an opportunity to practice and apply their listening, speaking, reading, and writing skills.

Types of texts and purposes	Sample texts
Wordless Books • Allowing ELLs to write a description of an illustration on each page in a native language or in English. • Allowing ELLs to write a story based on illustrations in a native language or in English.	See Figure 6.8
Books with a few words • Allowing ELLs to expand the text (of a few words). • Allowing ELLs to demonstrate their comprehension.	Carlson, N. (1997). *ABC I like me!* New York: Viking. Kightley, R. (1986). *Opposites.* New York: Little, Brown. McMillan, B. (1991). *Eating fractions.* New York: Scholastic. Numeroff, L. (1998). *What daddies do best; What mommies do best.* New York: Simon & Schuster. Numeroff, L. (2000). *What grandmas do best; What grandpas do best.* New York: Simon & Schuster. Raschka, C. (1993). *Yo! Yes?* New York: Orchard Books.
Community artifacts • Allowing ELLs to write about something familiar to them.	See Figure 6.8.

FIGURE 6.9. Texts for inviting ELLs to write.

Mrs. McBride, a kindergarten teacher, set up a science center (see Figure 6.10) in which she displayed a set of texts related to hermit crabs—a tank with hermit crabs, hermit crab food, hermit crab shells, several magnifying glasses, and books about hermit crabs. During the center time, Mrs. McBride modeled how to observe a hermit crab and describe it; how to use information in the books to help identify types of hermit crabs; and how to report an observation of hermit crabs back to the whole class. Mrs. McBride then let her students work in groups to explore the science center.

Figure 6.11 lists some sample text sets. We encourage teachers to collect books and other texts related to a content concept. A text set on a content concept provides ELLs with various text types to explore the

FIGURE 6.10. The text set in Mrs. McBride's science center.

Math (shapes)

Baker, A. (1994). *Brown rabbit's shape book*. New York: Larousse, Kingfisher, Chambers.

Dodds, D. A. (1994). *The shape of things*. Cambridge, MA: Candlewick Press.

Falwell, C. (1992). *Shape space*. New York: Houghton Mifflin.

Greene, R. G. (1997). *When a line bends . . . A shape begins*. New York: Houghton Mifflin.

Hoban, T. (1986). *Shapes, shapes, shapes*. New York: Morrow.

Scarry, R. (1998). *Lowly worm's shapes and sizes*. New York: Simon Spotlight.

Serfozo, M. (1996). *There's a square: A book about shapes*. New York: Scholastic.

Thong, R. (2000). *Round is a mooncake: A book of shapes*. San Francisco: Chronicle Books.

Science (color)

Baker, A. (1994). *White rabbit's color book*. New York: Kingfisher Books.

Carle, E. (1998). *Hello, red fox*. New York: Simon & Schuster.

Emberley, R. (2000). *My colors/Mis colores*. Boston: Little, Brown.

Heller, R. (1995). *Color*. New York: Grosset & Dunlap.

(continued)

FIGURE 6.11. Sample text sets.

Kissinger, K. (1994). *All the colors we are: The story of how we get our skin color*. St. Paul, MN: Redleaf Press.

McMillan, B. (1988). *Growing colors*. New York: Lothrop, Lee & Shepard Books.

Robbins, K. (1998). *Autumn leaves*. New York: Scholastic.

Seuss, Dr. (1996). *My many colored days*. New York: Knopf.

Walsh, E. S. (1989). *Mouse paint*. Orlando, FL: Harcourt Brace.

Social studies (people)

Carlson, N. (1988). *I like me!* New York: Viking Penguin.

Carlson, N. (1997). *ABC I like me!* New York: Viking Penguin.

Cheltenham Elementary School Kindergartners. (1991). *We are all alike . . . we are all different*. New York: Scholastic.

Curtis, J. L. (2002). *I'm gonna like me: Letting off a little self-esteem*. New York: Joanna Cotler Books.

Fox, M. (1997). *Whoever you are*. San Diego: Harcourt Brace.

Hudson, C. W., & Ford, B. G. (1990). *Bright eyes, brown skin*. South Orange, NJ: Just Us Books.

Marzollo, J. (1998). *How kids grow*. New York: Scholastic.

Rudko, C. (2000). *Flags of the world*. New York: Scholastic.

Spier, P. (1980). *People*. Garden City, NY: Doubleday.

FIGURE 6.11. (*continued*)

content and to practice and learn academic language (e.g., expository text structures and content-specific vocabulary).

> **TAKE A MOMENT**
>
> Now that you have finished reading this chapter, think about what you might do differently this school year in terms of selecting instructional texts for your ELLs. Jot down these differences and compare your choice of the texts with those you used last year. How are the texts selected different from those you used last year? What are the differences? What impact do you think these choices will have on your ELLs?

FINAL THOUGHTS

In the first half of this chapter, we discussed the differences between oral and written language and the effect of such differences on increased difficulty level a written text might pose for ELLs. We also explained various structure and content factors of a text and the intersection of both structure and content factors that can increase the difficulty level of a text for ELLs. In the second half of this chapter, we focused on presenting instructional texts for developing ELLs' listening, speaking, reading, and writing proficiency. To conclude this chapter, we caution teachers about the following: In selecting materials, teachers need to consider both the text factors (structure, content, and intersection of structure and content) that have an impact on text difficulty levels *and* an instructional purpose for using one particular text. Texts factors and instructional purpose should go hand in hand. Paying attention to one while overlooking the other may result in a selected text that is too hard or too easy for ELLs to serve any instructional purpose.

CHAPTER 7

Phonics, Spelling, and Vocabulary

> Children learning English may acquire literacy skills in
> English in a similar manner as native speaking children,
> although their alphabetic knowledge (i.e., their knowl-
> edge of the English alphabet and letter sound correspon-
> dences in English) may precede and facilitate the acqui-
> sition of phonological awareness in English.
> —CHIAPPE, SIEGEL, AND WADE-WOOLEY (2002. p. 369)

The issue of order of learning related to phonological awareness and
phonics is an important one for ELLs, as it varies from what is typically described for native English speakers. For English speakers, early-
childhood teachers primarily focus on phonological awareness and
phonemic awareness activities before moving to phonics activities or
activities where sound is connected to its symbolic representation. Because phonological awareness and in particular phonemic awareness
may develop later for ELLs, teachers would include more typical phonics
activities in their curriculum before they see mastery of phonological
understandings or phonics and phonemic awareness activities may occur simultaneously (Chiappe et al., 2002), unlike what is typically
taught to monolingual children.

In this chapter, we focus on word-level knowledge—that is, an
exploration of phonics, spelling, and vocabulary for ELLs. It is important for young children to understand the alphabetic code or how
sounds map to letters or letter groups in English. This knowledge
supports the decoding of words in text and facilitates comprehension

171

and spelling achievement (Strickland & Riley-Ayers, 2006). We then move to an exploration of vocabulary and its particular importance for ELLs and supporting instruction. Chapter 4 provided a more thorough discussion of phonological awareness and supporting instructional activities.

At the end of this chapter, you will be able to:

- Describe important language knowledge of ELLs and how it supports or hinders phonics instruction in English.
- Describe strategies and activities to help ELLs develop phonics knowledge.
- Describe how ELLs develop as spellers and how teachers can support them in gaining spelling proficiency.
- Describe the importance of vocabulary to reading comprehension.
- Describe strategies to support vocabulary knowledge.

PHONICS

Early reading achievement is highly dependent on word decoding skills (Juel, 1988; Stanovich, 1986). These skills develop in preschool, kindergarten, and first grade (sometimes later for ELLs who enter U.S. schools for the first time) as teachers support students in understanding phonological awareness (Lonigan, Burgess, & Anthony, 2000), letter knowledge (Adams, 1990), and vocabulary (Share, Jorm, MacLean, & Mathews, 1984). Recently, the *Report of the National Literacy Panel on Language-Minority Children and Youth* (August & Shanahan, 2006b) supported instruction for ELLs in phonemic awareness, phonics, and vocabulary among other reading components. The authors recommended that teachers consider the phonemes and combinations of phonemes that students may not have in their home language as a way to modify current phonemic awareness and phonics programs. More is shared about this later in this chapter.

Phonics refers specifically to teaching children about the code of the English language and its relationships in the spelling of words (Stahl, 1992). Stahl further described what exemplary phonics instruction would entail:

1. Phonics instruction builds on a child's understanding of how print functions. The child must know how print functions, what reading is, and so on. Stahl recommends that teachers help children develop this knowledge by reading to them and engaging them in language experience (see Chapter 4) and writing activities (see Chapter 5).

2. Phonics instruction builds on a foundation of phonemic awareness. For ELLs, teachers work on phonemic awareness as they also work on phonics activities.

3. Phonics instruction is clear and direct. Stahl recommends that teachers provide the written representation as children focus on individual sounds. Thus the children would see the word *ball* as they studied the initial consonant *b*. For ELLs, teachers may want to include the picture as well.

4. Phonics instruction is a part of a whole reading program. Here Stahl cautions teachers about an overreliance on worksheets to teach phonics. Rather, he sees phonics instruction directly integrated with the reading children are doing.

5. Phonics focuses on reading words, not learning rules. Stahl cautions readers not to rely on rules to decode a word; rather, they recognize new words by comparing them to known words or spelling patterns.

6. Phonics instruction may include an investigation of onsets and rimes. Stahl suggests that students explore rimes as a way to expand students' decoding skills. For example, they can generate new words from the rime *-ack*.

7. Phonics may include invented spelling practice. As children work on spelling a word, they are practicing what they know about phonics. As children write, they often sound out each letter orally as they record it.

8. Phonics instruction develops independent word recognition strategies, focusing attention on the structure of words. In this situation, children rely on the rime of a word, for instance, and do not decode that part of the word in a letter-by-letter way. Thus a word like *pack* would be decoded as *p + ack*.

9. Phonics instruction develops automatic word recognition so that students can focus their attention on comprehension.

The expectations for quality phonics instruction are not different for ELLs. It is important for teachers to know something about the home language of children so that they can build explicit connections between languages and also understand when an ELL represents a word based on first-language learning.

Structure of Languages

To begin, not all languages are alphabetic in structure. English has 26 letter symbols to represent more than 36 phonemes. Spanish, French, and Italian are also alphabetic languages and rely on approximately 26 symbols; however, they include diacritics or accent marks as special symbols that indicate different pronunciations. Other languages might be syllabic (e.g., Cherokee). Syllabic languages have a symbol for each syllable, not each phoneme. Besides syllabic languages there are logographic languages. The languages in China and Japan rely on characters; to read a newspaper a person needs to know approximately 5,000 characters. Whereas many Asian languages use a logograhic system, Vietnamese uses an alphabetic system with accompanying differences in its symbol representation. To further complicate the picture, there are combinations of these representations; for instance, in Japan they use both syllabic and logographic symbols (Strickland & Snow, 2002). Furthermore, some Asian languages use a phonic script for young learners (e.g., Pinyin in China) as a transition to learning to read and write characters.

Beyond the structure of symbols used, some languages are not read from left to right and top line to bottom line as is done with English. In Chinese, readers read down a column moving from right to left across a page (Wong & Kao, 1991) (see *zhongwen.com* for examples of characters and how to navigate text). Modern Hebrew is also written from right to left using the Hebrew alphabet (see *www.jewishvirtuallibrary.org/jsource/Judaism/alephbet.html* for examples). For children coming to U.S. schools with a home language such as Chinese or Hebrew, teachers need to explicitly teach the orientation of reading print and writing in English. For early-childhood teachers this is just part of their routine curriculum as they teach children about print and book awareness. Teachers of second grade and above may need to include this instruction as they help ELLs decode words and learn the alphabetic code so that they examine parts of words in a left-to-right orientation.

There are other language transfer issues for teachers as they embark on phonics instruction with ELLs (Kress, 1993). Teachers need to consider:

- Phonic elements that may have negative transfer from a child's first language. For instance, *v* is pronounced as a *b* in Arabic, Chinese, Spanish, and Vietnamese.
- English phonic elements that are unique to English. For example, in English vowels have a multitude of sounds and letter combinations; however, in Spanish vowels have a single sound.
- Difficult English sounds for speakers of other languages (see Table 7.1).

In Spanish, the alphabet is composed of the following symbols: *a, b, c, ch, d, e, f, g, h, i, j, k, l, ll, m, n, ñ, o, p, q, r, s, t, u, v, w, x, y, z*. English consonant sounds that also occur in Spanish are *n, p, k, f, y, b, g, s, ch, t, m, n, l,* and *h*. There are also shared blends such as *pl, pr, bl, br, tr, dr, cl, cr, gl, gr, fl,* and *fr*. There are English consonant blends not present in Spanish, such as *st, sp, sk/sc, sm, sl, sn, sw, tw, qu, scr, spr, str,* and *squ*. There are also English vowels sounds that are not present in Spanish, such as short *a* (*man*), *i* (*bit*), and *u* (*up*), *r*-controlled vowels (*girl*), schwa sound (*away*), and vowel sounds in *caught, could,* and *use*. Sounds that are difficult for Spanish speakers of English are *d*, often pronounced as *th, y* or *ch* for *j* in *juice*, a rolled *r* for the *r* in *rope*, a *b* sound for the *v* in *van*, an *s* sound for the *z* in *zipper,* a *ch* sound for the *sh* in *shell,* and a *t* sound for the *th* in *then* (see *Spanish.about.com* for details about Spanish).

Few words in Spanish end with *t*. This sound requires explicit teaching for students whose home language is Spanish as it is not in

TABLE 7.1. Difficult English Sounds

Native language	Difficult English Sounds
Chinese	*b, ch, d, g, f, m, n, ng, ō, sh, s, th, v, z, l*-clusters, *r*-clusters
Japanese	*d, g, f, h, l, th, oo, sh, s, v, w,* schwa, *l*-clusters, *r*-clusters
Korean	*b, l, ō, ow, p, r, sh, t, v,* schwa, *l*-clusters, end clusters
Spanish	*b, d, dg, h, j, m, n, ng, sh, th, v, w, y, z, s*-clusters, end clusters
Urdu	*ā, a, d, ē, f, n, ng, s, sh, t, th*
Vietnamese	*ā, ē, k, l, ng, p, r, sh, s, y, l*-clusters, end clusters
	In Vietnamese, *th* sounds like *t* in English and *t* sounds like *th*.

their Spanish-language repertoire. While this one sound at the end of a word seems minor, most early readers begin with students exploring short-*a* words such as *cat, mat,* and *fat.* To complicate matters, there are also no words in Spanish that end with *p* (Rodriguez-Galindo & Wright, 2006).

In Asian languages, there are no clusters that contain *l*. Words with *l*-blends like *sled* and *clock* will pose difficulty for Asian students (see *en.wikipedia.org/wiki/Chinese_language* for details about Chinese). Although teachers may be overwhelmed by the language nuances that help or hinder phonics knowledge and decoding, there are many websites that provide this information. We listed two in this section focused on Spanish and Chinese. Information about hundreds of languages is available at *en.wikipedia.org/wiki/List_of_languages.*

Moreover, students with different home languages will pronounce words differently. Differences in pronunciation do not mean that students are not aware of the sound–symbol connections; they may just be difficult for them to produce. We are sure that many teachers in their foreign language classes found it difficult to pronounce certain sounds in learning a new language. For some sounds not found in English, they may never have been successful. This situation is no different for children learning to speak, read, and write in a new language. Children can listen to how words are pronounced in English through the use of *www.thefreedictionary.com* where by clicking an icon the word is pronounced.

Teachers should also be aware that in many countries children learn English in their schools. For example, in Taiwan all children are instructed in English in the fifth grade, and many preschools and kindergartens are systematically bringing English into their curricula (Oladejo, 2006). These children would then have experiences with their home language and English as they enter U.S. schools, and they would have an understanding of how sounds map to letters or characters.

TAKE A MOMENT

Think about how a teacher can support students who come to school with a home language other than English in phonics knowledge. How might teachers use older students or family members to help?

Phonics Instruction

Learning the Alphabet

ALPHABET BOOKS

One of the easiest ways to help children learn the alphabet is to read alphabet books to them. If the teacher highlights each letter, children begin to identify the letter and perhaps begin to connect the item connected to the letter. In Figure 7.1 we included several alphabet books that we think are appropriate for children just learning the alphabet, including a few books that have bilingual representations of words so that students can connect their home language and letters and sounds with English letters and sounds.

Alphabet books serve many purposes. They provide a vehicle for explicit instruction in the alphabet. They also provide informal instruction in the relationship between sound and symbol. Finally, they provide opportunities for ELLs to learn English vocabulary.

Alphabet books in English

Aylesworth, J. (1992). *Old black fly*. New York: Holt.

Ehlert, L. (1989). *Eating the alphabet: Fruits and vegetables from A to Z*. New York: Harcourt Brace.

Hague, K. (1984). *Alphabears: An ABC book*. New York: Holt, Rinehart & Winston.

Hoban, T. (1982). *A, B, see!* New York: Greenwillow Books.

Hoban, T. (1987). *26 letters and 99 cents*. New York: Greenwillow Books.

Isadora, R. (1983). *City seen from A to Z*. New York: Greenwillow Books.

Jay, A. (2003). *ABC: A child's first alphabet book*. New York: Penguin.

Kitchen, B. (1984). *Animal alphabet*. New York: Dial.

Martin, B., & Archambault, J. (1989). *Chicka chicka boom boom*. New York: Simon & Schuster.

Miller, J. (1987). *The farm alphabet book*. New York: Scholastic.

Bilingual alphabet books

Rosa-Mendoza, G. (2000). *The alphabet. El alfabeto*. Wheaton, IL: me + mi Publishing.

www.asianparent.com for English–Asian alphabet books.

FIGURE 7.1. Alphabet books.

Children can also create their own alphabet books. Teachers can encourage very young children to write or cut out letters for each page. They can also find pictures in catalogues to glue on each letter page. Often children locate environmental print that they can read with the logo present, such as McDonald's or Trix, or they can include classmate's names or pictures. Teachers may need to scaffold this activity when children are first learning about sound–symbol relationships. With more sophisticated alphabet knowledge, children can write each letter and draw representative pictures for each page.

Children can also create multilanguage alphabet books. Through this type of cross-language endeavor children learn that even though the item is the same, the way it is represented can be very different. For instance, if *eagle* is chosen as the English word for the letter *e*, the Spanish equivalent is *águila*, the Italian equivalent is *áquila*, the Japanese equivalent is *i-guru*, and in Chinese 名鷹 .

SAND, CLAY, AND OTHER MEDIA

Young children can also make letters in sand or with clay. Often preschool teachers have children glue objects onto a letter pattern. The object is connected to the sound of the letter—for example, gluing feathers on the letter *f*. Teachers also have children form the letters with their bodies, use water on the playground to form letters, or paint letters. Each of these activities supports children's learning of the alphabet.

LETTER SORTING

Children find specific letters and sort them. For instance, a teacher may request students to look through magazines and find the letters *a* and *m*. See Figure 7.2 for an example of this sorting. Through this activity, children come to notice the various ways a single letter can be formed.

WEBSITES

In our search for alphabet websites, we were surprised at how many are available. We list several, some of which identify letters and have games to facilitate letter identity.

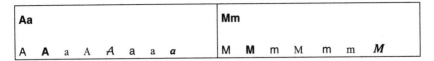

Aa	Mm
A **A** a A *A* a a *a*	M **M** m M m m *M*

FIGURE 7.2. Letter sorting.

- *www.computerlab.kids.new.net/abc_sites.htm* (alphabet websites)
- *www.tccsa.net/websites/k/* (alphabet activities and websites for kindergarten children)
- *www.billybear4kids.com/games/online/alphabet/abc.htm* (alphabet games)
- *www.muddlepuddle.co.uk/Resources%20and20%Themes/Alphabets.htm* (alphabet letter games)
- *www.apples4theteacher.com/coloring-pages/interactive-alphabet/index. html* (alphabet games)
- *www.sesameworkshop.org/sesamestreet/coloringpages* (pages for children to color)
- *www.learningplanet.com/act/fl/aact/index.asp* (alphabet games)
- *www.pbskids.org/lions/games* (alphabet games and other word games)

This last website offers a view of the alphabet in numerous languages. Children can compare or at least see the differences among alphabets (*www.ask.com/*) and then type in the alphabet.

Mapping Letters and Sounds

As children develop some knowledge of letters, they can be instructed in sound–symbol instruction explicitly. Typically teachers use the following sequence for instruction:

- Initial consonants
- Short vowels, including word families (onset–rime)
- Blends and digraphs
- Long vowels (Peregoy & Boyle, 2005)

USING PICTURES

As children recognize letters and start making connections with sound, teachers can have students compare pictures for initial consonant sounds or find pictures that begin with a certain sound. See Figure 7.3 for examples of these activities. If children do these activities in a small group, they can chat about the pictures and the sounds they begin with.

As children acquire rich knowledge about initial consonant sounds, they can do similar activities with pictures where they find words that have short *a* in them, like *bat,* or a digraph in them, like *ch* in *chip,* and so on. Picture support is particularly beneficial to ELLs who may not easily be able to identify words alone that exemplify a sound.

USING LETTERS

Teachers can start by having children show a magnetic letter that begins with the targeted consonant, short vowel, blend, and so on. The child just moves the letter up or down from the full alphabet. For very young children, the teacher might limit the full range of letters to about five for this process. As the child develops letter–sound knowledge, the teacher can ask the child to form words with the letters. See Figure 7.4 for an example of this process.

This photo shows Micah building words with the rime of *at.* He changes the beginning consonant as he constructs words. His teacher has limited the letters he can choose from so that they all form real *at* words like, *cat, hat, mat, sat,* and *bat.* In order for Micah to be successful with this task, he must understand the sounds of the initial consonants—

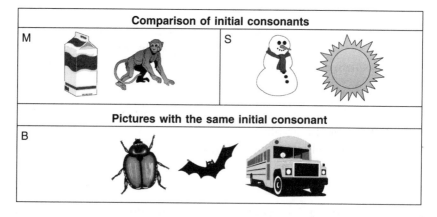

FIGURE 7.3. Picture activities.

FIGURE 7.4. Micah forming words.

the short-*a* sound, the sound of the ending *t* consonant—and he must blend these sounds to form words.

ELKONIN BOXES

We have observed teachers who have small individual chalkboards or whiteboards with three or four squares on them. When a child creates a word with letters, he or she puts each phoneme in a box. For example, if the child was asked to represent *map* with letters, he or she would put the *m* in the first box, the *a* in the middle, and the *p* in the last. Through this process children identify the individual phonemes that make up a word, often before they can easily write the letters.

COMPARING LANGUAGES IN BOOKS

Many books for young children have English and most often Spanish within them. These books offer children opportunities to compare the sounds in words between languages. For instance, they might notice that *red* begins with an *r* as does *rojo*, but yellow begins with a *y* and *amarillo* an *a*. We found the books *My House, Mi Casa* (Emberley, 1990a) and *Taking a Walk, Caminando* (Emberley, 1990b) quite helpful for this

exploration. For more sophisticated readers, *Pepita Talks Twice* (Lachtman, 1995) offers a resource for similar exploration.

WRITING

As mentioned in the discussion around phonological awareness, one
of the ways children learn about sound–symbol representation is by
writing. As children create their message, they experiment with letters
to represent sounds. Chapter 4 described the development of representing words. Children as young as 3 years can participate in daily
journal writing to sustain this practice and support sound–symbol
awareness. Teachers are able to see children moving from random representations for letter sounds to conventional representations of the
phonemes within words.

WORD WALLS

Word walls, where the teacher places words on the wall, are great support for ELLs. Here children can see words and analyze similar phonic
elements. Teachers might compare words that begin with the same initial consonant, such as *fat* and *far*. Students can also use these words in
their writing. In particular, we have seen teachers place pictures next to
words to help children secure the meaning as well as the spelling of
words.

WORD SORTS

Word sorts are similar to the earlier description of picture sorting.
Rather than children sorting pictures, they sort words. The words might
come from a teacher-created list, a teacher- and student-created list, or
children's exploration of text (Bear et al., 2003). For instance, if children are studying the short sound of *a*, they might sort words that the
teacher organized, they might create a list with their teacher's support,
or they might be sent to find short-*a* words in books they have read.
Figure 7.5 depicts a finished sorting activity accomplished by a first-
grade student. In this activity, the child sorted short-*a* words by ending
sound–letter and then had a crazy pile for words that did not fit these
patterns. This student's teacher provided each child with a notebook for
the recording of word sorts. By having the sorts organized in this way,

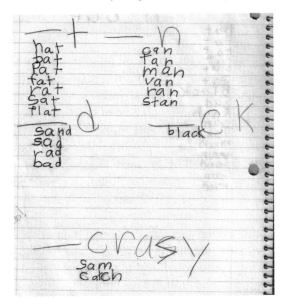

FIGURE 7.5. Short-*a* word sort.

children could return to previous sorts for other sorting activities. For instance, a child might compare the short-*a* word sort with a long-*a* word sort, noting differences in the words.

MAKING WORDS

Making words is a strategy developed by Cunningham (1991). When using this strategy, teachers provide students with individual letters such as *t, s, a, e, b,* and *k.* The teacher might begin by asking students to form the word *bat,* then *sat, set, ask, base,* and finally *basket.* The first words are always the easiest and represent short-vowel, consonant–vowel–consonant (CVC) words. As students are successful with these words, the teacher nudges them to more complex words and ends with a mystery word that uses all the letters.

What is important about teaching phonics is that teachers explicitly focus on how sounds are represented with letters. ELLs need this explicit instruction to learn the alphabetic code of the English language. This foundational knowledge is critical to their future reading and writing success.

SPELLING

Spelling instruction builds on the phonics section we presented earlier in this chapter. To learn to spell, children first learn about letters, letter–sound combinations, and how to map single-syllable short-vowel words—known as the *alphabetic element* of spelling (Bear et al., 2003). This part of spelling centers on the alphabet and a very straightforward representation of letter sounds in words (as can be seen in CVC words like *cat, hop,* or *red*). The next level of exploration involves studying blends like *pr* or *sl* where both letters are sounded. Children then explore digraphs where two or more letters represent one sound, like *sh, ch,* or *tch.*

Once students understand the alphabetic layer of spelling, they are ready to deal with the variability of spelling that moves beyond such straightforward representation of sound to symbol. The second level for exploration is the *pattern layer* where children learn about groups of letters or patterns that may have a single sound but various representations. Children learn about silent letters as in *know* and long-vowel patterns such as those for long *a: make, steak, rain, may, they,* and *neighbor.* They also explore homophones, words that sound the same—but have different meanings—like *meat* and *meet.* They begin this exploration in single syllable words and then consider multisyllabic words, although this spelling instruction is beyond what is typical for most young children in the primary grades (Templeton, 1997).

The third layer of spelling is the *meaning layer* and ties directly to vocabulary instruction. Within this level, children learn about the meaning aspects of words and how the sound may change but the spelling remains consistent (Templeton, 1997) (e.g., words like *sign* and *signal*). Younger children might learn about how *tri* means three as they explore a tricycle and a triangle.

TAKE A MOMENT

Think about instruction to support ELLs before reading the next section. Write down activities that you use or are familiar with. Then, when you finish the spelling instruction section, complete your list of possible activities to use to support spelling knowledge.

Spelling Instruction

Instruction in spelling begins with the phonics activities we described earlier. The importance of this early instruction is that children examine similarities and differences in words and then write them, rather than memorizing a list of words. For instance, when a teacher instructed a group of children in how to represent short-*a* CVC words, she modeled how to write one short-*a* word, then students examined other words with the same rime pattern like *at, an,* or *ap.* As children recorded short-*a* words with the *at* rime, they noticed that for the most part the words stayed the same, just the initial consonant changed. For spelling, these children would be expected to spell any CVC word with the *at* pattern. Following these lessons, teachers expand their investigation of short-*a* with other rimes. Then students compare these words, sort them as seen in Figure 7.5, and can be expected to spell them correctly.

Word Sorts

Word sorts were described under phonics and they play an important part with spelling. By sorting words and representing them, students have multiple opportunities for practice with word patterns. These practice activities involve children in physically sorting words, which relies on children's ability to read the word and analyze where it fits. Thus if the categories for sorting (determined by the teacher, students and teacher, or students) are *ot* and *op,* children read words from small

op	ot
mop	pot
hop	hot
top	dot
stop	not

FIGURE 7.6. Short-*o* word sort.

word cards or from their reading and place them in the appropriate column. See Figure 7.6 for an example. In this example, the teacher has provided pictures so that students, especially ELLs, can refer to them when comparing sounds in words. A shift is seen in this sort as the children are sorting words without picture support. When children can do this easily, they can expand this sort to include other short-*o* words. As children achieve mastery on short-vowel words, they consider long- and short-vowel words and then they move to long-vowel, single-syllable word exploration.

Word Games

Word games are just that, games that focus on the representation of words or elements within words.

■ Teachers can create simple *game boards* that follow a path. Children roll a die to determine how many places to move and they read a word on the spot where they land. If the board is blank, teachers can put in any word cards to fit the pattern they are studying. For example, if students are learning about short-*a,* each space would have a short-*a* word on a card on it. Other students can use the same board with different word cards.

■ *Bingo games* also help with spelling. Again, if teachers have blank bingo cards, they can enter the words they are studying.

■ *Word wheels* allow children to explore all the words with a similar pattern. For instance, the child turns the wheel and a new beginning initial consonant, blend, or digraph appears. The child then reads the word knowing that the end remains the same.

■ *Letter cube games* allow children to create words and read them. Children might also be asked to record the words they form. And, perhaps, the teacher might expect a student to sort these recorded words.

Student-Created Spelling Books

For this activity children create either individual, small-group, or whole-class books. For example, students may create a short-i book where each child contributes a page with a short-i word and an illustration. As children mature in their knowledge of words, they could create long-vowel books, homonym books, compound words, and so on.

These books then serve as a spelling support in the classroom and are very useful for ELLs as they have word and picture support.

Word Walls

The word wall serves as a classroom support for the spelling of words. This is also a great place to put sight words or words that cannot be decoded, such as *of, a, the,* and so on. These words require memorization.

Simple Phonics Readers

Most reading programs have supplementary phonics readers. These readers are written to allow children to practice reading a simple text that repeats a phonics competency. For example, a book might be written about a cat with many short-*a* words within it. Books with limited vocabulary, constructed to repeat phonic elements, offer support and success for children who are beginning readers. Importantly, these books would only comprise a small part of a child's reading material.

Websites

Numerous websites support phonics development. We provide a few for exploration.

- *teacher.scholastic.com/reading/bestpractices/phonics/teach.htm.* This site offers a sequence of phonics competencies from preschool through sixth grade. It has activities as well.
- *www.readingrockets.org.* This site provides numerous articles centered on various elements of reading, in particular phonics.
- *www.starfall.com.* This site provides phonic readers for young children so they can practice their current knowledge of phonics.
- *www.readwritethink.org.* This site provides lessons in phonics based on the age of the student. All the materials for each lesson are downloadable and the lessons have been created by teachers.

The spelling activities we have described all require active engagement on the part of students. We do not believe that having students memorize a list of words supports their long-term spelling development. Rather, we believe that exploring words and questioning what is similar or different about words and the way they are represented supports students in their acquisition of spelling knowledge. ELLs can offer additional information during these comparisons as they also document similarities and differences in spelling of words between their home language and English.

VOCABULARY

Students' vocabulary grows at an astonishing rate each year, approximately 3,000 words, many more words than any one teacher can teach directly in a single school year (Nagy & Herman, 1987). Children begin to learn words at home, as has been documented by Hart and Risley (1995). They studied 42 families and their young 1- or 2-year-old children as they talked with their parents until the children were 3. They discovered that by age 3, children's vocabularies closely matched the size of their parents'. They also grouped children and their families by parent status: welfare, working class, or professional. They noted that professional families talked to their child more than three times as much as welfare parents did (i.e., 2,153 words per hour compared with 616 words per hour). This difference resulted in discrepancies in vocabulary size from 500 words to 1,000 when the children were 3. These early differences are magnified as children get older. In their study, Hart and Risley (1995) documented the words that children acquired (basic names and categories) and how these words created "the foundations for the complex concepts and relationships the children will be asked to understand later on" (pp. 98–99).

The Hart and Risley study documents how children acquire English vocabulary through the support of their families. Certainly, ELLs acquire their first vocabulary from their parents and family members in a similar way. However, when ELLs step into their first U.S. classrooms, they are expected to acquire the social and academic vocabulary necessary to become a successful reader and writer of English, a language that is different from the one with which they are familiar.

For young children, teachers are important for the learning of vocabulary beyond that typically shared in their families. They highlight school words like *desks, room, office, cafeteria, pencil,* or *crayons* throughout the day. They support students in learning how to say "Hello," "I need the bathroom," and so on. They offer students opportunities to talk with fellow students to practice their new words and ideas. They bring in objects or use photos or video to help students acquire important words for classroom content. For instance, we saw a first-grade teacher bring in sandpaper when a poem students were exploring discussed how a cat's tongue felt like sandpaper. Students rubbed their fingers on the sandpaper to learn about sandpaper and simultaneously to learn how the cat's tongue felt.

Teachers of young children also extend children's vocabularies through the reading of narrative and informational text. Beck, McKeown, and Kucan (2002) suggest the following way of categorizing words so that the most important words are selected from books and targeted in instruction:

■ *Tier 1 words.* These are words that ELLs typically know in their first language, like *hop* or *house.* Typically a picture or quick acting out of the word helps the ELL understand the meaning. We have used *googleimages.com* to find pictures of words that may be more abstract in understanding. At this site you can type in a word such as *smooth* and many photos representing this word appear. Sometimes the use of a Spanish cognate helps children whose home language is Spanish (e.g., the comparison of *family* with *familia*). A source for Spanish/English cognates is *www.colorincolorado.org.*

■ *Tier 2 words.* These words tend to be more complex and abstract than Tier 1 words. They include words tied to text, such as character, setting, and plot. They include more specific nouns, verbs, and adjectives, such as *frustrated.* These words are the ones that Beck et al. (2002) recommend teachers select in text to highlight. They are important words for students to learn, as they are used often in narrative and informational texts that students encounter. These words require more instruction from teachers. Spanish-speaking children may have an advantage here because many of these words include Spanish cognates such as *industrious/industrioso.*

■ *Tier 3 words.* These words are found mostly in content books for older students. They are infrequently encountered in the primary grades.

When considering vocabulary instruction for ELLs, there have been few studies. Shanahan and Beck (2006) reviewed these studies and noted that the results are similar to what is reported for native speakers. That is, vocabulary instruction leads to deeper processing of word meanings that in turn support reading comprehension. Fitzgerald (1995a) concurs that there are few studies targeted to vocabulary instruction for ELLs and that the results of the few studies converge with the results of what is reported for English speakers. She supports the important connection between vocabulary knowledge and comprehension. Moreover, Fitzgerald suggests that students whose first languages have cognates in English have an advantage in learning English vocabulary.

Beck, McKeown, and Omanson (1987) explored what it means to know a word. They identified four levels in the development of full word understanding:

1. *No knowledge.* The child has never heard the word before.
2. *General sense.* The child believes he or she has seen or heard the word before.
3. *Partial knowledge.* The child knows something about the word. He or she might be able to relate it situationally.
4. *Full knowledge.* The child can explain the word's meaning and use it correctly.

Teachers can use this developmental progression when targeting new words for children to learn. They can create a simple chart where children check what they know about a word. If the teacher uses Post-it Notes, he or she can get an idea of children's knowledge of words targeted for instruction.

The tricky part of vocabulary knowledge and instruction is that although it is critical to develop in young children, its importance does not show up until around second grade, when there is more of a focus on comprehension and the words students encounter in reading are not as familiar. Moreover, the need for vocabulary instruction is especially significant for preschoolers who are considered at risk for grade-level reading achievement, which certainly includes ELLs (Roth, Speece, & Cooper, 2002; Strorch & Whitehurst, 2002). Thus preschool and kindergarten teachers will find that they will not see the direct results of the amount of time spent in vocabulary instruction, and they will have to be intractable in their valuing of such instruction so that it does not disappear from their instruction.

TAKE A MOMENT

As a teacher, how would you decide on the words that you will use to directly instruct students? Look at a reading selection and select four words that would require direct instruction. What words do you notice that ELLs struggle with? How would you help ELLs learn these words?

Beck et al. (2002) help teachers with the sources of words for young children. For the most part, books that young children can read are not a good source. These books focus on words already in most young children's vocabularies, such as *dog, family, sun, snow,* and so on. They recommend that teachers rely on children's books beyond the reading level of students, as they are one of the major sources of rare words for students—about 31 per 1,000 words (Cunningham & Stanovich, 1998). In addition to these books, teachers also serve as a model for language learning through their own conversations with students. They might do this modeling with *on-the-spot* explanations of words from books so that students can comprehend text. For example, they might say, "Brilliant means very bright in this book so the sun is very bright or brilliant." This supportive instruction occurs quickly and teachers can help students with multiple words as they read. The goal is to focus on comprehension as students are given quick, student-friendly definitions. Teachers also take time after reading a book to engage students in an active discussion of several words. Importantly, this discussion focuses on the meaning of words that require thinking on the part of students and will be seen multiple times in other reading and is fast paced.

Gersten, Baker, Haager, and Graves (2005) described the strategies that effective teachers used with ELLs that resulted in high growth of vocabulary. These teachers emphasized vocabulary throughout their entire teaching day: "Vocabulary served as a kind of anchor around which many other activities revolved" (p. 203). Teachers chose words that were engaging and essential for story or informational text understanding. In addition to these words, they taught words that they believed were essential for ELLs and would not necessarily be explicitly taught to monolingual children. Gersten et al. provided an example of students learning about a valley, where the teacher explained what *high* and *low* meant. They found that most teachers relied on books or pictures to teach vocabulary and one teacher also acted out words. Importantly, they noted that most of the vocabulary instruction did not require extensive preparation on the part of teachers. However, teachers were mindful of the importance of students understanding words, not just pronouncing them correctly.

The remainder of this chapter focuses on activities to support the acquisition of vocabulary for ELLs.

Vocabulary Instruction

We begin this section with descriptions of more informal, on-the-go kinds of vocabulary activities. Then we consider more formal, thought-out activities to support vocabulary growth.

Conversations

The teacher can highlight words or substitute simple words with more complex ones as he or she is interacting with students. For example, the teacher can use the word *ajar* for an open door or *aghast* when she or he is surprised. Children can be asked to repeat this word and use it throughout the day. Another way to support children's vocabulary through conversation is by having one area of the classroom serve as a talking center. The teacher or an instructional aide can facilitate conversation with a small group of students in this center. They might talk about an item brought for show-and-tell, or the teacher might supply an item that stimulates conversation such as shells, an insect, or a small animal. The teacher could also use any established center in the room to extend children's language. For instance, if a child is painting, the teacher might comment on the *texture* of the paint rather than just the content of the painting. Another way to interact with young children is to have a snack with them or eat lunch with them. If a few children are scheduled each day for this activity the teacher can engage them in conversation and nudge them to more complex word choice (Cote, 2001).

Teachers need to be mindful of the language they use in these conversations. Most preschool teachers provide positive comments to students which most often deal with routine matters but do not contribute to vocabulary growth (Dunn, Beach, & Kontos, 1994). Thus teachers will want to extend the word choice offered by students with more complex terminology.

Text Talk

Beck et al. (2002) describe a process of reading aloud that targets vocabulary. The teacher introduces the story. Then the teacher stops and asks questions and receives responses from the children while reading. The teacher also highlights pictures and how they support comprehension. Following a wrapup of the text, the teacher engages students in vocabulary exploration. Following is an example of the vocabulary part of text talk. We used the book *Russell the Sheep* (Scotton, 2005) for this example.

TEACHER: It says that Russell was too cramped. I think *cramped* is an interesting word. How about we say it together?

CHILDREN: *Cramped.*

TEACHER: *Cramped* means that he was squeezed into a very small space and he was uncomfortable. Look at the picture and you can see that he was cramped. I wonder where else someone might be cramped. I think if you crawled under my desk, you would feel cramped. Can you think of a place where you felt cramped?

CHILD: I felt cramped when I was too big for my crib.

Children learn about the meaning of a word through the contextualization of the text. First the teacher explains the word; then students follow up with their own examples. Through this process, students gain an understanding of the word and practice using it repeatedly in sentences that they construct.

Text talk is not limited to fictional text. Teachers can use this same strategy with informational text. Following is an example using the informational book *Night Wonders* (Peddicord, 2005).

TEACHER: This book begins with, "Beside a dark and quiet sea beneath a starlit canopy." The word *canopy* confused me a bit. I thought it was like a canopy over my bed. You know some beds have cloth over them. We can look in this book and see a canopy over a bed. The author is using this idea of a canopy, something over our head, but she means the sky. She is talking about the sky filled with stars as a canopy. How about if we all say *canopy.*

CHILDREN: *Canopy.*

TEACHER: So we now know an interesting way a writer used the word *canopy.* Can you think of a way to use *canopy?* Share a way with your neighbor.

CHILD: I have a canopy bed.

CHILD: The ceiling is a canopy in my house.

Rereading Books

Sénéchal (1997) writes about how preschoolers learn new words by re-reading books. On the first reading, children might be expected to attend to meaning. On a second or subsequent reading, children's attention can be drawn to the interesting words.

Centers

Teachers place interesting items in centers for which children may not know the label. For instance, they may place a stethoscope, spatula, receipt, or other items in centers for children to explore and to learn the label. Having the real objects present will support ELLs in acquiring this vocabulary.

Quick Sketch

Children quickly sketch a representation of a word. Importantly, this is not an art lesson. It is best if children use pencils and are given a limited amount of time for each sketch.

Word of the Day

The teacher or teacher and students together decide on a word each day that they will use repeatedly throughout the day. For instance, they might choose *refreshed* from *Caps for Sale* (Slobodkina, 1987). After snack a child might say, "I am so refreshed." This idea might be combined with Beck's (2003) "word wizard" activity. In this activity, the teacher or children identify a word for the day. The teacher places student names on a chart. Each time a student says the word, he or she puts a Post-it Note next to his or her name. There is some identified number of repetitions and the child is then honored as a word wizard.

Acting Out a Word

Once a word is explained, children might act it out. For example, if the word is *hysterical*, children could pretend to cry.

Word Clusters

The child, with teacher support, explores the meaning of a word by describing it with related words in a cluster. See Figure 7.7 for an example.

Word Collections or Word Consciousness

Children collect words related to a category. For example, young children might add fairytale words to a poster. The list might include *tiny, wee, gigantic, fierce, huge,* or *puny.* As this list grows large, children might categorize the words into big and small words, scary words, and so on.

Semantic Maps of Words

In this activity, children organize words around a topic of study. Figure 7.8 displays a semantic chart for the night sky. Children learn about one

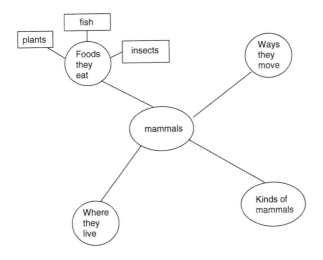

FIGURE 7.7. Word cluster of mammals.

Parts	People in sky	Galaxy
Stars Planets Moon	Pilots Astronauts	Dust Gas Stars Milky Way
Moon	**Stars**	**Planets**
Comes out at night Gets bigger and smaller	Twinkle Bright Lots of them	Earth Pluto Mars

FIGURE 7.8. Semantic chart for the night sky.

topic and the many vocabulary words related to it. A chart allows students to return to it to check on current knowledge or to add to it.

Content Word Walls

Content word walls are similar to word walls, except that they target current instruction. For instance we observed a teacher create a content word wall centered on butterflies and moths. Figure 7.9 shows an early form of this expanding word wall. This chart hung throughout the study, and students referred to it during reading or while writing. Picture support would have provided more support for ELLs.

Student-Created Vocabulary Explorations

In this activity, the child writes the new vocabulary word, guesses at its meaning, then checks out the context in which it was found and, finally,

A antennae	B butterfly	C caterpillar cocoon chrysalis	D	E eggs	F	G	H
I	J	K	L larvae	M migration	N nectar	O	P
Q	R	S	T	U	V	W	XYZ

FIGURE 7.9. Content word wall.

a dictionary. Young children could participate in this activity with the teacher writing or independently through the use of pictures. See Figure 7.10 for an example.

A variation of this activity can be used in content areas such as math. For instance, the word might be *sum*. The child writes *sum* in the first box, then describes what *sum* is in the second box (answer in addition), and then in the third box shows a sum (4 + 4 = 8).

Academic Vocabulary

ELLs also need to learn words that teachers use routinely, such as page, chart, author, and so on. While monolingual students may understand the use of *first, then,* and *finally,* ELLs may not understand how these words are used in reading and writing for organization. This vocabulary requires that as teachers consider the content they teach, they must also think of the vocabulary expectations. They must scan a lesson and determine whether there are words that may be confusing to ELLs. Echevarria et al. (2004) describe the Sheltered Instruction Observation Protocol (SIOP) model, which helps teachers consider the content and the language expectations within lessons for ELLs. Importantly, teachers need to think carefully about the content they are teaching and any problem places that ELLs may have because of word understanding. For instance, an ELL may struggle with the word *sequence,* although he or she may understand the concept of sequencing. A quick drawing on the board may be all the child needs to understand this concept.

groom	brushing your hair	It means to clean up
keen	squinting	Great—he liked it.
scorching	bugging someone	burning
scorching		

FIGURE 7.10. Student vocabulary exploration.

Websites

As in other areas, numerous websites are targeted to vocabulary. Following are a few we found that are rich with activities for young children.

- *www.vocabulary.com.* This website includes lists of words and multiple activities to support vocabulary for children in grades 1 through 10.
- *www.lessonplancentral.com.* This site offers activities for word learning and integrates vocabulary with writing and listening exercises.
- *www.eslflow.com/vocabularylessonplans.html.* This site offers vocabulary activities targeted to the needs of ELLs.
- *www.ohiou.edu/esl/english/vocabulary.html.* This site offers games and pictures to support ELLs' vocabulary development.
- *www.eslbears.homestead.com/Contact_Info.html.* This site provides vocabulary activities for the youngest students.

Similar to other word-level investigation, we see vocabulary as an active process where children manipulate objects, pictures, and text to acquire meaning. We value the work that teachers of very young children provide to students in vocabulary so that comprehension of text is facilitated.

FINAL THOUGHTS

In this chapter, we considered letter- and word-level knowledge. Although we have isolated this knowledge, we understand that it is just a part of the learning that children need to accomplish to become fully literate. The phonics, spelling, and vocabulary instruction shared in this chapter is expected to be embedded in rich literacy curricula that explore a wide variety of texts for reading and writing. We also expect that word-level instruction requires active engagement on the part of students. For example, students sort words or students respond frequently as they collaborate with their teachers on word meanings. Finally, we see word-level knowledge as fundamental to reading fluency and comprehension.

CHAPTER 8

Engaging English Language Learners in the Comprehension Process

Good readers set a purpose for reading and bring several knowledge resources to bear upon the comprehension process, among them: decoding ability, language knowledge, background knowledge, written genre knowledge, familiarity with text structures, and comprehension-monitoring abilities. Non-native English readers engage in a similar reading process, with certain important differences . . . (a) English language proficiency, (b) background knowledge, and (c) literacy knowledge and experience in the primary language.
—PEREGOY AND BOYLE (2000, p. 239)

The reading process, as Peregoy and Boyle stated, involves several subprocesses such as decoding words; applying background knowledge of the topic of a text, text genre, and text structures to text being read; and self-monitoring to construct meanings from the text. The subprocesses occur simultaneously and mostly automatically to make the comprehension process successful. If several subprocesses are not automatic, a reader has to divide his or her cognitive resources among tasks of attending to these subprocesses. For example, if a reader cannot decode words fast enough, he or she must focus on decoding words, assigning a meaning to each word, and putting meanings of words together to form a meaning for a sentence. The reader then constructs meaning for a paragraph based on a meaning of each sentence. Given that this subprocess of decoding is not automated but laborious, the reader's cognitive capacity for constructing meanings from the text is limited, and the comprehension process cannot be successful (Fitzgerald & Graves, 2004).

Besides complexity of the comprehension process, other unique factors, as outlined by Peregoy and Boyle, present additional challenges to ELLs who must develop their language proficiency while becoming literate in English. By contrast, their English-speaking peers, who have developed a fairly good command of the English language before coming to school, can focus on learning how to decode words in a text and comprehend the text (Mora, 2006). Although we agree with Peregoy and Boyle (2000), among others, on the impact of English-language proficiency on ELLs' comprehension, we have decided not to discuss it in this chapter, as we presented a more elaborate discussion of this factor in Chapter 4. ELLs' ability to decode words and their vocabulary knowledge, both of which are also related to the comprehension process, are discussed in Chapter 7. We also believe that the comprehension process is a process of an active transaction between a reader and a text (Pearson, 1985; Pilgreen, 2006; Rosenblatt, 1978). Acknowledging an important role that a text plays in a reader's successful comprehension (Fitzgerald & Graves, 2004; Lesaux, Koda, Siegel, & Shanahan, 2006), in Chapter 6 we have focused on a wide range of instructional materials supportive of ELLs' development of English language proficiency and literacy development.

In this chapter, we focus on ELLs and the teacher who guides them through the comprehension process. Specifically, we first describe the subprocesses involved in the comprehension process and the challenges of these subprocesses for ELLs. Next, we differentiate comprehension strategies ELLs use to facilitate their comprehension process (*reader comprehension strategies*) and comprehension strategies teachers use to facilitate ELLs' comprehension process (*instructional comprehension strategies*). This discussion is followed by the presentation of specific reader comprehension strategies and instructional strategies. While reading this chapter to gain knowledge of what the comprehension process means to ELLs and how to effectively teach ELLs comprehension, it is helpful for you to constantly relate other factors, as discussed, respectively, in Chapters 4, 6, and 7, to what is being discussed here.

At the end of this chapter, you will be able to:

- Explain the comprehension process and the challenges that ELLs face in comprehending a text.
- Understand the difference between reader comprehension strategies and instructional comprehension strategies.
- Understand a wide range of comprehension strategies ELLs use to facilitate their comprehension strategies.
- Understand and apply a wide range of instructional comprehension strategies teachers use to facilitate ELLs' comprehension process.

COMPREHENSION PROCESS
AND ITS CHALLENGES FOR ELLs

In the beginning of this chapter, Peregoy and Boyle (2000) reminded us that ELLs go through a similar process of reading a text, except for three factors that affect their comprehension: English-language proficiency; background knowledge on a topic; and literacy knowledge, skills, and experiences in a first language. The reading process Peregoy and Boyle described is similar to what others say about the process (e.g., Duke & Pearson, 2002; National Institute of Child Health and Human Development, 2000). It includes:

- Setting a purpose for reading about a topic.
- Activating prior knowledge and connecting it to the topic.
- Assigning meaning to words and chunks of words.
- Applying knowledge of sentence and text structure and text genre.
- Organizing, elaborating, and revising ideas.
- Applying strategies to constructing meanings.

In this section, we talk about the reading process with special attention to comprehension. In discussing each step of the process, we point out areas difficult for ELLs.

Setting a Purpose for Reading about a Topic

Good readers have a clear purpose for reading a text. One reads a storybook for enjoyment, an informational book for learning about the topic the book is presenting, and a poem for enjoyment or information. Because good readers have developed, based on some experiences with various texts, knowledge of text genres, they select a text to serve their purpose. At school, teachers have often set a purpose for children's reading, based on curricular standards. It is important, however, that teachers communicate with children about the purpose for reading books so that children can establish their *own* purpose for reading.

Setting a purpose for reading is often hard for young ELLs, who, like their native English-speaking peers, lack experiences with different types and functions of text genres. In addition, in learning English, they are focusing on its linguistic elements. Setting a purpose of reading for meaning by themselves seems to make less sense. Older ELLs who have developed knowledge of text genres and functions in English and/or in a native language may experience less difficulty in setting a purpose. However, if the topic of a book is quite unfamiliar to ELLs, the purpose they have set would not motivate them to construct meanings from the book. For example, we all have a story to tell: We become excited about learning about a new topic (we have a purpose), we locate resources related to it, we start exploring the topic only to find that we cannot make sense of what we have read (due to limited background knowledge and possibly unfamiliarity with text genre and structure), and we give up learning about this topic.

Activating Prior Knowledge and Connecting It to the Topic

After setting a purpose and before reading a text, readers activate in their brain any prior knowledge related to the topic they are reading. Just consider our brain as a huge warehouse for storing information—*schemas* (prior knowledge or background knowledge) about a topic. Readers' schemas on the topic develop through direct personal experiences (e.g., a child knows how a swing functions because he or she has been on one before) and/or through secondary experiences (e.g., reading a book in which children played on a swing, or watching a TV show or a movie in which children played on a swing).

Before and throughout reading, readers constantly relate a schema to the topic. If a reader learns new information, he or she adds this information to the existing schema. Sometimes, he or she needs to revise the old schema to reflect newly gained knowledge (Anderson, 1994;

Anderson & Pearson, 1984; Rumelhart, 1975). In addition to its content-specific nature, the schema is also (sub-)culturally related (Bransford & Johnson, 1972; Steffensen, Joag-Dev, & Anderson, 1979). For instance, a student (in our class) from New York once called a Pizza Hut to order a "pizza pie." She was told to call Marie Callender's (a restaurant and bakery known for its pies). This student had no schema about what a pizza is called on the West Coast (definitely not *pizza pie*) and the Pizza Hut employee had no schema that a pizza is called a *pizza pie* in New York; he or she mistakenly thought that the student wanted a pie. The differences in subculture of the East and West Coast can cause a native English-speaking student to lack a schema about a proper term for pizza. Just imagine how the differences in two cultures (a culture in the United States and a native culture of an English learner) would impact the schemas of ELLs.

One of the challenges that ELLs face in constructing meanings of a text is a lack of prior knowledge on a topic (Fitzgerald & Graves, 2004; García, 2000; García, 2005). The topics in many books are unfamiliar to them to various degrees. Take a look at the opening sentences of *Geoffrey Groundhog Predicts the Weather* (Koscielniak, 1995): "One morning, after a long winter's nap, Geoffrey Groundhog popped out of his burrow to look for his shadow. It was February 2, Groundhog Day" (p. 5). The words present concepts confusing or difficult to ELLs—*long winter's nap, groundhog, burrow,* and *Groundhog Day*. Given this situation, this reader has to rely heavily on the contextual clues to make sense of the text, including inferring information not written in the text.

As shown in Figure 8.1, while he or she is constructing meanings out of the text, the reader also raises questions based on what he or she has gathered from the text on this page. The reader may find answers to these questions directly or inferred on the next page or pages or from pictures on the same page or the following pages. Making inferences also requires a reader to have some prior knowledge of the topic.

Even when ELLs have a schema about the topic, their schema can be different from the one that the author of the book expects them to have. Before reading Riley's (1997) *Mouse Mess* (a mouse made a big mess while searching for his snack), an ELL from an Asian country may predict that the mouse may make a mess out of a bag of rice, a staple in most Asian countries. It would be hard for this child to associate cheese with a mouse in this story.

Word or Phrase from the Text	Meaning	Questions
nap	1. The animal slept.	1. Does it mean the same nap people take? 2. Is it like a nap a cat takes?
after a long winter's nap	1. The animal only takes the nap during winter. 2. It is long (not like a short cat's nap). 3. It is now spring (the reader may not be able to infer that spring follows winter if the seasons in his or her home country include only spring and summer).	1. But how long is the nap? Several hours, several days, several months?
popped out of his burrow	1. The animal was inside the burrow during the long winter's nap.	1. But where is the burrow? On the ground or underground? (The picture on this page does not show that the burrow is underground. The picture on the next page does show that Geoffrey lived underground).
It is February 2, Groundhog Day.	1. February 2 is Groundhog Day.	1. What does *Groundhog Day* mean? 2. Is it the animal's birthday?

FIGURE 8.1. Making sense of written text.

TAKE A MOMENT

Think back to the last school year. How much prior knowledge related to the readings in the curriculum did your ELLs have? In which area are they lacking prior knowledge? What was the impact of students' lack of prior knowledge on their understanding of readings? What was the impact of their lack of prior knowledge on your teaching?

Assigning Meaning to Words and Chunks of Words

After activating prior knowledge on the topic, readers begin to read words in a left-to-right, top-to-bottom, and left-page-to-right-page fashion. While reading each word, good readers automatically decode it and assign a meaning to it and then quickly move onto the next word. They read words by chunks (a meaningful unit). For the sentence "Yesterday, I played tether ball with Maria, Ann, and Jose," it takes much more time for a reader to read the sentence word by word than to read by chunks: *yesterday—I played tether ball—with Maria, Ann, and Jose.* Reading by chunks not word-by-word enables readers to not use too much cognitive energy and time in decoding.

If ELLs have limited decoding skills and strategies, they would spend most of their cognitive energy on decoding words, leaving little energy to making sense of what they have read. On the other hand, if ELLs are skillful at decoding words but lack prior knowledge or are not good at other steps we are about to discuss, they also can fail to comprehend the text. (For details about how to teach phonics to ELLs, refer to Chapter 7.)

Teachers can also support students in developing reading fluency by having them reread text, text at their independent or instructional level. Through rereading, students become more automatic in decoding words. Other strategies include students reading and rereading texts with partners or listening to a tape-recorded text and echo-reading or simultaneously reading with it.

A final strategy involves students charting their reading progress. This strategy can be completed in several ways. One way is for a teacher to select a text at a student's independent or instructional reading level. The teacher marks 100 words. The student reads the passage and is timed to determine how many words he or she reads in 1 minute. This process is repeated with the same text until the child reaches a goal of 100 words in 1 minute. Another way to chart progress is to have a student read a text (approximately 100 words) and put a blue Post-it Note where he or she finishes in 1 minute—this is a cold read. Then the child practices the text, perhaps reading with a partner. At the end of this practice the child once again reads the passage. This time he or she records the last word read in a minute with a red Post-it note—the hot read. The child should quickly note his or her improvement.

Fluency in reading is a critical element in comprehension. Without it students, and in particular ELLs, spend all their time focused on decoding. This singular focus on reading words inhibits meaning making.

Applying Knowledge of Sentence and Text Structure, and Text Genres

Even after readers can decode words and understand meanings of words and chunks of words, they may not be successful at comprehending a text if they are not familiar with sentence and text structure and text genres. The text written in English varies in sentence structures, which can increase the reading difficulty level. Consider the two sentences in the beginning of *Corduroy* (Freeman, 1968), a classic for primary-grade children: "Corduroy is a bear who once lived in the toy department of a big store. Day after day he waited with all the other animals and dolls for somebody to come along and take him home" (p. 5). The first sentence includes a relative clause, *who once lived in the toy department of a big store,* which modifies *a bear.* In the second sentence, an infinitive phrase *to come along and take him home,* whose subject is *somebody,* tells readers what Corduroy's wish is. If a reader cannot understand the structure of these two sentences (i.e., the relationship among these phrases and clauses), he or she would fail to extract meaning from the sentences.

Similarly, a reader's knowledge of text genres and structures plays an important role in comprehension. Readers can identify a text genre through a title (e.g., a title of *Corduroy* most likely tells a story about "Corduroy," whereas a book with a title of *Frogs* is probably an informational book on frogs) and/or by leafing through the book. Once readers know what genre the text is, they activate prior knowledge about the structure of this text genre—narrative text, expository text (one or more of the structure patterns or poetry). (Refer to Chapter 6 for details about text structures.) With familiarity with a text structure, readers can make predictions about what is coming in the text (Kintsch & Van Dijk, 1978; Pearson & Camperell, 1994).

For example, the sentences in the opening of *Corduroy* (Freeman, 1968) explicitly inform readers of a story problem: "Corduroy is a bear who once lived in the toy department of a big store. Day after day he waited with all the other animals and dolls for somebody to come along and take him home" (p. 5). Readers who are familiar with story grammar anticipate that Corduroy comes up with some solutions to his problem. In reading through the book, readers pay closer attention to how Corduroy solved his problem. While reading an informational text, readers go through a similar process. Knowing that the book *Shadows* (Otto, 2001) is an informational book, readers anticipate learning information from this book, such as what a shadow is, how a shadow is formed, and what different kinds of shadows are. As Peregoy and Boyle (2000) contend, readers' knowledge of text genre and structure is useful "for predicting and confirming meaning across sentences, paragraphs, and passages that comprise a text" (p. 239).

English sentence and text structure and text genres present a challenge to ELLs who are in a Catch-22 situation. For ELLs to become familiar with a wide range of sentence structures in English, they must practice reading and writing. On the other hand, they become successful at reading and writing after they have developed some knowledge of English sentence structures. This situation holds true for a close relationship between ELLs' knowledge of text genres and structures and their understanding of varied genres of text. To complicate this situation, variability within one text genre and its structure requires ELLs to have extensive exposure to English language through reading and writing. Let's take a moment to explore the examples presented in Figure 8.2.

TAKE A MOMENT

Read the examples in Figure 8.2. Think about the following questions.

1. How is an example from the first page of each story book different from other examples in sentence structure and information presented (i.e., characters, setting, and problem)?
2. How might this difference present an additional challenge to ELLs in their comprehension?
3. How is an example of description from the first page of each informational book different from other examples in sentence structure and information presented (i.e., an introduction of a topic and a description of the topic)?
4. How might this difference present additional challenge to ELLs in their comprehension?

Organizing, Elaborating, and Revising Ideas

While reading through a text, good readers organize information they have read such as categorizing and listing ideas, and identifying a rela-

Examples of a narrative text (from the first page of the text)	Examples of a descriptive text (from the first page of the text)
Corduroy (Freeman, 1968) Corduroy is a bear who once lived in the toy department of a big store. Day after day he waited with all the other animals and dolls for somebody to come along and take him home. (p. 5)	*Let's Go Rock Collecting* (Gans, 1984) People collect all kinds of things. They collect coins, stamps, baseball cards, shells, toys, bottles, pictures, and cats. Some people collect things that are very old—the older the better. (p. 5)
Geoffrey Groundhog Predicts the Weather (Koscielniak, 1995) One morning, after a long winter's nap, Geoffrey Groundhog popped out of his burrow to look for his shadow. It was February 2, Groundhog Day. (p. 5)	*Gulls . . . Gulls . . . Gulls . . .* (Gibbons, 1997) Gulls are among the most common birds seen along seashores. We see them feeding on sandy beaches, following fishing boats, and perching on rooftops in perfectly straight lines. (n.p.)
Swimmy (Lionni, 1963) A happy school of little fish lived in a corner of the sea somewhere. They were all red. Only one of them was as black as a mussel shell. He swam faster than his brothers and sisters. His name was Swimmy. (n.p.)	*The Best Book of Weather* (Adams, 2001) Earth is wrapped in a thick layer of air called the atmosphere. The air is made up of gases, and it can be hot or cold, wet or dry, and can move fast or stay still. . . . (p. 4)

FIGURE 8.2. Variability within one text genre and structure.

tionship among the ideas. For example, after reading the text on the first page of *Geoffrey Groundhog Predicts the Weather* (Koscielniak, 1995) (see Figure 8.1), readers identify "Geoffrey Groundhog" as a main character, the time setting of the story (i.e., on the morning of February 2), and an event (i.e., he popped out of his burrow to look for his shadow). In addition, readers elaborate on what they have read—connecting to prior knowledge and making inferences. For example, readers link their prior knowledge of *a nap* to the nap Geoffrey took, and question themselves if Geoffrey's nap is similar to or different from a human's long nap. Meanwhile, readers make inferences—identifying information not explicitly stated by the author. Readers, for example, need to infer, based on "after a long winter's nap," that the time setting for the story is spring.

In addition to organizing and elaborating on what they have read, another ongoing subprocess in which readers actively engage is revising ideas they have formulated based on previous text. For example, readers may need to revise what they have inferred from "after a long winter's nap," about the time setting of the story, spring, after reading the text on the following page: "Geoffrey remembered what his mother had told him. "If you see your shadow on Groundhog Day, go back to sleep, because winter will last six more weeks." "If there is no shadow, spring will soon be here" (p. 7). By now readers probably have learned that the time setting for this story can still be in winter, and that they will learn about the true time setting as the story develops.

At this comprehension stage, ELLs must be actively engaged in three different subprocesses—organizing, elaborating, and revising ideas. If ELLs have a hard time comprehending what they have read, organizing ideas is a tough task to undertake. Moreover, as discussed earlier, ELLs often lack prior knowledge on culture-specific topics as well as on content-specific topics. The task of elaborating on ideas, which involves making inferences, would present a challenge to ELLs. Without organized and detailed information about what has been read, ELLs are less likely to become aware of what information needs to be revised.

Applying Strategies to Constructing Meanings

As documented in existing research (Block & Pressley, 2002; Duke & Pearson, 2002; Paris, Lipson, & Wixson, 1994), good readers use strategies at various stages of the comprehension process to help them construct meanings of a text being read (e.g., previewing a text and activating and connecting prior knowledge to the topic). While reading, good readers use strategies such as organizing ideas, determining important details, and sequencing to categorize information in a way that is easy for readers to remember. Good readers are conscious ones; that is, they are aware of what and how they are reading. They, for example, would notice a difficult, confusing part of the text and immediately apply fix-up strategies in response to the situation. They may reread the previous text to see if they have missed certain content or have misread the content, or they examine their own prior knowledge to identify the part that has misled them in comprehending the text. (For a detailed description of each strategy, see the following section.)

Young ELLs begin developing reader strategies while becoming proficient in the English language. They shoulder a double burden. Only through immersion in the English language do ELLs learn strate-

gies and later apply them in reading. Their developing English proficiency, however, can limit the quality of such immersion. Older ELLs
may have developed certain reader strategies in a native language,
which can be transferred to reading an English text (August & Shanahan, 2006a; Cummins, 1979, 1986). However, if they are skillful at only
a few strategies, older ELLs face a challenge very similar to that of their
younger peers.

READER COMPREHENSION STRATEGIES

In the entry "Comprehension Strategies" in *Literacy in America: An
Encyclopedia of History, Theory, and Practice*, Dole (2002) stated that
the term *comprehension strategies* can refer to two sets of strategies—
strategies readers use and strategies teachers use. *Reader comprehension
strategies*, as we call them, are procedures readers use to help them
comprehend what is being read. Reader comprehension strategies are
"conscious processes under the direct control of readers. . . . Over
time, however, and with practice, comprehension strategies can become automatic procedures that readers use without conscious learning" (Dole, 2002, p. 85). Some examples of reader comprehension
strategies are previewing a text, predicting what is coming next in a
text, organizing and summarizing ideas, asking questions, and rereading part of a text. Figure 8.3 explains each reader comprehension
strategy.

Instructional comprehension strategies are procedures or activities
that teachers use to help readers comprehend a text they are reading.
"The teacher completes the activity directly with students. As a result of
completing the strategy or activity, students understand a particular text
better" (Dole, 2002, p. 87). Instructional comprehension strategies are
directly under the control of teachers. Some examples of instructional
comprehension strategies are reading aloud, shared reading, guided
reading, think-aloud, questioning, graphic organizers, and reading workshop. We focus on instructional comprehension strategies in the section
of instructional comprehension strategies.

In literature, reader comprehension strategies can be divided into
two categories—*cognitive* strategies, which directly assist readers in
making sense of a text (Block & Pressley, 2002; Chamot & O'Malley,
1994; Duke & Pearson, 2002; Pressley & Afflerbach, 1995; Weinstein

Strategy	Explanation
Cognitive reader comprehension strategies	
Setting a purpose	Readers identify a purpose for reading a text, either for enjoyment/pleasure or for information.
Previewing	Readers look at the book title, front and back cover of a storybook to get a general sense of what the book is about. If they are reading an information book, they may also scan the table of contents and index (if the book has these two sections) to gain some background knowledge about the topic of the book. For either genre, readers may leaf through the book.
Activating prior knowledge	Once readers know about the topic of a book, text genre, and text structure, they search and identify in their schema relevant information related to the topic. Readers use this strategy throughout the comprehension process.
Predicting	Based on what they have gathered from previewing and activating prior knowledge, readers predict what is going to happen in the book. Throughout the comprehension process they make predictions, confirm predictions if they are similar to the author's, or revise their predictions if they are different from the author's.
Visualizing	Readers make mental, visual images of what they have read. They can visualize any story element (e.g., a setting—in a hot, isolated desert, a character—a very happy boy) in a storybook or any content or concept in an informational book (e.g., a difference among drizzle, a short rainfall, and a downpour). When readers are visualizing, they are also making a connection between their prior knowledge on the topic and what they are reading.
Making connections	Different from activating prior knowledge, this strategy enables readers to survey what they have already known about the topic, text genre, and text structure and identify a relationship between what is known and the topic. For ELLs, the relationship can be formed between a native language and English.
Applying knowledge of text genre and structure	Readers use their knowledge of text genre and structure to guide them in reading a text. If they are reading a story, they pay attention to story elements; if they are reading an informational book, such as a descriptive text, they look for details about a topic. *(continued)*

FIGURE 8.3. Reader comprehension strategies.

Strategy	Explanation
Determining important details	Readers use their prior knowledge on the topic and text genre and structure in the text to determine what is important. While reading a story, readers note details about a setting, characters (e.g., appearance and actions), plot, and problem solutions. While reading an informational book on weather with a cause-and-effect structure, readers pay attention to causes for different types of weather.
Organizing ideas	As a flow of ideas comes to mind, readers categorize and sequence them so that they are easier for readers to identify and remember. These organized ideas are added to their schemas, becoming part of prior knowledge for readers as they read on in the text.
Summarizing ideas	Readers formulate a main idea of what they have read and identify supporting details. They come up with a summary based on organized ideas and important details.
Making inferences	Readers infer information that is not stated in the text. There are two types of inferences—schema-based and/or text-based inferences (Winne, Graham, & Prock, 1993). To make a schema-based inference, readers rely on their prior knowledge whereas in making a text-based inference, readers extract information from what an author has implied in the text.
Transferring literacy knowledge and strategies learned from a native language	This strategy is unique to ELLs. They use what they know about functions and conventions of print in a native language to help them with reading English. For example, a Spanish-speaking ELL knows about the concepts about print in Spanish, and he or she applies the concepts in reading an English text. They also apply reader comprehension strategies gained from their experiences reading texts in a native language to reading an English text. For example, they survey a text to develop a general idea of the topic and then activate prior knowledge about the topic before and during reading.
Metacognitive strategies	
Self-monitoring	Readers self-monitor the reading process by asking themselves questions (e.g., "Is my prediction similar to the author's?"). They also stop to think about what they have read and to decide which strategies need to be used to facilitate comprehension.

FIGURE 8.3. (*continued*)

Strategy	Explanation
Regulating	Readers vary how they read a text, depending on text type. If a text is easy, they read fast; if a text is hard, they slow down and constantly self-check to make sure that they understand. In reading for pleasure, they may not pay too much attention to all details; in reading for information, they pay closer attention to important details.
Applying fix-up strategies	Once they have realized that they are not making sense of the text, readers know which fix-up strategies to apply (e.g., rereading a previous part of the text and looking at a picture to identify the meaning of a word).

FIGURE 8.3. (*continued*)

& Mayer, 1987), and *metacognitive* strategies, which enable readers to become conscious of their own comprehension process (Baker & Brown, 1984; Chamot & O'Malley, 1994; Dole, Duffy, Roehler, & Pearson, 1991). (See Figure 8.3 for each cognitive and metacognitive strategy.) Research on the comprehension process of ELLs has shown that ELLs use a similar set of comprehension strategies (e.g., Chamot & O'Malley, 1994; O'Malley & Chamot, 1990; Watts-Taffe & Truscott, 2000) with some strategies unique to ELLs, such as translating a word/phrase/text from English to a native language or vice versa, and recognizing cognates in English such as *artist* and *artista* (*ist* to *ista*) or *famous* and *famoso* (*ous* to *oso*) (Jiménez, García, & Pearson, 1996).

While we list each strategy separately in Figure 8.3, readers often use more than one strategy simultaneously and subconsciously (i.e., without their own awareness). Often, readers use a set of strategies throughout the comprehension process.

TAKE A MOMENT

Now you have read about reader comprehension strategies. Think about your knowledge of your ELLs' use of strategies. Which strategies are they skillful at applying? Which strategies are they developing? Which strategies are unfamiliar to them at all? Keep this information in mind while reading the section on "Instructional Comprehension Strategies."

INSTRUCTIONAL COMPREHENSION STRATEGIES

In writing this section, we are mindful of several important things. We are aware that limited research has been done about second-language reading instruction and that no current research has shown much difference in teaching reading to ELLs and to their native English-speaking peers (Fitzgerald, 1995b; Fitzgerald & Graves, 2004). Researchers (e.g., Fitzgerald, 1995b; García, 2000; Gersten & Baker, 2000; Lesaux et al., 2006), however, do remind classroom teachers to pay attention to certain areas (e.g., prior knowledge of a topic) while teaching ELLs how to read. This reminder echoes what Peregoy and Boyle (2000) stated about the three differences in ELLs' reading process: English-language proficiency, background knowledge, and literacy experience in a native language. In presenting each strategy, we take into consideration areas unique to ELLs in their comprehension process.

We also agree with Anderson and Roit (1998), Fitzgerald and Graves (2004), and Mohr (2004), among others, that reading instruction for ELLs should be closely tied to promoting their English-language development and engaging them in actively constructing meanings from a text. Roit (2006) explained:

> Key to successful reading comprehension is student engagement. When students are genuinely engaged in the comprehension process, not only are they learning about strategies and using them intentionally to make sense of text, but they are also continually using language, learning vocabulary, sharing experiences, discussing text, collaboratively solving problems, elaborating on ideas, and engaging in meaningful conversations. Teaching reading comprehension creates the perfect environment for English language learners not only to learn how to derive meaning from text but also to learn how to talk about text and about what they are learning. (p. 80)

In support of Roit's view, Shanahan and Beck (2006) stated, based on a literature review, that "efforts to provide students with substantial experience with English . . . has shown some value. This pattern of results is evident in studies that encouraged students to read as well as in those aimed at developing more thorough discussion routines around literature" (p. 448).

Finally, in presenting a set of instructional strategies, we focus on modeling for ELLs how to read and comprehend the English language and scaffolding ELLs' comprehension process (Cappellini, 2006; Fitzgerald & Graves, 2004; Roit, 2006). This focus is consistent with what Shanahan and Beck (2006) suggested: "Common instructional routines may need to be adjusted to make instruction in the literacy components maximally effective with English-language learners" (p. 437). With that in mind, we categorize strategies into five categories, each of which serves a *specific* purpose in *facilitating* ELLs' comprehension processes (see Figure 8.4).

Modeling and Scaffolding the Comprehension Process: Read-Aloud and Guided Reading

All the instructional comprehension strategies in this category have been used by teachers with native English-speaking children. Their use with ELLs has also been documented in literature. For example, in her summary of research related to reading instruction for young children, García (2000) found that storybook reading can benefit ELLs if children can relate to the book being read and if teachers use sheltered English techniques (e.g., using realia and involving learners' multiple senses). Cappellini (2006) considered guided reading a strategy that "provides [ELLs] plenty of opportunities for practice with the guidance of an expert" (p. 114). Shared reading (including buddy reading—a student chooses a buddy to read with—and paired reading—a teacher pairs one student with another), as Boyd-Batstone (2006)

Category	Instructional comprehension strategy
Modeling and scaffolding the comprehension process	Read-aloud Guided reading
Presenting information visually	Graphic organizers
Elaborating on comprehending the text	Questioning
Facilitating comprehension via the use of linguistic cueing systems	Cloze technique
Promoting metacognition	Think-aloud

FIGURE 8.4. Categories of instructional comprehension strategies.

pointed out, allows ELLs practice reading in a nonthreatening environment.

Read-Aloud

In a read-aloud, the teacher directs ELLs' attention to the conventions and functions of a text, activating their prior knowledge, and assisting children in constructing meanings of the text. Many sheltered English techniques, such as involving five senses, repetition, and using books with a pattern, are incorporated into a read-aloud to make it effective for ELLs. Figure 8.5 illustrates an example of a read-aloud with Kalan's (1978) *Rain*, which introduces the common concept of rain and has repetitive patterns. In this read-aloud of a big-book version of *Rain*, the teacher used only English. This reflects a reality in many classrooms—teachers do not speak ELLs' native language and/or ELLs speak different native languages, and the use of a native language is not practical. Of course, if ELLs share a native language, and if their teacher is fluent in the language, the teacher is encouraged to use a native language within a read-aloud to provide support for children.

Guided Reading

Unlike a read-aloud, in guided reading ELLs read a text and practice skills and strategies they have learned, and a teacher provides support in guiding through ELLs' reading processes. Cappellini (2006) presented three kinds of guided reading lessons based on ELLs' language proficiency— Emergent and early guided reading lesson: Emphasis on talk; early fluent guided reading lesson: Sustaining and expanding meaning; and fluent guided reading lesson: Focusing on higher level comprehension strategies.

In a 15- to 20-minute emergent and early guided reading lesson, Cappellini (2005, 2006) suggested the following steps:

> Introduction: Teacher solicits language
> Orientation: Teacher guides students through first viewing of the text
> First Reading: Students read the text by themselves
> Discussion: Students respond to the text
> Students re-read the text (on their own or in buddy reading)
> Students respond to the text on their own (p. 116)

Steps and purpose	Modeling and scaffolding
• Teaching book conventions • Activating prior knowledge	• Today, we are going to read a new book. It is called *Rain* (*pointing at the book title, showing several pictures of rain, and asking children to listen to the sound of rain available on the Internet*). [If Internet is not available, pretape the the sound and then play it.] • Robert Kalan wrote the words in the book (*pointing at the name and then the text on the first several pages, and doing the action of writing*). • Donald Crews drew the pictures (*pointing at the name and then the pictures on the first several pages, and doing the action of drawing*). [The teacher may say the word *rain* in a native language.]
• Teaching book conventions • Previewing the book	• Let's look at the front cover of the book (*pointing at the title, author, illustrator, and rain formed by the word* rain). • Now, let's look at the back cover (*pointing at rain formed by the word* rain *and words on the cover*).
• Previewing the book	• Now let's see what is inside the book. Here is a picture of the blue sky (*pointing at the words* blue sky *and showing another picture of the blue sky from a magazine or from the Internet*). • Here is a picture of the yellow sun (*pointing at the words* yellow sun *and showing another picture of the sun from a magazine or from the Internet*). [The teacher does the same for the rest of the book.]
• Modeling concepts about print	• Now, I am going to read the book (*pointing at him- or herself, his or her mouth, and then the book*), and you are listening to me (*pointing at children, doing an action of listening*). • *Rain* (*pointing at the title*), written by Robert Kalan (*pointing at the author*), and illustrated by Donald Crews (*pointing at the illustrator*). • Now we are at the title page. It says similar things on the front cover (*showing both pages, pointing out what is the same and what is different*). • *Rain* (*pointing at the title*), written by Robert Kalan (*pointing at the author*), and illustrated by Donald Crews (*pointing at the illustrator*). • Here is a dedication page. It says, "With love to my parents. R. K." *R* is the first letter in *Robert* (*pointing at* (*continued*)

FIGURE 8.5. A read-aloud with Kalan's (1978) *Rain*.

Steps and purpose	Modeling and scaffolding
	the word). *K* is the first letter in *Kalan* (*pointing at the word*). " . . . *and to mine D. C."* *D* is the first letter in *Donald* (*pointing at the word*). *C* is the first letter in *Crews* (*pointing at the word*). [The teacher may skip talking about a dedication page if it overwhelms ELLs.]
• Modeling concepts about print • Facilitating comprehension	• "Blue sky" (*pointing at each word while reading and then the picture of blue sky*). [The teacher repeats the same step with the following pages till the page "Rain on the green grass"] • "Rain on the green grass" (*pointing at each word while reading; showing a picture of grass as this page does not show grass*). • "Rain on the green grass" (*overlapping lower bottom part of a picture of rain with the upper top part of a picture of grass to show the meaning of "rain on the green grass"*). • "Rain on the black road" (*pointing at each word while reading; pointing at the rain and then at the road*). [The teacher repeats the same step with the following pages till the page "rain."] • Rain," "Rain" (*pointing at each word while reading; comparing this page with the previous page to show that things disappear due to the heavy rain*). • "Rainbow" (*pointing at each word while reading; showing other pictures of rainbow*).
• Reviewing	• I am going to read this book again (*repeating Step 4*).
• Checking for comprehension	• I am going to read this book again. But I need your help (*pointing at the children*). When I read words on each page, I want you to point at the picture. [The teacher asks a child to stand next to the big book easel. The teacher first points at the words *blue sky*, then gives a pointer to the child, and holds the child's hand to point at the picture of blue sky on that page. The teacher repeats the steps with the next page, "yellow sun."] • Are you ready? Let's start? • "Blue sky" (*pointing at each word while reading*). Who wants the pointer (*waving the pointer at the children*)? [If nobody volunteers, the teacher may call a child who the teacher thinks can point at the picture. Or the teacher can have several children come up to the front to point at the picture. The teacher repeats the same step with the rest of the book.]

FIGURE 8.5. (*continued*)

Steps and purpose	Modeling and scaffolding
• Reinforcing comprehension	The read-aloud does not stop here. Children's experience with it needs to be carried out throughout the day and the week. During a center time, the teacher can work with a small group of children to reinforce their comprehension of the book. Each child is given a set of pictures related to the pictures in the book (e.g., rain, blue sky, a road, a house, a car, and trees). • Do you remember what you read about this book this morning (or yesterday) (*holding up the book*)? I am going to read this book again, and you will show me the pictures. • I am reading "blue sky." You will show me a picture of blue sky (*finding the picture, putting it in a child's hand, and holding up the child's hand while saying "blue sky"*). "Blue sky" (*pointing at children, and signaling them to hold up the picture of blue sky*). [The teacher repeats the same step with the following text until the page of "gray sky" and "rain."] • "Rain on the green grass" (*holding up a picture of rain and a picture of grass; overlapping lower bottom part of a picture of rain with the upper top part of a picture of grass to show the meaning of "rain on the green grass"*). • "Rain on the green grass" (*signaling children to do the same as the teacher has modeled*). [During this activity, the teacher pays attention to who is able to hold up the correct picture(s) and who is not able to.]
• Inviting children to practice reading through echo reading, shared reading, and choral reading	On the next day or later in a week, the teacher invites children to do echo reading, shared reading, and choral reading. These carefully scaffolded reading experiences provide children with an opportunity to practice reading aloud with teacher's support. *Echo reading:* • We are going to read the book again. This time, you can read *after* me: "Rain" [The teacher starts pointing at the title of the book, signaling to ask children to read after the teacher.] [The teacher repeats the same step with the rest of the book.]

FIGURE 8.5. (*continued*)

Steps and purpose	Modeling and scaffolding
	Shared reading: • We are going to read the book again. This time, you can read with me if you want to: "Rain." [The teacher starts pointing at the title of the book, signaling to ask children read if they want to. Otherwise, the teacher reads it.] [The teacher repeats the same step with the rest of the book.] *Choral reading:* • We are going to read the book again. This time, you can read with me (*pointing at self and the children*). "Rain." [The teacher starts pointing at the title of the book, signaling to ask children to read.]

FIGURE 8.5. (*continued*)

Figure 8.6 lists questions that teachers can ask at each stage of the lesson and the purpose for the questions. A teacher encourages children to respond in the language they find most comfortable. If a native language is used, the teacher can enlist help from children who speak that language. If no children in the class share that language, the teacher can still allow a child to respond in a native language if that child is not ready to produce English.

In an early fluent guided reading lesson, as Cappellini (2005, 2006) described, a teacher goes through similar steps used in an emergent and early guided reading lesson, except the text ELLs are reading is longer. In addition, a teacher focuses on scaffolding the process of figuring out unknown words in the text. Cappellini suggested the use of a focus sheet on which a student writes down each unknown word (or phrase), states what he or she knows about each word (or phrase) or what his or her guess is about it, and explains how each word (or phrase) is used.

A 25- to 30-minute fluent guided reading lesson is appropriate for ELLs who have developed their fluency in decoding. In addition to following some steps in an emergent and early fluency that focus on meaning construction, Cappellini (2005, 2006) recommended that teachers focus on assisting children in understanding the author's intent. In a focus sheet, a teacher wants an ELL to write down—

Steps and purpose	Questions
Introduction: • Activating prior knowledge • Setting a purpose • Predicting	1. (*pointing at the title*) What does this say? 2. Do you know anything about . . . Question 3. What do you know about . . . Question 4. What other words can you use for . . . Question 5. (*showing the front and back cover*) What is this book about? 6. What is going to happen in the book? How do you know that?
Orientation: • Modeling concepts about print • Identifying vocabulary unfamiliar to students • Confirming or disconfirming prediction	1. Where do you start reading on this page? 2. What is in the picture? 3. Which words (or word) are (or is) about the picture? 4. Did you predict what is happening in this picture? Why or why not?
First reading: • Practicing reading independently • Constructing meanings	When a student stops during reading, the teacher asks these questions. 1. Is this word hard for you? 2. Read to the end of the sentence. Does your reading of the word make sense? (meaning cue) 3. Does your reading of the word look like the word on the page? (visual cue) 4. Does your reading of the word sound like the word on the page? (sound cue) 5. Can the picture tell you about this word? What is this word? 6. What does this sentence tell you? 7. What does the picture tell you?
Discussion: • Elaborating on the text • Making inferences • Making connections	1. What does the book tell you? 2. Can you tell me . . . Question 3. Is your prediction similar to the author's or different from the author's? 4. What in the book supports your prediction? 5. What does the book remind you of . . . in your life? (text-to-self connection) 6. What does the book remind you of . . . in other books you read? (text-to-text connection) 7. What does the book remind you of . . . in the world? (text-to-world connection) (*continued*)

FIGURE 8.6. Questions to ask during an emergent and early guided reading lesson.

Steps and purpose	Questions
Students reread the text (independently or buddy reading): • Practicing independent reading	The teacher asks students to keep in mind these questions while reading independently or with a buddy. 1. Which part of the book do you know better now? 2. Which part of the book is still hard for you?
Students respond to the text on their own: • Making connections	The teacher asks students to respond to the book by using these guiding questions. 1. What does the book remind you of . . . in your life? (text-to-self connection) 2. What does the book remind you of . . . in other books you read? (text-to-text connection) 3. What does the book remind you of . . . in the world? (text-to-world connection)

FIGURE 8.6. (*continued*)

What was the purpose of the story? (What was the author trying to say?)

    Problem:

    Character—What I know about the character (What is the character like in the beginning of story?)

    Character—What I learned about the character (How does the character change?)

    Solution:

    What did I learn from the story? (What was the author trying to say?) (Cappellini, 2006, p. 126)

Presenting Information Visually: Graphic Organizers

While listening to a teacher read a book aloud or reading a book independently, ELLs need to remember and organize what has been read. Because ELLs are developing literacy skills, this process can be eased by the use of graphic organizers which present information visually (Boyd-Batstone, 2006; Soltero, 2004). As Soltero (2004) stated, "graphic organizers provide a visual organizational frame for making sense of concepts and knowledge. More importantly, when students themselves utilize graphic organizers as a tool to make connections, summarize, or sequence ideas and concepts, they begin to move toward becoming strategic and independent learners" (p. 118). Following is a list of websites of graphic organizers. Teachers can download the ones appropriate for their ELLs' needs.

- *www.eduplace.com/graphicorganizer/*
- *www.teachervision.fen.com/graphic-organizers/printable/6293.html*
- *www.teach-nology.com/web_tools/materials/timelines/*
- *www.region15.org/curriculum/graphicorg.html*
- *www.enchantedlearning.com/graphicorganizers/*

Figure 8.7 lists and displays several commonly used graphic organizers that can be used before, during, or after reading.

Unorganized Semantic Mapping (Cluster, Webbing)

This graphic organizer is used before reading to activate ELLs' prior knowledge about a topic and/or after reading to help ELLs to summarize what has been read. It supports beginning ELLs in the sense that they usually list whatever they know about the topic.

Organized Semantic Mapping (Cluster, Webbing)

Organized semantic mapping is used in the same way as unorganized semantic mapping, except that ELLs need to supply information related to a specific category, which can present a challenge to beginning ELL readers.

Pictorial Map

Pictorial maps allow ELLs, and especially those beginning readers who are developing their English-language proficiency, to express their ideas using pictures. With a pictorial map, ELLs can demonstrate their understanding of a text even though they have limited English-language proficiency.

KWL Chart

The *K* column of the KWL chart (Ogle, 1986) helps ELLs activate prior knowledge and make connections between prior knowledge and the text being read. The *W* column encourages ELLs to set a purpose for reading by asking questions related to the topic; the questions can also be associated with predicting. In completing the *L* column ELLs summarize what they have read, and the summary is composed of details.

Graphic organizer	Example
Unorganized semantic mapping (cluster, webbing)	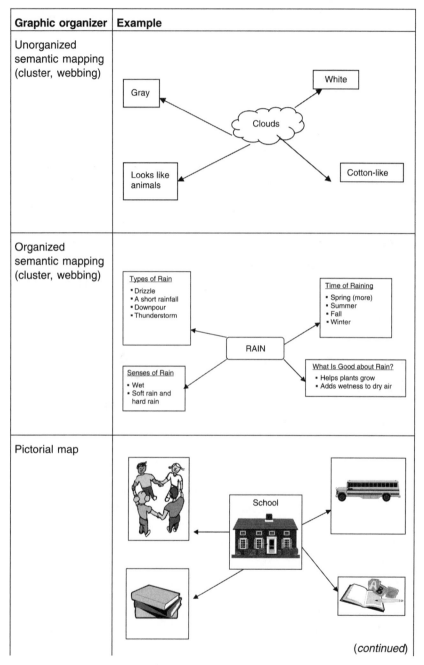
Organized semantic mapping (cluster, webbing)	
Pictorial map	

(continued)

FIGURE 8.7. Common graphic organizers.

Graphic organizer	Example
Beginning–middle–end story map (*The Three Little Pigs* [Galdone, 1970])	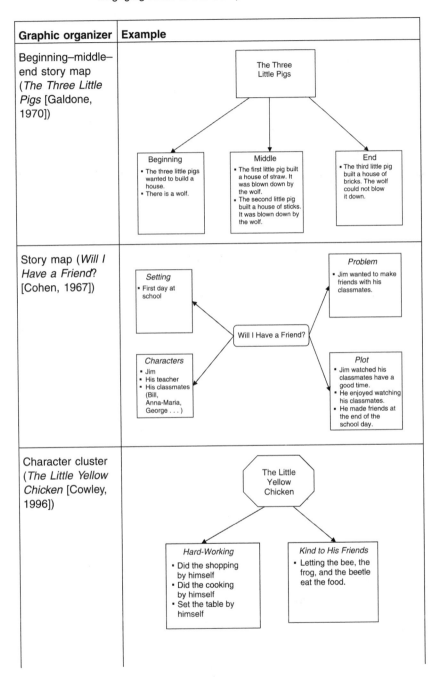
Story map (*Will I Have a Friend?* [Cohen, 1967])	
Character cluster (*The Little Yellow Chicken* [Cowley, 1996])	

FIGURE 8.7. (*continued*)

Graphic organizer	Example

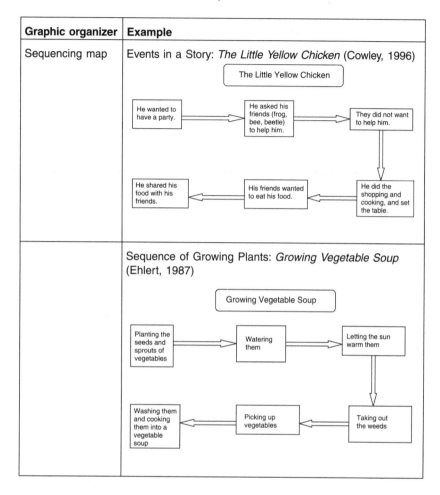

FIGURE 8.7. (*continued*)

A KWL chart can be used with a storybook or with an informational book. For a storybook, this chart engages ELLs in thinking about (1) what they *know* about a story after reading the title, and looking at the front and back cover; and (2) what they *want to know* about the story. After finishing reading the book, ELLs summarize what they *have learned* (see Figure 8.8). For an informational book, ELLs think about (1) what they *know* about the topic of the book, and (2) what they *want to know* about it. After reading the book, they summarize what they *have learned* (see Figure 8.9).

K (what I know)	W (what I want to know)	L (what I have learned)
• A lady is wearing a straw hat. • She is holding strawberries. • She is in the strawberry field.	• Who is this lady? • Why is she holding strawberries and in the strawberry field? • Does she own the strawberry field? • Is she checking the strawberries?	• This lady is probably the author's mother. • She plants strawberries, takes care of them, picks them up, and packs them. • She often works in hot sun. • She also plants other crops (beets, lettuce, artichokes) • She is happy when people enjoy strawberries. • She does not live with me, and hopes to come home soon.

FIGURE 8.8. A KWL chart for Ada's (1995) *My Mother Plants Strawberries* (narrative text).

Beginning–Middle–End Story Map

A beginning–middle–end story map helps ELLs develop a general sense of a story that is comprised of a beginning (where characters, and setting are introduced), middle (where characters try to solve a problem), and end (where a problem is solved).

Story Map

Story maps help ELLs identify story elements and develop a more elaborate sense of story elements: setting, character(s), and plot (problem, problem solution).

Character Cluster

Character clusters allow ELLs to demonstrate their understanding of traits of a character in the book and details/evidence supporting the traits.

K (what I know)	W (what I want to know)	L (what I have learned)
• Shadows are dark. • Anything can form a shadow. • A hand can form a shadow. • A person can form a shadow.	• How is a shadow formed? • Why are some shadows bigger than others? • Why can't I see my shadow all the time? • Why does a shadow change?	• A shadow moves with an object, a person, or an animal. • When there is sun, if you move, your shadow moves. • Light is needed to make shadows. • When light is blocked by something, a shadow is made. • If the sun shines on you in the front, your shadow is behind you. • If the sun shines on you in the back, your shadow is ahead of you. • If the sun shines on your head, there is no shadow of you. • Shadows change their shapes.

FIGURE 8.9. A KWL chart for Otto's (2001) *Shadows* (expository text).

Sequencing Map

Sequencing maps allow ELLs to list the sequence of events in a story and steps of doing something. Other sequencing maps include a timeline chart which documents what happens during each period of time and a cycle map which presents a life cycle of a living thing.

Venn Diagram

Venn diagrams allow ELLs to compare and contrast two things, such as two similar books, two characters, and two people (see Figure 8.10).

Elaborating on Comprehending the Text: Questioning

In talking about the benefits of using questions in reading instruction for ELLs, Fitzgerald and Graves (2004) contended that "questions can

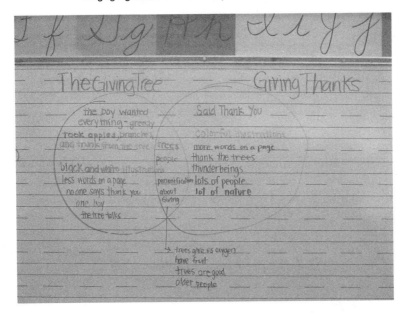

FIGURE 8.10. A Venn diagram on Silverstein's (1964) *The Giving Tree* and Swamp's (1995) *Giving Thanks.*

encourage and promote students' higher order thinking, and they can nudge students' interpretations, analysis, and evaluation of the ideas created and gleaned from reading" (p. 25). They further noted that questions also invite students to provide personal responses to what they have read. While all teachers' manuals for their reading programs (for native English-speaking children as well as for ELLs) list questions for each reading selection, it is important for teachers to formulate questions geared toward students' background experiences and English-language proficiency levels. Pilgreen (2006) suggested using detail questions that would guide students to identify important details in a text. Although Pilgreen was referring to *wh-* questions for expository texts, we think that her idea of detail questions can be easily applied to narrative texts. Furthermore, she advised teachers to add an icon (or a picture) next to a question, providing a visual aid for students. For example, a picture of a clock is put next to a *when* question, and next to a *who* question is a picture of a group of people. When ELLs have developed some level of reading competence, they are encouraged to ask one another questions (Fitzgerald & Graves, 2004).

Instead of discussing *wh-* questions (*Who? What? When? Where? Which? Why? How? How much?* and *How many?*), we present three types of questions with different levels of cognitive demands for ELLs: literal questions, inferential questions, and critical thinking questions.

Literal Questions

The answer to a literal question can be directly found in a text. At times, readers need to put together pieces of information found in different parts of a text in order to answer a literal question. But the answer is still written in the text. Two literal questions related to *The Three Little Pigs* (Galdone, 1970) are:

> How many pigs were in the story?
> What kind of house did each pig build?

Inferential Questions

The answer to an inferential question is not explicitly stated by the author(s). Readers must combine their prior knowledge (including life experiences) with a sentence or two in a text to figure out an answer. At times, there can be more than one answer to the question. Two inferential questions related to *The Three Little Pigs* (Galdone, 1970) are:

> Which pig was smartest?
> Why could the wolf not blow down the house of bricks?

Critical Thinking Questions

A critical thinking question is related to a text but also beyond the text. The question, for example, is about a character and partially related to a plot; but the question asks something that did not really happen in the text. In answering a critical thinking question, readers must combine their prior knowledge, a good understanding of a text, and critical thinking skills. Two critical thinking questions related to *The Three Little Pigs* (Galdone, 1970) are:

> What other kinds of house might the third little pig build?
> What would the third little pig do if the wolf blew down his house of bricks?

Facilitating Comprehension via the Use of Linguistic Cueing Systems: Cloze Technique

Since its first introduction by Taylor (1953), the cloze technique/procedure has become a common instructional strategy used at all grade levels. In a cloze, every nth word (e.g., every 5th, 7th, 9th, or 11th word) in a 250- to 350-word text is deleted, and students are asked to fill in the blanks (Tierney & Readence, 2005). In order to fill in each blank with an appropriate word that is syntactically, semantically, and pragmatically accepted, a student needs to pay attention to linguistic cueing systems, draws from his or her background information about the topic of a text, and develops a general understanding about the text. Given the process involved in a reader's completing a cloze text, cloze technique is recommended as a useful strategy for ELLs who are developing or fine tuning their English-language skills and developing and applying their reader comprehension strategies (Chamot & O'Malley, 1994; Echevarria et al., 2004; Pilgreen, 2006).

In using the cloze technique with ELLs, we recommend that teachers develop a cloze text based on readings ELLs have done so that unfamiliarity with content can be less of an issue. Teachers can vary the ways of deleting words (which are later to be filled in by students), depending on instructional goals and student needs. In the beginning, teachers use a text with a repetitive linguistic pattern which is easier for ELLs to predict. Difficulty level can be increased with a text without any patterns. Also remember not to delete words in beginning sentences which can be the topic sentence or a presentation of a linguistic pattern used throughout the text. Students can complete a cloze text orally after their teacher has read aloud a text on which a cloze is developed and after students have become familiar with the text. The teacher can cover words with sticky notes that students supply. Figure 8.11 lists some sample cloze texts.

Promoting Metacognition: Think-Aloud

Think-aloud, a metacognitive strategy, requires "a person to verbalize his or her thought process while working on a task (Chamot, Barnhardt, El-Dinary, & Robbins, 1999, p. 68). Think-aloud has long been used with native English-speaking children to improve skills for monitoring their comprehension process (Flower & Hayes, 1980; Gordon, 1985). As Chamot et al. (1999) and Roit (2006) argued, think-aloud is valuable for English language learners who need teachers to model and

Purpose	Cloze text
Focusing on parts of speech or grammar	
Color words	Brown Bear, Brown Bear, What Do You See? (Martin, 1983) Brown bear, brown bear, what do you see? I see a red bird looking at me. Red bird, _____ bird, what do you see? I see a _____ duck looking at me. _____ duck, _____ duck, what do you see? I see a _____ horse looking at me. (n.p.)
Verbs	*I Like Me!* (Carlson, 1988) I have a best friend. That best friend is me! I do fun things with me. I draw beautiful pictures. I ride fast! And I _____ good books with me! I _____ to take care of me. I _____ my teeth. (n.p.)
Past tense	The Little Yellow Chicken (Cowley, 1996) The little yellow chicken thought he'd have a party. He said to his friends, "Will you help me do the shopping?" His friends _____ at him. "Hop it!" _____ the frog. "Buzz off!" _____ the bee. And the big brown beetle _____, "Stop bugging me!" So the little yellow chicken _____ shopping by himself. (pp. 2–3)
Focusing on overall comprehension	
	The Little Yellow Chicken (Cowley, 1996) The little yellow chicken thought he'd have a party. He said to his friends, "Will you help me do the shopping?" His _____ laughed at him. "Hop it!" _____ the frog. "_____ off!" said the bee. And the big brown beetle _____, "Stop bugging me!" So the little yellow chicken went _____ by himself. (pp. 2–3)

FIGURE 8.11. Sample cloze texts.

demonstrate the thinking process and, in particular, reader comprehension strategies used while constructing meanings from the text.

Roit (2006) identified several steps in planning a think-aloud with ELLs:

■ Teacher shares how to use different strategies at various parts of a text for different purposes.

■ Teacher names a strategy used and explains a rationale for its use and steps of using it.

- During a think-aloud, teacher uses language comprehensible to students.
- Teacher uses think-aloud to address ELLs' linguistic needs.

Figure 8.12 illustrates an example of a think-aloud with *Pip's Magic* (Walsh, 1994). We focus on the book title and the text on the first page of the story. Teachers can vary the steps and language used in the think-aloud process, depending on ELLs' English-language proficiency and comprehension levels.

After a first think-aloud modeling, a teacher should list the reader comprehension strategies on the chart and display the chart in a salient area of the whiteboard. In the subsequent modeling, the teacher tries not to tell students a strategy being used. Instead, the teacher invites them to identify it from the chart. The teacher then asks students to do a think-aloud related to the text on one page or even a sentence on the page to provide them with a guided-practice opportunity. Later on, students experience guided-practice again in a small-group setting where the teacher can pay closer attention to each student. The teacher encourages students to use the think-aloud checklist (Figure 8.13) to record strategies they have used and to identify strategies they need to learn. The information from the checklist becomes assessment data from which a teacher can diagnose which reader comprehension strategies one particular student is skillful at using and which ones the student has not mastered.

TAKE A MOMENT

Now you have read about instructional comprehension strategies. Think about how you used strategies in your teaching last year. Which strategies would you keep using in this year's teaching? Why? Which new strategies would you adopt? Why?

FINAL THOUGHTS

Although instructional comprehension strategies are important to use in teaching ELLs, we need to be cognizant of opportunities for ELLs to practice reading (Shanahan & Beck, 2006). Without these opportunities, ELLs would have limited time to practice reader comprehension

Text	Teacher modeling	Reader comprehension strategy
Title: *Pip's Magic*	Today, I am going to show you how I think when reading a new book. I first look at the title. It says, "Pip's Magic." I then look at the front and back cover of the book. On the front cover, I see an animal, and it looks like a lizard. I use a strategy of looking at the title and pictures on the cover. (For older students, the teacher says, "I preview the book cover.")	• Previewing the text
	How do I know it looks like a lizard? I have seen lizards in my life and also in pictures in books. I search in my brain for what I know about lizards. I use a strategy called "activating or getting background information." I use what I know to help me figure out what I am reading. (For older students, the teacher says, "I use a strategy of making a connection between what I know and this book.")	• Getting/ activating background information • Connecting prior knowledge to the text
	I guess that this lizard's name is Pip. I am guessing or predicting, that's *the* strategy I am using.	• Predicting
"I am afraid of the dark," said Pip. "Even shadows scare me." His friends did know how to help. (n.p.)	Now I see water and pebbles. Now I remember what I read before. Salamanders are one kind of lizard. They go to water to lay their eggs. Now, I am getting my background information about salamanders from my brain. So Pip is not a lizard. He is a salamander. This happens all the time. You read and you think you understand the meaning. Then you read the next page, and you say to yourself what I learned on the previous page is wrong or not completely correct. It is okay to change your meaning. Now I know Pip is a salamander. Here, I again use the strategy of connecting to my background knowledge about lizards and salamanders. I also use a strategy of changing (or revising, modifying) meanings. What I did is what a good reader does.	• Getting/ activating background information • Connecting prior knowledge to the text • Revising meanings
	"I am afraid of the dark," said Pip. So this story begins with a problem. Pip's problem is "he is afraid of the dark." I can't wait to see how Pip	• Applying knowledge of text structure *(continued)*

FIGURE 8.12. Think-aloud with Walsh's (1994) *Pip's magic.*

Text	Teacher modeling	Reader comprehension strategy
	solved his problem. I have read stories before. So I know each story has a character, and sometimes more than one characters. A story also has a problem, and then a character or characters try to solve the problem. I use what I know about a story to help me find a character, Pip, a problem—he is afraid of the dark.	
	"Even shadows scare me." I think that Pip has a big problem. Because he thinks shadows are scary. When I was young, like my friends, we were all afraid of darkness, but not shadows. The sentence "Even shadows scare me." tells me more about Pip's problem. This sentence is important. So I know now, Pip's problem is not a little one. We have a name for sentences that tell readers important things. The name is "detail." My strategy here is noticing important details.	• Connecting prior knowledge to the text • Determining/ noticing important details
	His friends didn't know how to help. I look at the picture on the left page and I see three salamanders. So I know that his friends are also salamanders. Here is an interesting thing about how authors write a story. They do not tell you everything, and for a lot of things, you must figure them out on your own. Ms. Walsh (the author) did not need to tell you who Pip's friends are, because the picture tells you that. You figure out information that authors do not tell. While you are doing this, you use the strategy of making inferences.	• Making inferences
	His friends didn't know how to help. Help Pip with what? Again Ms. Walsh did not tell us. But I can guess (or, with older ELLs, "make an inference"). How? I know Pip has a problem of being afraid of the dark. Other salamanders must want to help him solve his problem. Just like sometimes, your friend does not know how to read certain words in a book. You would say to him or her, "I do not know how to help you." This means you do not know how to help him or her read words. Here, I again use the strategy of guessing (or making inferences).	• Making inferences

FIGURE 8.12. (*continued*)

Name: _____

Date: _____

Book Title: _____

Strategies I used in think-aloud	**Strategies I still need to learn**
__ Previewing the text	__ Previewing the text
__ Getting/activating background knowledge	__ Getting/activating background knowledge
__ Making connections	__ Making connections
__ Predicting	__ Predicting
__ Visualizing	__ Visualizing
__ Applying knowledge of text genre and structure	__ Applying knowledge of text genre and structure
__ Determining important details	__ Determining important details
__ Organizing ideas	__ Organizing ideas
__ Summarizing ideas	__ Summarizing ideas
__ Making inferences	__ Making inferences
__ Transferring literacy knowledge and strategies learned from a native language	__ Transferring literacy knowledge and strategies learned from a native language
__ Self-monitoring	__ Self-monitoring
__ Applying fix-up strategies	__ Applying fix-up strategies

FIGURE 8.13. Think-aloud checklist.

strategies, and, consequently, they would have a hard time developing and honing their strategies. Using instructional comprehension strategies to model and scaffold ELLs' comprehension process would become fruitless without time for ELLs to practice reading. We would expect that during independent time when the teacher is working with a small group, students have the opportunity to read and reread multiple texts organized in plastic baggies or tubs. Having multiple opportunities to read with support from teachers and/or peers and to read independently is necessary for students to enhance their reading ability.

CHAPTER 9

Visits to Classrooms
and Schools

To watch a master teacher in action is like watching an artist immersed in her discipline, drawing on an array of techniques, skills, and visions of beauty to create distinct pictures with each boy and girl.
—STRICKLAND AND SNOW (2002, p. 2)

Strickland and Snow (2002) capture both the importance of teachers to student learning and the importance of the art of teaching. This chapter provides vignettes of exemplary teachers who are artists in supporting the learning needs of ELLs. Each vignette centers on a different grade level and a teacher's strength in a particular area. We narrowed the view to classrooms so that across the vignettes a rich variety of instructional strategies and organizations is shared. Although only one or two exemplary practices are shared, each teacher displayed a rich repertoire of practices to support the learning of all students and in particular ELLs. We also present one exciting foray into bringing parents into a school so they can more effectively work with their children in literacy activities at home.

PRESCHOOL

We chose Veronica Larson as the preschool teacher. Veronica teaches 15 ELLs in her classroom of 4-year-olds. Most of her students are ELLs who speak Spanish as their home language. Veronica finds that having so many ELLs who speak the same language presents unique difficulties in extending the language repertoires of her students. For instance, she says:

> "Whenever they are in centers, they always speak Spanish. They are getting better at chatting with each other in Spanish, but their English language conversation is not developing very rapidly."

To solve this problem, Veronica has her aide work with one group of students and a parent with another. Through this additional adult support, she nudges students to practice their novice English oral language skills.

When a visitor enters Veronica's preschool classroom, he or she primarily notices children actively working in centers. Veronica uses centers as one of the principal structures to engage children in conversation while they are learning about literacy and content. When we observed in her room, we noticed the following centers:

■ *Listening center.* On this day children listened to an informational book about baby animals that Veronica had read earlier in the day. When they finished listening, each child was expected to draw a baby animal and label it. Some children scribbled their label and others used the initial letter of the animal's name.

■ *Letter center.* In this center, a parent worked with children. They were looking for the letter *m*. Each child talked about this letter as they looked through catalogues and newspapers. Frequently, we heard Michael's mother comment in Spanish and English on items they found in the text. For example, when two boys talked about the picture of a *carro*, she replied with the word *carro* and that in English it is called a *car*. While the task was to find the letter m, cut it out, and glue it on a chart, this mother simultaneously extended the children's vocabulary in English.

■ *Phonemic awareness lesson.* Veronica worked with a small group of students on phonemic awareness. In her lesson, each child had a chart with three Elkonin boxes on it. Veronica said a CVC word and the children dragged a chip to the corresponding box to match each phoneme. For instance, Veronica said *mud,* and the children dragged a chip to the first box for the *m* sound, a second to the middle box for the *u* sound, and a third to the last box for the *d* sound. The children repeated this activity with other words.

■ *Theater center.* In this center, children worked with an aide on acting out the book *Mrs. Wishy-Washy* (Cowley, 1999). The aide read a simple board book version of this story to the children. After they discussed the story, each child was given a part to act out from the story. Each child had a simple part, such as "And she jumped in." The text was simple and offered the children many opportunities to practice it through choral reading. The children enjoyed performing the play for the other students.

■ *Library center.* In this center, children perused many books about baby animals. Veronica placed favorite books on the bookshelves, but she highlighted books about baby animals—the current topic for instruction. These books along with small plastic baby animals were placed on the table so that students could play with the figures as they looked through the books.

■ *Science center.* In this center, children observed a closed jar with water and dirt in it. When they shook it, they discovered how these two elements became mud. She also had the book *Mud, Mud, Mud* (Meharry, 2001) at the center. In this book a variety of animals are shown who live in mud, such as pigs and frogs. Unlike *Mrs. Wishy-Washy*, this book is an informational text about mud. This center had a journal for students to record their observations. Each child drew and wrote to the best of his or her ability about his or her discoveries. The children enjoyed seeing what other students recorded.

■ *Computer center.* On this day two children worked at one computer where they used Kid Pix Deluxe software to write and draw about baby animals. Their work was printed and displayed for students to read.

In chatting with Veronica about her centers, she conveyed that she wanted each center to be a rich literacy experience. She carefully selected materials that engaged children through content and provided multiple opportunities for reading and writing. She said:

"Using parents and aides, I am able to nudge the children to talk in English. They also have more chances to talk when they are in small groups. When we are all together, even if I ask them to talk to a partner, I don't feel they get enough practice."

Following are just a few of the exemplary practices displayed by Veronica in her instructional content and organization:

1. She organized the children in small groups with an adult to support early efforts in communicating in English.
2. She provided activities that allowed students to read, write, and draw.
3. She engaged students in active activities such as the play, where they practiced retelling a story. This activity allowed ELLs multiple opportunities to practice English.
4. She provided opportunity for children to read both narrative and informational text.
5. She supported students in acting like scientists and they observed and recorded their observations in journals.
6. She encouraged children to use technology as a tool to share their messages.
7. She provided direct instruction in letter recognition and phonemic awareness to strengthen these important, fundamental reading skills.
8. She supported bootstrapping English by providing Spanish/English comparisons.

KINDERGARTEN

Eileen Morris teaches kindergarten in a school considered at risk because of a long history of poor test scores and because of the home backgrounds of the children who attend her school. Over 80% of the students have a home language other than English and most receive free or reduced lunch. As in Veronica's classroom, most of Eileen's students have a home language of Spanish, and few have had any formal preschool experience.

Eileen is most concerned about making her students and their families feel welcome in her school. Before school begins, she sends each family a letter inviting them to visit the school the week before classes start. She wants families to visit her room before the first day of school so that they are comfortable in the new surroundings and comfortable with Eileen being their children's teacher.

When we visited on the first morning of kindergarten, Eileen was at her classroom door welcoming families and their children. Although most had been there before, the children were hiding behind parents when they entered the room. Their eyes lingered on their parents as they sat in a circle on the floor. Eileen welcomed parents to bring their children to the circle and then she asked them to leave so that their children could begin the first day of kindergarten. Eileen recalled later:

> "I wanted the children to feel welcomed and I wanted parents to know that they were too, but I also needed the parents to leave on the first day so that children could learn the routines of the classroom. In our earlier meeting, I told them that I wanted them in my room, just one at a time. And we scheduled their first day to visit."

While Eileen demonstrated many exemplary teaching practices, we are targeting her connections to parents and the way she supported students' home language in her classroom. From that very first day of school, the children had journals that they took home each day. Each night they were to write and draw in their journal. Eileen encouraged them to use English or their home language for writing. Then when they arrived in school, she had several children share what they had written. Later in the day, each child shared his or her journal with a parent helper. Most parents did not speak English fluently, but they could listen to a child's writing and chat with the child in his or her home language or English.

Throughout the room, Eileen had text support. After they read a book about polar bears, they created the chart:

A polar bear likes to eat, swim, and play. The polar bear is big.

She and the children returned to this chart when they read books about other animals and added to it. Later her plan was for them to compare animals orally and in writing.

She also shared poetry and rhymes with children. For each one, she created a poster with a Spanish and English version. For example, for the poem "The Wind," from her basal text she wrote:

| I whistle without lips. | Silbo sin labios. |
| I fly without wings. | Vuelo sin alas. |

Later in the year, we observed Eileen as she engaged all of her students in reading a message she wrote. Her message was:

Raindrops fall on my head.

She first asked her students to quietly read this message. She then pointed to each word as children quietly read each one. The word *raindrops* caused difficulty for many children. To help them she said, "In English, the first sound of this word is like the sound in *run* or *rat*. Who knows that sound?" Children responded. Then she helped them with *ai* and they provided the *n* sound. Then they all read the first part of this word together. One child figured out the *dr* sound and offered it to the group and soon all the children had deciphered *raindrops*. When one child struggled with fall, she had him refer to the word wall and he found the word card and was able to read it. They also used the word wall for *on*. Eileen then paused and let the children read the remaining part of the message. As we watched this small lesson, we understood how Eileen supported her children in independent learning. She patiently waited and provided support so that all of her students could decode this message—a message that was repeated in a book she would read to them a bit later.

We also learned about Eileen's take-home literacy program. Each student took home a baggie with a book and an activity in it each day. The books related to her themes for instruction such as friends, animals, helpers, and so on. At first, she used leveled text from her reading program to send home but found that her students wanted to keep the books at home and it was difficult to get them back. So she investigated possible inexpensive books that she could send home and the children could keep. She asked her school to subscribe to Reading A–Z (*www. readinga-z.com*) so she could print leveled text in English and Spanish to send home. The site also has French versions but none of her students had a home language of French. As a result, each day children took home two books (e.g., *What Is at the Zoo?* and *¿Qué hay en el zoológico?*). Children were expected to read these books with their parents and then to write or draw something about their book. Often these writings showed up in their home–school journal. Children kept these books in a special shoebox that was decorated as a book box. Throughout the year they saw their at home library grow and they discovered how they developed as readers.

Following are just a few of the exemplary practices Eileen displayed in her instructional content and organization:

1. She made parents and students comfortable with kindergarten even before the first day of school.
2. She found ways to use parents in her classroom even when they were not proficient English speakers.
3. She validated the home language of her students through her translations of poems and in the books she sent home.
4. She found ways to connect home and school literacy. She sent books home in English and Spanish.
5. She provided extensive text support in her room for her students.
6. She valued the intelligence of her students as she provided them the time and strategies to decode a message.

FIRST GRADE

Maria Lopez teaches a first-grade class with 13 Spanish-speaking children and 7 children who speak other languages (Vietnamese, Thai, and Farsi) in a Title I school. Most of her students are at the late-beginning English proficiency level, and some are at the immediate level. Maria finds it challenging to work with students who speak a language unfamiliar to her and different from a language shared by most students in her class. To address this challenge, Maria focuses her instruction on capitalizing on students' *funds of knowledge* and on scaffolding the process of oral and written language development.

On the day we visited Maria, we observed how she brought students' funds of knowledge to her class to best support her students' learning (Moll et al., 1992). In a daily show-and-tell, five students were sharing artifacts from their home, community, or home country (e.g., a toy, a book, a photo, an ad written in Vietnamese, and a piece of clothing). During sharing, each student used the sentence patterns on a chart that Maria prepared for them. The patterns guided students through the show-and-tell experience, allowing them to be successful in sharing their message. Here are some examples of what Maria wrote on her chart:

1. What is it?
   This is a . . .
   It is a
2. Why do you like it?
   . . . gave . . . to me.
   It tastes good.
   It is fun to play with it.
   This is a picture of me and my . . .
   It is from my country.

While each student was sharing, Maria wrote down what the student said. If the student was speaking Spanish, Maria wrote down the words in Spanish. If the student was speaking another language, Maria tape-recorded that student's show-and-tell. She later asked a parent who was proficient both in English and in the student's native language to translate the tape. At the end of the sharing, the student called on three peers for questions and/or comments. Again, Maria wrote a set of questions and sentence starters to help students ask good questions and make an interesting, and relevant comment on a peer's sharing. These language supports helped children as they developed English oral skills. For example, Maria wrote:

Questions:
1. Can you tell us more about . . . ?
2. Where did . . . get it?
3. How much was it?
4. How do you take care of it?

Comments:
1. Thank you for sharing your . . . with us.
2. I like your . . .
3. Your is very interesting.
4. Your . . . looks very nice.

Maria shared how she would use the text produced by each student during the show-and-tell.

"I like to use a lot of children's picture books with predictable patterns. But they can be too hard for my students, because the vocabulary, content, and/or linguistic structures are beyond their levels. So I use texts produced by children as supplementary materials for individual guided reading. The texts are at their proficiency level."

At the end of the day, Maria typed up the students' words on a computer and printed out two copies of the text. One copy was for the student and the other copy was for Maria to keep in the student's portfolio. On the following day, Maria asked each student who did show-and-tell on the previous day to read the text with her. Maria chose to read only a few sentences that were grammatically correct with the student. She also chose one or two sentences where she modeled correct structure. For example, José produced these four sentences:

It is a toy.
Me like toy.
Papí buy for me.
It is fun.

Maria selected *It is a toy* to read with José, and highlighted on José's copy of the text the word *toy*. She then pointed at the sentence *It is fun*, asking José if he meant "It is fun to play with the toy.". Maria then added *to play with the toy* at the end of *It is fun.* on José's copy of the text. She asked José to highlight the words *fun*, *play*, and *with*. These three words and the word *fun* were then added to José's personal word book. These words became part of José's weekly homework—he was to write a sentence using each of the four words. Each student's word book served as a resource that was referred to when writing in a journal and when finding words that fit a phonemic awareness or phonics concept. For example, José found the word *play* to fit the *-ay* pattern for the long-*a* sound he was learning.

During this show-and-tell, Maria scaffolded students' learning, and nicely integrated oral language, reading, writing, and grammar instruction. In addition to this unique variation of show-and-tell (similar to the language experience approach [Stauffer, 1980]), Maria engaged her students in different types of reading and writing. For each core text in the basal reader, Maria modeled fluent reading by reading aloud when the text was new to students. She then went back to the text and explained sentences on each page and showed students how a picture on the page supported the sentences. In addition, Maria used simple *wh-* questions to check for her students' comprehension of the text. On following days, Maria echo-read with her students and asked students about what they could remember from the text. If there was some confusion about the storyline, Maria modeled the strategy of going back to the text for clarification. She also pulled out words central to the storyline and added them to the class word wall. Later in the week, Maria invited students to do shared reading. In particular, she encouraged students to join in her reading by reading a sentence or even a few words. After that, Maria wanted her students to volunteer to retell the story. Maria considered retelling a way to assess students' comprehension. During the following week, Maria encouraged her students to read the text introduced the previous week. After this series of scaffolding events, Maria used this text for buddy or paired reading and independent reading.

As for writing, Maria had students write in a journal everyday. She alternated between allowing students to choose a topic and giving them a topic to write about. If she gave students a topic, it was often related to what they were reading or to what students had experienced in life (e.g., family gathering and celebrating a birthday). Everyday, Maria had five students share their journal with the class. She asked a student about how he or she came up with the topic, and what part of the journal he or she thought was the best. She also pulled from the journals grammatically incorrect sentences and misspelled words that were later used as a focus for grammar and spelling instruction.

Following are just a few of the exemplary practices displayed by Maria in her instructional content and organization.

1. She capitalized on students' funds of knowledge by asking students to bring artifacts for show-and-tell.
2. She provided language scaffolds for her students' show-and-tell.
3. She worked with her students on vocabulary and sentence structure at the individual's level.
4. She connected oral language, vocabulary, and grammar instruction.
5. She focused on fluency, comprehension, and vocabulary in her scaffolded reading instruction.
6. She struck a balance between giving students a choice of topic and inviting students to write about a topic she had chosen.
7. She embedded grammar and spelling instruction in writing instruction.

SECOND GRADE

Mary Smith teaches second grade with 20 students who speak a wide range of native languages. Some home languages spoken in her class are Arabic, Chinese, Farsi, Korean, Japanese, Spanish, Russian, and Vietnamese. Her students' English proficiency levels also vary from beginning to early advanced levels. Some of her students are newcomers. Mary's school is not a Title I school, but she does have an instructional aide in her class. Neither Mary nor her aide speak any of the home languages of the students.

Mary considered it very challenging to teach her students, who had a wide range of English proficiency levels and native language backgrounds. She was most concerned about getting all her students at grade level for reading and writing. She stated:

> "It is hard to teach this class. I rely on a group of people who speak my students' native languages—parents, other students in upper grades at my school, people from the community, and even students from a nearby university. I teach reading and writing through content. I find this is helpful even for newcomers. They have some knowledge of content in their native language. Now they only need to know the English equivalents for these concepts."

On the day we visited Mary, we observed how she used content to teach reading and writing (Freeman & Freeman, 2005; Houk, 2005; National Council of Teachers of English, 2006). There were three parent helpers in her class on this day. After a short trip to the school playground where the class observed the sky and different clouds, Mary guided students to talk about what they had observed. She recorded what students said on a chart paper. For example, she wrote:

The sky is as blue as sea.
There are different clouds.
Clouds are white.
Some clouds are big.
Some clouds are small.

Based on students' sentences, Mary came up with a semantic map, including these categories: color of clouds, shapes of clouds, and location of clouds. She took phrases from students' sentences and filled the map.

After this prereading activity, Mary read aloud *The Cloud Book* (dePaola, 1975) and her students followed along in their own copy of the book. After reading the words on each page, Mary pointed out the illustration that matched the words. For example, on the first page of the book, it says, "Almost any time you go outside and look up at the sky, you can see clouds" (n.p.). After reading this sentence, Mary pointed at the word *sky* and then the blue sky in the picture and the word *clouds* and then the clouds in the picture. While matching the phrase *look up* to the picture of a boy who was looking up at the sky, Mary also performed the action of looking up. Mary repeated this process for sentences on each page of the book.

After she finished reading the whole book, she asked students to talk in groups about what they had learned from this book about clouds. She encouraged students to write down key information related to clouds in English or in their native language. They could even draw pictures to represent the information learned.

Mary then asked a student from each group to provide her with one piece of new information and she wrote it down on the semantic map. Parents helped translate the information written in a native language. They also wrote down the English version of the information on the student paper. Later during the day, Mary asked students to do buddy reading or independent reading of the book.

During recess, Mary shared what she and her students would do with the book for the next few days. Students would first work in pairs to complete a semantic map on clouds based on the book and their prior knowledge. In pairing up students, Mary took into consideration students' proficiency levels in English and their native language background. Specifically, she paired up two students who spoke the same native language but were at different proficiency levels. Once students finished their map, they shared their map with the class.

For one of the follow-up activities, Mary pulled out two sets of words from the book: one set was high-frequency words and the other was words related to clouds. Some examples of high-frequency words were *time, outside, look up, see, little, drop, hang, high,* and *above.* Examples of content words of clouds included *cloud, water, ice, atmosphere, cirrus, cumulus, stratus, puffy,* and *feathery.* Both sets of words were then displayed on a word wall. Mary also asked students to copy down the words in their individual word books. She encouraged students who were at the beginning English proficient level to write a native language equivalent next to an English word to better help them remember the word meaning.

Another follow-up activity was for students to write about what they had learned about clouds. Mary allowed those who were at the beginning English proficiency level to use pictures to demonstrate their understanding of the content. During small-group activity time, Mary worked with this group of students on their writing. Specifically, she dictated what students described in the pictures they drew on the computer; later she printed out the dictated text for each picture and pasted it under the picture. If a student dictated in his or her native language, Mary had a parent type up the dictation and then translate it into English. In this student's journal, there was a dictated text in English and in a native language under each picture.

In addition to the activities described using content to teach reading and writing, Mary's teaching of ELLs reflected several exemplary practices. For example, she had a wide range of children's books on different topics and at different reading levels available to students. She also kept collecting as many books and other print materials written in a variety of languages as she could. These books and materials helped students become aware of what they knew about literacy in their native language and also served as a way to create a welcoming environment for them. While emphasizing content to teach reading and writing, Mary also used storybooks in her teaching with a consideration that each story focused on an experience relatively familiar to *all* students in her class (e.g., eating, making friends). When it came to teaching phonics, in addition to the materials listed in her teacher's manual, Mary encouraged her students to bring words from their environmental print such as candy bar wrappers, cereal labels, or signs.

Following are just a few of the exemplary practices Maria displayed in her instructional content and organization.

1. She scaffolded her teaching by modeling and guided practice and by building on students' prior knowledge.
2. She made an effective connection between reading and writing instruction.
3. She provided students with authentic and meaningful experiences with reading and writing.
4. She effectively used parents to enhance her teaching and students' learning.

5. She taught language and literacy through content which is familiar to her students.
6. She provided students with a wide range of print materials.
7. She capitalized on and respected students' literacy knowledge in their native language.
8. She practiced an effective way of grouping students.

WHOLE-SCHOOL CONNECTIONS WITH PARENTS

Fernley Elementary School started Parent University to improve the home–school connection. In past years the school held academic fairs, literacy nights, and other family events. While many family events were well attended by parents, literacy nights resulted in few parents turning out. Although the teachers, coaches, and principal were disappointed with the low turnout, they decided the difficulty was with the format, not with parents' involvement. So they set about discovering a new format for literacy events.

The first change was that parent nights were now called Parent University, so that parents would attach a new importance to these events. The second change was the addition of a bilingual paraprofessional. Her job was to work with ELL parents and students. She personally contacted the families of ELL students before the first Parent University meeting to let them know that she was available for interpreting and that she would be working with some of their children during the event and at school. Moreover, she interpreted all of the handouts that were used during the session and translated during the entire session.

The third change involved the time of the event. The school principal and coaches moved Parent University to the morning, before the schoolday began. For the first Parent University they chose picture day, as many parents bring their children to school on this day so that they stay clean for their photos.

The fourth change was the addition of food and other surprises. They served a continental breakfast—juice, coffee, donuts, bagels, and fruit. Prizes were given during the session. At the end of the session parents received a plastic container with scissors, glue, crayons, pencils, and flashcards. Parents now had materials to take home and school personnel hoped they would be more able to engage their children in literacy activities at home.

Long before the first Parent University, the literacy coaches notified parents with fliers (in English and Spanish), by discussions at PTA meetings, and by personal invitation. They encouraged parents to attend back-to-school night. Finally, a bulletin board was placed in a hallway near the coaches' room, so that whenever parents walked by they saw the notice of the first university event.

The first event began with parents, teachers, the paraprofessional, coaches, and the principal eating breakfast and chatting. As they ate, parents made folders to store materials for the class. One activity was a mixer activity where parents had to find a person to sign up on a sheet written in Spanish and English to discuss a hobby, book, or their family. For instance, one box on the sheet stated hobby and each person had to find someone in the room who had a hobby and would sign his or her name. This activity involved parents interacting with all of the parents and staff and served as a way to relax the parents and to allow them to meet other parents even if they did not speak the same language. The coaches noted:

> "This was hard for the parents—until we said that the person with the most signatures would win a prize. That broke the ice."

The coaches also introduced the principal, vice principal, ELL teacher, ELL aide, ELL paraprofessional, and themselves.

After parents were comfortable, the coaches shifted the focus to literacy. They modeled a picture walk. They used the same book in English and in Spanish: *How Do Dinosaurs Play with Their Friends? ¿Cómo juegan los dinosaurios con sus amigos?* (Yolen & Teague, 2006). The coaches noted:

> "Parents appreciated hearing the benefits of a picture walk and seeing how it was done. They knew they could do it in English or Spanish and they enjoyed using the pictures to tell the story."

Following the picture walk, they broke the group into four smaller groups for more activities. Each station had reading materials in English and Spanish so parents could practice the different reading strategies. Parents spent about 20 minutes at each station. There was a staff person at each station to chat with parents as they engaged in the activities. The activities were:

■ *Comprehension glove.* Parents wrote story elements on a plastic glove. They labeled each finger (setting, problem, events, and solution) and the thumb (characters) and drew a heart on the palm—the heart of the story (main idea).

■ *Word study.* Three levels of word study activities were provided:

1. The paraprofessional used an alphabet activity with ELL parents. She had a chart that showed the differences between the English and Spanish alphabet.
2. A matching game was included that addressed letter name, letter sound, and initial sound.
3. Short-vowel words were sorted by each short vowel.

■ *Bedtime reading strategies.* Handouts were made available for parents to learn about the benefits of reading before bedtime and strategies for talking about what they have read. The suggestions included:

1. Younger children can be encouraged to read by pushing back bedtime by 20 to 30 minutes. Ask an older child to read to a younger child.
2. Cooking together can build reading and math skills. Read the recipes aloud as you measure the ingredients together.
3. Take your child to storytelling time at your local library. This will make reading a fun activity.
4. Let your children pick out their own books. Books with humor can make even the most reluctant reader see that there is enjoyment in reading.
5. Read everything you see from directories to maps to labels and recipes. This helps your children see that reading is important in everything that you do.
6. Encourage your children to make their own books as gifts. They can write and draw a story on pieces of paper stapled together.

■ *Graphic organizers.* Parents were given different types of organizers for working with story elements. They had an opportunity to read a book and practice completing one of the graphic organizers. These included:

1. *A head outline.* Children wrote or drew what they were thinking.
2. *A circle divided into four sections.* Children drew or wrote what

they thought about the story. They might write about the
characters or plot for instance.

3. *A rectangle divided into three sections*. Children wrote or drew
   about the beginning, middle, and end of the story.

Fernley Elementary was pleased with the success of the event. In
the past, few parents had appeared for literacy events. However, at the
first Parent University 25 parents and 10 children attended. The
coaches have learned that these parents have shared how wonderful this
event was with friends, and they expect bigger turnouts at successive
Parent University meetings. They are also formally and informally assessing their ELL students whose parents attended this event to see if
these students achieve at higher rates in literacy.

The family–school literacy program at Fernley is exemplary for
many reasons:

1. Even with low turnout, the staff at Fernley considered it their
   problem and they changed the format of literacy events.
2. They used a paraprofessional so that parents had at least one
   person who could help them access English.
3. They prepared all materials in English and Spanish.
4. They used multiple ways to bring parents to Parent University.
5. They provided parents with activities that could easily be completed at home and that supported literacy development.
6. They provided all the necessary materials so that parents could
   complete the activities with their child.

FINAL THOUGHTS

Each of the teachers profiled in this chapter carefully thought about
ways to best support the learning needs of her students. In addition to
the content expected through district curricula and standards, they analyzed the language strengths and needs of their students. Each lesson
and activity targeted content knowledge as well as language expectations. Many of the teachers used language frames to support novice oral
language abilities in English.

These teachers also found ways to value parents and to authenti-
cally use their language expertise to support student learning. Parents

listened to students and served as language brokers throughout the day. Students and parents understood that all languages were valued as teachers supported students in acquiring oral and listening capabilities and reading and writing proficiency in English.

Perhaps most important is that each of these teachers established high expectations for their students. Then they set about discovering ways for their students to achieve these standards. They utilized parents, aides, materials, technology, and their own expertise to support the learning needs and strengths of their students, and in particular their ELLs.

References

Abedi, J. (2004). The No Child Left Behind Act and English language learners: Assessment and accountability issues. *Educational Researcher, 33,* 4–14.

Adams, M. (1990). *Beginning to read: Thinking and learning about print.* Cambridge, MA: MIT Press.

Alvermann, D. E., Moon, J. S., & Hagood, M. C. (1999). *Popular culture in the classroom.* Newark, DE: International Reading Association.

Anderson, R. C. (1994). Role of the reader's schema in comprehension, learning, and memory. In R. B. Ruddell, M. R. Ruddell, & H. Singer (Eds.), *Theoretical models and processes of reading* (4th ed., pp. 469–482). Newark, DE: International Reading Association.

Anderson, R. C., & Pearson, D. P. (1984). A schema-theoretic view of basic processes in reading comprehension. In P. D. Pearson, R. Barr, M. L. Kamil, & P. Mosenthal (Eds.), *Handbook of reading research* (Vol. 1, pp. 255–291). Mahwah, NJ: Erlbaum.

Anderson, V., & Roit, M. (1998). Reading as a gateway to language proficiency for language-minority students in the elementary grades. In R. M. Gersten & R. T. Jimenez (Eds.), *Promoting learning for culturally and linguistically diverse students: Classroom applications from contemporary research* (pp. 42–54). Belmont, CA: Wadsworth.

Applebee, A. (1978). *A child's concept of story.* Chicago: University of Chicago Press.

Arab-Moghadam, N., & Sénéchal, M. (2001). Orthographic and phonological processing skills in reading and spelling in Persian/English bilingual. *International Journal of Behavioral Development, 25,* 140–147.

Archer, A. (2007, February). *Reading comprehension in the primary grades.* Paper presented at the National Reading First Comprehension Conference, San Francisco.

Armbruster, B. (2000). Responding to informational prose. In R. Indrisano & J. Squire (Eds.), *Perspectives on writing: Research, theory, and practice* (pp. 140–161). Newark, DE: International Reading Association.

Armbruster, B., Lehr, F., & Osborn, J. (2001). *Put reading first: The research building blocks for teaching children to read.* Washington, DC: National Institute for Literacy and Center for the Improvement of Early Reading Achievement.

Asher, J. (1977). *Learning another language through actions.* Los Gatos, CA: Sky Oaks Productions.

Au, K. H. (2000). A multicultural perspective on policies for improving literacy achievement: Equity and excellence. In M. L. Kamil, P. B. Mosenthal, P. D. Pearson, & R. Barr (Eds.), *Handbook of reading research* (Vol. 3, pp. 835–851). Mahwah, NJ: Erlbaum.

Au, K. H. (2002). Multicultural factors and the effective instruction of students of diverse backgrounds. In A. E. Farstrup & S. J. Samuels (Eds.), *What research has to say about reading instruction* (3rd ed., pp. 392–413). Newark, DE: International Reading Association.

August, D. (2002). *From Spanish to English: Reading and writing for English language learners kindergarten through third grade.* Pittsburgh: University of Pittsburgh.

August, D., & Shanahan, T. (Eds.). (2006a). *Executive summary for developing literacy in second-language learners: A report of the National Literacy Panel on language-minority children and youth.* Available at *www.cal.org/natl-lit-panel/reports/Executive_Summary.pdf*

August, D., & Shanahan, T. (Eds.). (2006b). *Developing literacy in second-language learners: Report of the National Literacy Panel on language-minority children and youth.* Mahwah, NJ: Erlbaum.

Baker, L., & Brown, A. L. (1984). Metacognitive skills and reading. In P. D. Pearson (Ed.), *Handbook of reading research* (pp. 353–394). New York: Longman.

Barone, D. (2006). *Narrowing the literacy gap.* New York: Guilford Press.

Barone, D. M., Mallette, M. H., & Xu, S. H. (2005). *Teaching early literacy: Development, assessment, and instruction.* New York: Guilford Press.

Barone, D., & Taylor, J. (2006). *Improving students' writing, K–8.* Thousand Oaks, CA: Corwin Press.

Bartolomé, L. (1998). *The misteaching of academic discourses: The politics of language in the classroom.* Boulder, CO: Westview Press.

Bear, D., & Barone, D. (1989). Using children's spelling to group for word study and directed reading in the primary classroom. *Reading Psychology, 10,* 275–292.

Bear, D., & Barone, D. (1998). *Developing literacy: An integrated approach to assessment and instruction.* Boston: Houghton Mifflin.

Bear, D., Caserta-Henry, C., & Venner, D. (2004). *Personal readers for emergent and beginning readers.* San Diego: Teaching Resource Center.

Bear, D., Helman, L., Invernizzi, M., Templeton, S. R., & Johnston, F. (2007). *Words their way with English learners: Word study for spelling, phonics, and vocabulary instruction.* Upper Saddle River, NJ: Prentice Hall.

Bear, D., Invernizzi, M., Templeton, S., & Johnston, F. (2003). *Words their way* (3rd ed.). New York: Prentice Hall.

Beck, I. (2003, October). *Bringing words to life in kindergarten and first grade classrooms.* Paper presented at the Focus on Vocabulary Forum, Pacific Resources for Education and Learning, Dallas.

Beck, I., McKeown, M., & Kucan, L. (2002). *Bringing words to life: Robust vocabulary instruction.* New York: Guilford Press.

Beck, I., McKeown, M., & Omanson, R. (1987). The effects and uses of diverse vocabulary instructional techniques. In M. McKeown & M. Curtis (Eds.), *The nature of vocabulary acquisition* (pp. 147–163). Hillsdale, NJ: Erlbaum.

Benard, B. (1997). *Turning it around for all youth: From risk to resilience* (ERIC/CUE Digest No. 126). New York: ERIC Clearinghouse on Urban Education.

Benard, B. (2004). *Resiliency: What we have learned.* San Francisco: WestEd.

Binkley, M. R. (1988). New ways of assessing text difficulty. In B. L. Zakaluk & S. J. Samuels (Eds.), *Readability: Its past, present, and future* (pp. 98–120). Newark, DE: International Reading Association.

Bissex, G. (1980). *GNYS AT WORK: A child learns to read and write.* Cambridge, MA: Harvard University Press.

Blachman, B., Ball, E., Black, R., & Tangel, D. (2000). *Road to the code: A phonological awareness program for young children.* Baltimore: Brookes.

Block, C. C., & Pressley, M. (Eds.). (2002). *Comprehension instruction: Research-based best practices.* New York: Guilford Press.

Bloodgood, J. (1999). What's in a name? Children's name writing and literacy acquisition. *Reading Research Quarterly, 34,* 342–367.

Boyd-Batstone, P. (2006). *Differentiated early literacy for English language learners: Practical strategies.* Boston: Allyn & Bacon.

Bransford, J. D., & Johnson, M. K. (1972). Contextual prerequisites for understanding: Some investigations of comprehension and recall. *Journal of Verbal Learning and Verbal Behavior, 11,* 717–726.

Brennemann, K., Massey, C., Machado, S,, & Gelman, R. (1996). Notating knowledge about words and objects: Preschoolers' plans differ for "writing" and "drawing." *Cognitive Development, 11,* 397–419.

Brown, D. (2002). *Becoming a successful urban teacher.* Portsmouth, NH: Heinemann.

Button, K., Johnson, M., & Furgerson, P. (1996). Interactive writing in a primary classroom. *The Reading Teacher, 49,* 446–454.

Cappellini, M. (2005). *Balancing reading and language learning: A resource for teaching English language learners K–5.* Portland, ME: Stenhouse.

Cappellini, M. (2006). Using guided reading with English learners. In T. A. Young & N. L. Hadaway (Eds.), *Supporting the literacy development of English language learners: Increasing success in all classrooms* (pp. 113–131). Newark, DE: International Reading Association.

Carrasquillo, A., & Rodriquez, V. (2002). *Language minority student in the mainstream classroom* (2nd ed.). Philadelphia: Multilingual Matters.

Chamot, A. U., Barnhardt, S., El-Dinary, P. B., & Robbins, J. (1999). *The learning strategies handbook.* White Plains, NY: Addison-Wesley Longman.

Chamot, A. U., & O'Malley, J. M. (1994). *The CALLA handbook: Implementing the cognitive academic language learning approach.* Reading, MA: Addison-Wesley.

Chesterfield, R., Chesterfield, K., Hayes-Latimer, K., & Chavez, R. (1983). The influence of teachers and peers on second language acquisition in bilingual preschool programs. *TESOL Quarterly, 21,* 617–641.

Chi, M. (1988). Invented spelling/writing in Chinese-speaking children: The developmental patterns. *Yearbook of the National Reading Conference, 37,* 285–296.

Chiappe, P., Siegel, L., & Wade-Wooley, L. (2002). Linguistic diversity and the development of reading skills: A longitudinal study. *Scientific Studies of Reading, 6*, 369–400.

Christie, J., Vukelich, C., & Enz, B. J. (2006). *Teaching language and literacy: Preschool through the elementary grades* (3rd ed.). New York: Allyn & Bacon.

Clark, M. M. (1976). *Young fluent readers: What they can teach us.* London: Heinemann.

Clay, M. (1975). *What did I write?: Beginning writing behaviour.* Auckland, New Zealand: Heinemann.

Collier, V. (1987, April). *Age and rate of acquisition of cognitive–academic second language proficiency.* Paper presented at the annual meeting of the American Education Research Associations, Washington, DC.

Corson, D. (1997). The learning and use of academic English words. *Language Learning, 47*, 671–718.

Cote, L. (2001). Language opportunities during mealtimes in preschool classrooms. In D. Dickinson & P. Tabors (Eds.), *Beginning literacy with language* (pp. 205–221). Baltimore: Brookes.

Cummins, J. (1979). Linguistic interdependence and the educational development of bilingual children. *Review of Educational Research, 49*, 222–251.

Cummins, J. (1986). Empowering minority students: A framework for intervention. *Harvard Educational Review, 56*, 18–35.

Cummins, J. (1989). *Empowering minority students.* Sacramento: California Association for Bilingual Education.

Cummins, J. (1996). *Negotiating identities: Education for empowerment in a diverse society.* Ontario: California Association for Bilingual Education.

Cummins, J. (2003). Reading and the bilingual student: Fact and friction. In G. Garcia (Ed.), *English learners reaching the highest level of English literacy* (pp. 2–33). Newark, DE: International Reading Association.

Cunningham, A., & Stanovich, K. (1998). What reading does for the mind. *American Educator, 22*(1–2), 8–15.

Cunningham, P. (1991). *Phonics they use: Words for reading and writing.* New York: HarperCollins.

Davis, L., Carlisle, J., & Beeman, M. (1999). Hispanic children's writing in English and Spanish when English is the language of instruction. *Yearbook of the National Reading Conference, 48*, 238–248.

Delgado-Gaitan, C. (1994). Spanish speaking families' involvement in schools. In C. L. Fagnano & B. Z. Werber (Eds.), *School, family and community interaction: A view from the firing lines* (pp. 85–98). Boulder, CO: Westview.

Delgado-Gaitan, C. (2001). *The power of community: Mobilizing for family and schooling.* Denver, CO: Rowman & Littlefield.

Delpit, L. (1995). *Other people's children: Cultural conflict in classroom.* New York: New Press.

Dillon, D. (2000). *Reconsidering how to meet the literacy needs of all students.* Newark, DE: International Reading Association.

Dole, J. A. (2002). Comprehension strategies. In B. J. Guzzetti (Ed.), *Literacy in America: An encyclopedia of history, theory and practice* (pp. 85–87). Santa Barbara, CA: ABC-CLIO.

Dole, J. A., Duffy, G., Roehler, L., & Pearson, P. D. (1991). Moving from the old to the new: Research in reading comprehension instruction. *Review of Educational Research, 61*, 239–264.

Duke, N. K., & Pearson, P. D. (2002). Effective practices for developing reading comprehension. In A. E. Farstrup & S. J. Samuels (Eds.), *What research has to say about reading instruction* (pp. 205–242). Newark, DE: International Reading Association.

Dunn, L., Beach, S., & Kontos, S. (1994). Quality of the literacy environment in day care and children's development. *Journal of Research in Childhood Education, 9*, 24–34.

Dyson, A. (1988). Negotiating among multiple words: The space/time dimensions of young children's composing. *Research in the Teaching of English, 22*, 355–391.

Dyson, A. (1997). *Writing superheroes: Contemporary childhood, popular culture, and classroom literacy.* New York: Teachers College Press.

Dyson, A. (2001). Writing and children's symbolic repertoires: Development unhinged. In S. Neuman & D. Dickinson (Eds.), *Handbook of early literacy research* (pp. 126–141). New York: Guilford Press.

Dyson, A. H. (2003). *The brothers and sisters learn to write: Popular literacies in childhood and school cultures.* New York: Teachers College Press.

Echevarria, J., Vogt, M., & Short, D. (2004). *Making content comprehensible for English Language learners: The SIOP model* (2nd ed.). New York: Allyn & Bacon.

Echevarria, J., Vogt, M., & Short, D. J. (2008). *Making content comprehensible for English Language learners: The SIOP model* (3rd ed.). Boston: Allyn & Bacon.

Edelsky, C. (1982). Writing in a bilingual program: The relation of L1 and L2 texts. *TESOL Quarterly, 16*, 211–228.

Elley, W. (1998). *Raising literacy levels in third world countries: A method that works.* Culver City, CA: Language Education Associates.

Evans, J. (Ed.). (2005). *Literacy moves on: Popular culture, new technologies, and critical literacy in the elementary classroom.* Portsmouth, NH: Heinemann.

Faltis, C. J. (2001). *Joinfostering: Teaching and learning in multilingual classrooms* (3rd ed.). Upper Saddle River, NJ: Prentice Hall.

Ferreiro, E., & Teberosky, A. (1985). *Literacy before schooling.* Portsmouth, NH: Heinemann.

Fitzgerald, J. (1995a). English-as-a-second-language learners' cognitive reading processes: A review of research in the United States. *Review of Educational Research, 65*, 145–190.

Fitzgerald, J. (1995b). English-as-second language reading instruction in the United States: A research review. *Journal of Reading Behavior, 27*, 115–152.

Fitzgerald, J. (2001). Multilingual writing in preschool through 12th grade: The last 15 years. In S. Neuman & D. Dickinson (Eds.), *Handbook of early literacy research* (pp. 337–354). New York: Guilford Press.

Fitzgerald, J., & Graves, M. F. (2004). *Scaffolding reading experiences for English language learners.* Norwood, MA: Christopher-Gordon.

Fitzgerald, J., & Noblit, G. (1999). About hopes, aspirations, and uncertainty: First-grade English-language-learners' emergent reading. *Journal of Literacy Research, 31*, 133–182.

Flores-Gonzalez, N. (2002). *School kids/street kids: Identity development in Latino students.* New York: Teachers College Press.

Flower, L., & Hayes, J. (1980). The dynamics of composing: Making plans and juggling constraints. In L. W. Gregg & E. R. Steinberg (Eds.), *Cognitive processes in writing* (pp. 1–50). Hillsdale, NJ: Erlbaum.

Freeman, D., & Freeman, Y. (2000). *Teaching reading in multilingual classrooms.* Portsmouth, NH: Heinemann.

Freeman, Y. S., & Freeman, D. E. (2005). *Dual language essentials for teachers and administrators.* Portsmouth, NH: Heinemann.

Freire, P. (1987). The importance of the act of reading. In P. Freire & D. Macedo, *Literacy: Reading the word and the world* (pp. 29–36). South Hadley, MA: Bergin & Garvey.

Garcia, E. E. (2005). *Teaching and learning in two languages.* New York: Teachers College Press.

Garcia, G. E. (1991). Factors influencing the English reading test performance of Spanish-speaking Hispanic children. *Reading Research Quarterly, 26,* 371–392.

Garcia, G. E. (2000). Bilingual children's reading. In M. L. Kamil, P. B. Mosenthal, P. D. Pearson, & R. Barr (Eds.), *Handbook of reading research* (Vol. 3, pp. 813–834). Mahwah, NJ: Erlbaum.

Garcia, G., McKoon, G., & August, D. (2006). Synthesis: Language and literacy assessment. In D. August & T. Shanahan (Eds.), *Developing literacy in second-language learners: Report of the National Literacy Panel on language-minority children and youth* (pp. 583–624). Mahwah, NJ: Erlbaum.

Garcia, G., & Willis, A. (2002). Frameworks for understanding multicultural literacies. In P. Schmidt & P. Mosenthal (Eds.), *Reconceptualizing literacy in the sewage of pluralism and multiculturalism* (pp. 3–31). Greenwich, CT: Information Age.

Gates, A. I. (1947). *The improvement of reading* (3rd ed.). New York: Macmillan.

Gee, J. P. (2003). *What video games have to teach us about learning and literacy.* Hampshire, UK: Palgrave-Macmillan.

Genesee, F., Lindholm-Leary, K., Saunders, W., & Christian, D. (2005). English language learners in U. S. schools: An overview of research findings. *Journal of Education for Students Placed at Risk, 10,* 363–385.

Gersten, R. (1996). Literacy instruction for language-minority students: The transition years. *Elementary School Journal, 96,* 228–244.

Gersten, R., & Baker, S. (2000). What we know about effective instructional practices for English language learners. *Exceptional Children, 66,* 454–470.

Gersten, R., Baker, S., Haager, D., & Graves, A. (2005). Exploring the role of teacher quality in predicting reading outcomes for first-grade English learners. *Remedial and Special Education, 26,* 197–206.

Geva, E., & Petrulis-Wright, J. (1999). *The role of English oral language proficiency in reading development of L1 and L2 primary level children.* Unpublished manuscript, Department of Human Development and Applied Psychology, University of Toronto, Ontario, Canada.

Gibson, E., & Levin, H. (1980). *The psychology of reading.* Cambridge, MA: MIT Press.

Goldenberg, C. (1987). Low income Hispanic parents' contributions to their first-grade children's word-recognition skills. *Anthropology and Education Quarterly, 18,* 149–179.

Goldenberg, C., & Gallimore, R. (1995). Immigrant Latino parents' values and beliefs about their children's education: Continuities and discontinuities across cultures and generations. *Advances in Motivation and Achievement, 9,* 183–228.

Goldman, S. R., & Rakestraw, J. A. (2000). Structural aspects of constructing meaning from text. In M. L. Kamil, P. B. Mosenthal, P. D. Pearson, & R. Barr (Eds.), *Handbook of reading* research (Vol. 3, pp. 311–336). Mahwah, NJ: Erlbaum.

Goldstein, B. (2000). *Resource guide on cultural and linguistic diversity.* San Diego: Singular.

Gonzáles, N., & Moll, L. (1995). Funds of knowledge for teaching in Latino households. *Urban Education, 29,* 443–471.

Gonzáles, N., Moll, L., & Amanti, C. (2005). *Funds of knowledge: theorizing practice in households, communities, and classrooms.* Mahwah, NJ: Erlbaum.

Goodman, Y. (1986). Children coming to know literacy. In W. H. Teale & E. Sulzby (Eds.), *Emergent literacy* (pp. 1–14). Norwood, NJ: Ablex.

Goodman, Y. (1996). Revaluing readers while readers revalue themselves. *The Reading Teacher, 49,* 600–609.

Gordon, C. J. (1985). Modeling inference awareness across the curriculum. *Journal of Reading, 28,* 444–447.

Gordon, G. (1999). Teacher talent and urban schools. *Phi Delta Kappan, 81,* 304–307.

Grant, C. (2001). Teachers and linking literacies of yesterday and today with literacies of tomorrow: The need for education that is multicultural and social reconstructionist. In J. V. Hoffman, D. L. Schallert, C. M. Fairbanks, J. Worthy., & B. Maloch (Eds.), *50th yearbook of the National Reading Conference* (pp. 63–81). Chicago, IL: National Reading Conference.

Graves, D. (2004). *Teaching day by day: 180 stories to help you along the way.* Portsmouth, NH: Heinemann.

Guthrie, J. (2002). Engagement and motivation in reading instruction. In M. Kamil, J. Manning, & H. Walberg (Eds.), *Successful reading instruction* (pp. 137–154). Greenwich, CT: Information Age.

Gutiérrez, K. (1995). Unpacking academic discourse. *Discourse Processes, 19,* 21–38.

Gutiérrez, K. (2001). What's new in the English language arts: Challenging policies and practices. *Language Arts, 78,* 564–569.

Gutiérrez, K., Basquedano-Lopez, P., & Turner, M. (1997). Putting language back into language arts: When the radical middle meets the third space. *Language Arts, 74,* 368–378.

Hadaway, N., Vardell, S., & Young, T. (2004). *What every teacher should know about English learners.* Boston: Pearson/Allyn & Bacon.

Halliday, M. S. K. (1975). *Learning how to mean.* New York: Elsevier.

Harste, J., Woodward, V., & Burke, C. (1984). *Language stories and literacy lessons.* Portsmouth, NH: Heinemann.

Hart, B., & Risley, T. (1995). *Meaningful differences in the everyday experience of young American children.* Baltimore: Brookes.

Hart, B., & Risley, T. (1999). *The social world of children learning to talk.* Baltimore: Brookes.

Heath, S. (1983). A lot of talk about nothing. *Language Arts, 60*, 39–48.

Helman, L. (2004). Building on the sound system of Spanish: Insights from the alphabetic spellings of English-language learners. *The Reading Teacher, 57*, 452–460.

Henderson, E. (1990). *Teaching spelling* (2nd ed.). Boston: Houghton Mifflin.

Hiebert, E. H., Brown, Z. M., Taitague, C., Fisher, C. W., & Adler, M. A. (2004). Texts and English language learners: Scaffolding entrée to reading. In F. B. Boyd & C. H. Brock (Eds.), *Multicultural and multilingual literacy and language* (pp. 32–53). New York: Guilford Press.

Hiebert, E. H., & Raphael, T. E. (1998). *Early literacy instruction.* Fort Worth, TX: Harcourt Brace.

Houk, F. A. (2005). *Supporting English language learners: A guide for teachers and administrators.* Portsmouth, NH: Heinemann.

Hudelson, S. (1989). A tale of two children. In D. Johnson & D. Roen (Eds.), *Richness in writing* (pp. 84–99). New York: Longman.

Hurley, S. R., & Blake, S. (2000). Assessment in the content areas for students acquiring English. In S. R. Hurley & J. V. Tinajero (Eds.), *Literacy assessment of second language learners* (pp. 84–103). Boston: Allyn & Bacon.

International Reading Association (2001). *Resolution for second language literacy instruction.* Newark, DE: Author.

Jackson, N., Holm, A., & Dodd, B. (1998). Phonological awareness and spelling abilities of Cantonese–English bilingual children. *Asia Pacific Journal of Speech, Language, and Hearing, 3*, 79–96.

Jiménez, R. T. (2001). "It's a difference that changes us": An alternative view of the language and literacy learning needs of Latina/o students. *The Reading Teacher, 54*, 736–742.

Jiménez, R. T. (2004). More equitable literacy assessments for Latino students. *The Reading Teacher, 57*, 576–578.

Jiménez, R. T., Garcia, G. E, & Pearson, D. E. (1996). The reading strategies of bilingual Latina/o students who are successful English readers: Opportunities and obstacles. *Reading Research Quarterly, 31*, 91–112.

Johns, J. J. (2005). *Basic reading inventory* (9th ed.). Dubuque, IA: Kendall/Hunt.

Johnson, L. R. (2004). "The blood they carry": Puerto Rican mothers re-envisioning and reconstructing educational and cultural identities in a family literacy context. In J. Worthy, B. Maloch, J. V. Hoffman, D. L. Schallert, & C. M. Fairbanks (Eds.), *53rd yearbook of the National Reading Conference* (pp. 233–245). Oak Creek, WI: National Reading Conference.

Juel, C. (1988). Learning to read and write: A longitudinal study of 54 children from first through fourth grades. *Journal of Educational Psychology, 80*, 437–447.

Kintsch, W., & Van Dijk, T. A. (1978). Toward a model of text comprehension and production. *Psychological Review, 85*, 363–394.

Krashen, S. (1985). *The input hypothesis: Issues and implications.* New York: Longman.

Krashen, S. (2004). *The power of reading: Insights from the research* (2nd ed.). Portsmouth, NH: Heinemann.

Krashen, S., & Terrell, T. (1983). *The natural approach: Language acquisition in the classroom.* Englewood Cliffs, NJ: Alemany/Prentice Hall.

Kress, G. (1993). *Communication and culture*. New South Wales: University of New South Wales Press.

Kuby, P., & Aldridge, J. (2004). The impact of environmental print instruction on early reading ability. *Journal of Instructional Psychology, 31*, 106–114.

Labbo, L., Love, S., Prior, M., Hubbard, B., & Ryan, T. (2006). *Literature links: Thematic units linking read-alouds and computer activities*. Newark, DE: International Reading Association.

Ladson-Billings, G. (1994). *The dreamkeepers: Successful teachers of African American children*. San Francisco: Jossey-Bass.

Ladson-Billings, G. (2001). *Crossing over to Canaan: The journey of new teachers in diverse classrooms*. San Francisco: Jossey-Bass.

Landry, S. H., & Smith, K. E. (2005). The influence of parenting on emerging literacy skills. In D. K. Dickinson & S. B. Neuman (Eds.), *Handbook of early literacy research* (Vol. 2, pp. 135–148). New York: Guilford Press.

Lankshear, C., & Knobel, M. (2003). *New literacies: Changing knowledge amd classroom learning*. Buckingham, PA: Open University Press.

Lenski, S. D., Ehlers-Zavala, F., Daniel, M. C., & Sun-Irminger, X. (2006). Assessing English-language learners in mainstream classrooms. *The Reading Teacher, 60*, 24–34.

Lenters, K. (2004/2005). No half measures: Reading instruction for young second-language learners. *The Reading Teacher, 58*, 328–336.

Lesaux, N., Koda, K., Siegel, L., & Shanahan, T. (2006). Development of literacy. In D. August & T. Shanahan (Eds.), *Developing literacy in second-language learners* (pp. 75–122). Mahwah, NJ: Erlbaum.

Lessow-Hurley, J. (2005). *The foundations of dual language instruction* (4th ed.). Boston: Allyn & Bacon.

Li, G. (2004). Family literacy: Learning from an Asian immigrant family. In F. B. Boyd, C. H. Brock, & M. S. Rosendal (Eds.), *Multicultural and multilingual literacy and language: Contexts and practices* (pp. 304–321). New York: Guilford Press.

Liberman, E. (1985). *Name writing and the preschool child*. Unpublished doctoral dissertation. University of Arizona, Tucson.

Lipson, M. Y., & Wixson, K. K. (2003). *Assessment and instruction of reading and writing difficulty: An interactive approach* (3rd ed.). Boston: Allyn & Bacon.

Lonigan, C., Burgess, S., & Anthony, J. (2000). Development of emergent literacy and early reading skills in preschool children: Evidence from a latent-variable longitudinal study. *Developmental Psychology, 36*, 596–613.

Mandler, J. M., & Johnson, N. S. (1977). Remembrance of things passed: Story structure and recall. *Cognitive Psychology, 9*, 111–151.

Maniates, H., & Doerr, B. (2001). *Teach our children well*. Portsmouth, NH: Heinemann.

Marsh, J., & Millard, E. (Eds.). (2006). *Popular literacies, childhood and schooling*. New York: Routledge.

McCarthey, S. (2000). Home–school connections: A review of the literature. *Journal of Educational Research, 93*, 145–153.

McCarthey, S. (2002). *Students' identities and literacy learning*. Newark, DE: International Reading Association.

McGee, L., & Richgels, D. (1996). *Literacy's beginnings: Supporting young readers and writers*. Needham Heights, MA: Allyn & Bacon.

Meier, D. R. (2004). *The young child's memory of words: Developing first and second language and literacy.* New York: Teachers College Press.

Meyer, B. J. F., & Freedle, R. O. (1984). Effects of discourse type on recall. *American Educational Research Journal, 21*, 121–143.

Mohr, K. A. J. (2004). English as an accelerated language: A call to action for reading teachers. *The Reading Teacher, 58*, 18–26.

Moll, L. C. (1998). Turning to the world: Bilingual schooling, literacy, and the cultural mediation of thinking. In T. Shanahan & F. V. Rodriguez-Brown (Eds.), *47th yearbook of the National Reading Conference* (pp. 59–75). Chicago: National Reading Conference.

Moll, L. C., Amanti, C., Neff, D., & Gonzalez, N. (1992). Funds of knowledge for teaching: Using a qualitative approach to connect homes and classrooms. *Theory into Practice, 31*, 132–141.

Mora, J. K. (2006). Differentiating instruction for English learners: The four-by-four model. In F. A. Young & N. L. Hadaway (Eds.), *Supporting the literacy development of English learners: Increasing success in all classrooms* (pp. 24–40). Newark, DE: International Reading Association.

Morris, D. (1980). Beginning readers' concept of word. In E. Henderson & J, Beers (Eds.), *Developmental and cognitive aspects of learning to spell* (pp. 97–111). Newark, DE: International Reading Association.

Morris, D. (1993). The relationship between children's concept of word in text and phoneme awareness in learning to read: A longitudinal study. *Research in the Teaching of English, 27*, 133–154.

Morrow, L. (2005). *Literacy development in the early years* (5th ed.). Boston: Pearson.

Nagy, W., & Herman, P. (1987). Breadth and depth of vocabulary knowledge: Implications for acquisition and instruction. In M. McKeown & M. Curtis (Eds.), *The nature of vocabulary acquisition* (pp. 19–35). Hillsdale, NJ: Erlbaum.

Nagy, W. E., & Scott, J. A. (2000). Vocabulary processes. In M. L. Kamil, P. B. Mosenthal, P. D. Pearson, & R. Barr (Eds.), *Handbook of reading research* (Vol. 3, pp. 269–284). Mahwah, NJ: Erlbaum.

National Council of Teachers of English. (2006). *NCTE position paper on the role of English teachers in educating English language learners* (ELLs). Retrieved September 1, 2006, from *www.ncte.org/about/over/positions/category/div/124545.htm*.

National Institute of Child Health and Human Development. (2000). *Report of the National Reading Panel. Teaching children to read: An evidence-based assessment of the scientific research literature on reading and its implications for reading instruction* (NIH Publication No. 00-4769). Washington, DC: U.S. Government Printing Office.

Nespor, J. (1997). *Tangled up in school: Politics, space, bodies, and signs in the educational process.* Mahwah, NJ: Erlbaum.

Neufeld, P., & Fitzgerald, J. (2001). Early English reading development: Latino English learners in the "low" reading group. *Research in the Teaching of English, 36*, 64–105.

Neuman, S. (1999). Creating continuity in early literacy: Linking home and school with a culturally responsive approach. In L. Gambrell, L. Morrow, S. Neuman, & M, Pressley (Eds.), *Best practices in literacy instruction* (pp. 258–270). New York: Guilford Press.

Neuman, S. (2005). The knowledge gap: Implications for early education. In D. K. Dickinson & S. B. Neuman (Eds.), *Handbook of early literacy research* (Vol. 2, pp. 29–40). New York: Guilford Press.

Neuman, S., & Celano, D. (2001). Access to print in low-income and middle-income communities: An ecological study of four neighborhoods. *Reading Research Quarterly, 36*, 8–27.

Neuman, S. B., & Roskos, K. (1993). *Language and literacy learning in the early years: An integrated approach*. Fort Worth, TX: Harcourt Brace Jovanovich.

New London Group. (1996). A pedagogy of multiliteracies: Designing social futures. *Harvard Educational Review, 66*, 60–92.

Newmann, F., Wehlage, G., & Lamborn, S. (1992). The significance and sources of student engagement. In F. Newmann (ED.), *Student engagement and achievement in secondary schools* (pp. 11–39). New York: Teachers College Press.

Nieto, S. (1999). *The light in their eyes: Creating multicultural learning communities*. New York: Teachers College Press.

Ogle, D. (1986). K–W–L: A teaching model that develops active reading of expository text. *The Reading Teacher, 39*, 564–570.

Ogle, D. (2004). Meeting the challenges for all students in urban schools. In D. Lapp, C. Block, E. Cooper, J. Flood, N. Roser, & J. Tinajero (Eds.), *Teaching all children* (pp. 327–336). New York: Guilford Press.

Oladejo, J. (2006). Parents' attitudes towards bilingual education policy in Taiwan. *Bilingual Research Journal, 30*, 147–170.

O'Malley, J. M., & Chamot, A. U. (1990). *Learning strategies in second language acquisition*. New York: Cambridge University Press.

O'Malley, J. M., & Valdez-Pierce, L. (1996). *Authentic assessment for English language learners: Practical approaches for teachers*. Reading, MA: Addison-Wesley.

Padilla, A., & Liebman, E. (1975). Language acquisition of a bilingual child. *The Bilingual Review/La Revista Bilingüe, 2*, 34–55.

Paley, V. (1981). *Wally's stories*. Cambridge, MA: Harvard University Press.

Papandropoulou, I., & Sinclair, H. (1974). What is a word? An experimental study of children's ideas on grammar. *Human Development, 17*, 241–258.

Pappas, C., Kiefer, B., & Levstik, L. (1995). *An integrated language perspective in the elementary school* (2nd ed.). White Plains, NY: Longman.

Paratore, J. R. (2001). *Opening doors, opening opportunities: Family literacy in an urban community*. Boston: Allyn & Bacon.

Paratore, J. R., Melzi, G., & Krol-Sinclair, B. (2003). Learning about the literate lives of Latino families. In D. M. Barone & L. Morrow (Eds.), *Literacy and young children: Research-based practices* (pp. 101–118). New York: Guilford Press.

Paris, S. G., Lipson, M. Y., & Wixson, K. K. (1994). Becoming a strategic reader. In R. B. Ruddell, M. R. Ruddell, & H. Singer (Eds.), *Theoretical models and processes of reading* (4th ed., pp. 788–810). Newark, DE: International Reading Association.

Paterson, P. (1981). *Gates of excellence: On reading and writing books for children*. New York: Dutton Juvenile.

Pearson, D. P. (1985). Changing the face of reading comprehension instruction. *The Reading Teacher, 38,* 724–738.

Pearson, D. P., & Camperell, K. (1994). Comprehension of text structures. In R. B. Ruddell, M. R. Ruddell, & H. Singer (Eds.), *Theoretical models and processes of reading* (4th ed., pp. 448–468). Newark, DE: International Reading Association.

Peregoy, S. F., & Boyle, O. F. (2000). English learners reading English: What we know, what we need to know. *Theory into Practice, 39,* 237–247.

Peregoy, S., & Boyle, O. (2005). *Reading, writing, and learning in ESL* (4th ed.). New York: Allyn & Bacon.

Pérez, B. (2004). Literacy, curriculum, and language diversity. In B. Pérez (Ed.), *Sociocultural contexts of language and study* (2nd ed., pp. 339–375). Mahwah, NJ: Erlbaum.

Pérez, B., & Torres-Guzmán, M. (1992). *Learning in two worlds: An integrated Spanish/English biliteracy approach.* New York: Longman.

Pilgreen, J. (2006). Supporting English learners: Developing academic language in the content area classroom. In F. A. Young & N. L. Hadaway (Eds.), *Supporting the literacy development of English learners: Increasing success in all classrooms* (pp. 41–60). Newark, DE: International Reading Association.

Pinnell, G., & McCarrier, A. (1994). Interactive writing: A transition tool for assisting children in learning to read and write. In E. Hiebert & B. Taylor (Eds.), *Getting reading right from the start: Effective early literacy interventions* (pp. 149–170). Needham Heights, MA: Allyn & Bacon.

Pressley, M., & Afflerbach, P. (1995). *Verbal protocols of reading: The nature of constructively responsive reading.* Hillsdale, NJ: Erlbaum.

Prior, J., & Gerard, M. R. (2004). *Environmental print in the classroom: Meaningful connections for learning to read.* Newark, DE: International Reading Association.

Purcell-Gates, V. (1996). Stories, coupons, and the TV guide: Relationships between home literacy experiences and emergent literacy knowledge. *Reading Research Quarterly, 31,* 406–428.

Read, C. (1975). *Children's categorization of speech sounds in English.* Urbana, IL: National Council of Teachers of English.

Richgels, D. (2001). Invented spelling, phonemic awareness, and reading and writing instruction. In S. Neuman & D. Dickinson (Eds.), *Handbook of early literacy research* (pp. 142–155). New York: Guilford Press.

Richgels, D. (2005). Paying attention to language. *Reading Research Quarterly, 39,* 470–477.

Rodriguez-Brown, F. (1987). Questioning patterns and language proficiency in bilingual students. *NABE Journal, 13,* 217–233.

Rodriguez-Brown, F. V. (2003). Reflections on family literacy from a sociocultural perspective. *Reading Research Quarterly, 38,* 146–154.

Rodriguez-Galindo, A., & Wright, L. (2006, July). *English Language Learners: Teach them and they will learn.* Paper presented at the annual Reading First Conference, Reno, NV.

Roit, M. L. (2006). Essential comprehension strategies for English learners. In T. A. Young & N. L. Hadaway (Eds.), *Supporting the literacy development of English language learners: Increasing success in all classrooms* (pp. 80–95). Newark, DE: International Reading Association.

Rosenblatt, L. (1978). *The reader, the text, the poem: The transactional theory of the literacy work.* Carbondale: Southern Illinois University Press.

Roth, F., Speece, D., & Cooper, D. (2002). A longitudinal analysis of the connection between oral language and early reading. *Journal of Educational Research, 95,* 259–272.

Rumelhart, D. E. (1975). Notes on a schema for stories. In D. G. Bobrow & A. M. Collins (Eds.), *Representation and understanding: Studies in cognitive science* (pp. 211–236). New York: Academic Press.

Samway, K. (2006). *When English language learners write.* Portsmouth, NH: Heinemann.

Samway, K., & McKeon, D. (1999). *Myths and realities: Best practices for language minority students.* Portsmouth, NH: Heinemann.

Sénéchal, M. (1997). The differential effect of storybook reading on preschoolers' acquisition of expressive and receptive vocabulary. *Journal of Child Language, 24,* 123–138.

Shamir, A., & Korat, O. (2006). How to select CD-ROM storybooks for young children: The teachers' role. *The Reading Teacher, 59,* 532–543.

Shanahan, T. (2006). Relations among oral language, reading, and writing development. In C. MacArthur, S. Graham, & J. Fitzgerald (Eds.), *Handbook of writing research* (pp. 171–186). New York: Guilford Press.

Shanahan, T., & Beck, I. (2006). Effective literacy teaching for English-language learners. In D. August & T. Shanahan (Eds.), *Developing literacy in second-language learners* (pp. 415–448). Mahwah, NJ: Erlbaum.

Share, D., Jorm, A., MacLean, R., & Matthews, R. (1984). Sources of individual differences in reading acquisition. *Journal of Educational Psychology, 76,* 177–213.

Sleeter, C. E. (2001). Preparing teachers for culturally diverse schools. *Journal of Teacher Education, 52,* 94–106.

Smagorinsky, P., & Smith, M. (2002). Introduction. *Research in the Teaching of English, 36,* 305–308.

Smith, K. E., Landry, S. H., & Swank, P. R. (2000). The influence of early patterns of positive parenting on children's preschool outcomes. *Early Education and Development, 11,* 147–169.

Snow, C. E. (1986). Conversations with children. In P. Fletcher & M. Garmen (Eds.), *Language acquisition: Studies in first language development* (pp. 69–89). New York: Cambridge University Press.

Snow, C., Burns, M., & Griffin P. (Eds.). (1998). *Preventing reading difficulties in young children.* Washington, DC: National Academy Press.

Soltero, S. W. (2004). *Dual language: Teaching and learning in two languages.* Boston: Allyn & Bacon.

Stahl, S. (1992). Saying the "P" word: Nine guidelines for exemplary phonics instruction. *The Reading Teacher, 45,* 618–625.

Stanovich, K. (1986). Matthew effects in reading: some consequences of individual differences in the acquisition of literacy. *Reading Research Quarterly, 21,* 360–407.

Stauffer, R. (1975). *Directing the reading–thinking process*. New York: Harper & Row.

Stauffer, R. (1980). *The language experience approach to the teaching of reading* (2nd ed.). New York: Harper & Row.

Steffensen, M. S., Joag-Dev., C., & Anderson, R. C. (1979). A cross-cultural perspective on reading comprehension. *Reading Research Quarterly, 15*, 10–29.

Stein, N. L., & Glenn, C. G. (1979). An analysis of story comprehension in elementary school children. In R. O. Freedle (Ed.), *New directions in discourse processing* (Vol. 2, pp. 53–120). Norwood, NJ: Ablex.

Strickland, D., & Riley-Ayers, S. (2006). Early literacy: Policy and practice in the preschool years. *Preschool Policy Brief of the National Institute for Early Education Research, 10*, 1–3.

Strickland, D., & Snow, C. (2002). *Preparing our teachers: Opportunities for better reading instruction*. Washington, DC: Joseph Henry Press.

Strong, M. (1984). Integrative motivation: Cause or result of successful second language acquisition? *Language Learning, 34*, 1–13.

Strorch, S., & Whitehurst, G. (2002). Oral language and code-related precursors to reading: Evidence from a longitudinal structural model. *Developmental Psychology, 38*, 934–947.

Sulzby, E. (1985). Children's emergent reading of favorite storybooks: A developmental study. *Reading Research Quarterly, 20*, 458–481.

Taylor, D. (1983). *Family literacy: Young children learning to read and write*. Exeter, NH: Heinemann.

Taylor, W. L. (1953). Cloze procedure: A new tool for measuring readability. *Journalism Quarterly, 30*, 415–453.

Templeton, S. (1983). Using the spelling/meaning connection to develop word knowledge in older students. *Journal of Reading, 27*, 8–14.

Templeton, S. (1997). *Teaching the integrated language arts* (2nd ed.). Boston: Houghton Mifflin.

Tiedt, I. (1970). Exploring poetry patterns. *Elementary English, 45*, 1082–1084.

Tierney, R. J., & Readence, J. E. (2005). *Reading strategies and practices: A compendium* (6th ed.). Boston: Allyn & Bacon.

Tolchinsky, L. (2003). *The cradle of culture and what children know about writing and numbers before being taught*. Mahwah, NJ: Erlbaum.

Tolchinsky, L. (2006). The emergence of writing. In C. MacArthur, S. Graham, & J. Fitzgerald (Eds.), *Handbook of writing research* (pp. 83–95). New York: Guilford Press.

Tompkins, G. E. (2003). *Literacy for the 21st century* (3rd ed.). Upper Saddle River, NJ: Merrill.

Urzua, C. (1987). You stopped too soon: Second language children composing and revising. *TESOL Quarterly, 21*, 279–304.

U.S. Department of Education. (2002). *Survey of the states' limited English proficient students and available education programs and service*. Washington, DC: Author.

Valdés, G. (1996). *Con respeto: Bridging the distances between culturally diverse families and schools*. New York: Teachers College Press.

Valdez-Pierce, L. (2003). *Assessing English language learners*. Washington, DC: National Education Association

Wade-Woolley, L., & Siegel, L. (1997). The spelling performance of ESL and native speakers of English as a function of reading Skill. *Reading and Writing: An Interdisciplinary Journal, 9,* 387–406.

Watson, R. (2001). Literacy and oral language: Implications for early literacy acquisition. In S. Neuman & D. Dickinson (Eds.), *Handbook of early literacy research* (Vol. 1, pp. 43–53). New York: Guilford Press.

Watts-Taffe, S., & Truscott, D. M. (2000). Using what we know about language and literacy development for ESL students in mainstream classroom. *Language Arts, 77,* 258–266.

Waxman, H., Gray, J., & Padrón, Y. (2004a). Introduction and overview. In H. Waxman, Y. Padrón, & J. Gray (Eds.), *Educational resiliency: Student, teacher, and school perspectives* (pp. 3–10). Greenwich, CT: Information Age.

Waxman, H., Gray, J., & Padrón, Y. (2004b). Promoting educational resilience for student at-risk of failure. In H. Waxman, Y. Padrón, & J. Gray. (Eds.), *Educational resiliency: Student, teacher, and school perspectives* (pp. 37–62). Greenwich, CT: Information Age.

Weiner, L. (1999). *Urban teaching: The essentials.* New York: Teachers College Press.

Weinstein, C. F., & Mayer, R. F. (1987). The teaching of learning strategies. In M. C. Wittrock (Ed.), *Handbook of research on teaching* (pp. 315–327). New York: Macmillan.

Winne, R. H., Graham, L., & Prock, L. (1993). A model of poor readers' text-based inferencing: Effects of explanatory feedback. *Reading Research Quarterly, 28,* 536–566.

Wong, T., & Kao, S. (1991). The development of drawing principles in Chinese. In J. Wann, A. Wing, & N. Sovik (Eds.), *Development of graphic skills: Research perspectives and educational implications* (pp. 93–112). New York: Academic Press.

Xu, H. (1999). Young Chinese ESL children's home literacy experiences. *Reading Horizons, 40*(1), 47–64.

Xu, H. (2000a). Preservice teachers integrate understandings of diversity into literacy instruction: An adaptation of the ABCs model. *Journal of Teacher Education, 51,* 135–142.

Xu, H. (2000b). Preservice teachers in a literacy methods course consider issues of diversity. *Journal of Literacy Research, 32,* 505–532.

Xu, S. H. (2003). The learner, the teacher, the text, and the context: Sociocultural approaches to early literacy instruction for English language learners. In D. M. Barone & L. M. Morrow (Eds.), *Literacy and young children: Research-based practices* (pp. 61–80). New York: Guilford Press.

Xu, S. H. (2004). Teachers' reading of students' popular culture texts: The interplay of students' interests, teacher knowledge, and literacy curriculum. In C. M. Fairbanks, J. Worthy, B. Maloch, J. V. Hoffman, & D. L. Schallert (Eds.), *53rd yearbook of the National Reading Conference* (pp. 417–431). Oak Creek, WI: National Reading Conference.

Xu, S. H., & Rutledge, A. L. (2003). "Chickens start with Ch!": Kindergartners talk about print through environmental print. *Young Children, 58*(2), 44–51.

Xu, S. H., Sawyer, R., & Zunich, L. (2005). *Trading cards to comic strips: Popular culture texts and literacy learning in grades K–8.* Newark, DE: International Reading Association.

CHILDREN'S BOOKS CITED

Ada, A. F. (1995). *My mother plants strawberries*. Worthington, OH: SRA Macmillan/McGraw-Hill.

Adams, S. (2001). *The best book of weather*. New York: Kingfisher.

Aliki, B. (1986). *How a book is made*. New York: HarperCollins.

Bang, M. (1999). *When Sophie gets angry—really, really, angry . . .* New York: Blue Sky Press.

Berger, M., & Berger, G. (2002). *GRRR! A book about big cats*. New York: Scholastic.

Brett, J. (1989). *The mitten*. New York: Putnam's.

Brett, J. (1997). *The hat*. New York: Putnam's.

Carle, E. (1971). *Do you want to be my friend?* New York: HarperCollins.

Carlson, N. (1988). *I like me!* New York: Viking Penguin.

Choi, Y. (2001). *The name jar*. New York: Dell Dragonfly Books.

Cohen, M. (1967). *Will I have a friend?* New York: Aladdin Books.

Cole, J. (1996). *The magic school bus: Inside a beehive*. New York: Scholastic.

Cowley, J. (1996). *The little yellow chicken*. Bothell, WA: Wright Group.

Cowley, J. (1999). *Mrs. Wishy-Washy*. New York: Philomel.

dePaola, T. (1973). *Charlie needs a cloak*. New York: Simon & Schuster.

dePaola, T. (1975). *The cloud book*. New York: Holiday House.

de Regniers, B. S., Moore, E., White, M. M., & Carr, J. (1988). *Sing a song of popcorn: Every child's book of poems*. New York: Scholastic.

Ehlert, L. (1987). *Growing vegetable soup*. Orlando, FL: Harcourt Brace.

Ehlert, L. (1989). *Eating the alphabet: Fruits and vegetables from A to Z*. San Diego: Harcourt Brace.

Emberly, R. (1990a). *My house: A book in two languages—Mi casa: Un libro en dos lenguas*. New York: Little, Brown.

Emberly, R. (1990b). *Taking a walk: A book in two languages—Caminando: Un libro en dos lenguas*. New York: Little, Brown and Company.

Freeman, D. (1968). *Corduroy*. New York: Viking Penguin.

Galdone, P. (1970). *The three little pigs*. New York: Houghton Mifflin/Clarion Books.

Gans, R. (1984). *Let's go rock collecting*. New York: HarperCollins Children's Books.

Gibbons, G. (1997). *Gulls . . . gulls . . . gulls . . .* New York: Holiday House.

Kalan, R. (1978). *Rain*. New York: Greenwillow Books.

Kalan, R. (1981). *Jump, frog, jump*. New York: Greenwillow Books.

Koscielniak, B. (1995). *Geoffrey Groundhog predicts the weather*. New York: Houghton Mifflin.

Lachtman, O. (1995). *Pepita talks twice—Pepita habla dos veces*. Houston, TX: Piñata Books.

Levine, E. (1989). *I hate English!* New York: Scholastic.

Lionni, L. (1963). *Swimmy*. New York: Knopf.

Martin, B. (1983). *Brown bear, brown bear, what do you see?* New York: Holt, Rinehart & Winston.

Meharry, D. (2001). *Mud, mud, mud*. Washington, DC: National Geographic Society.

Metzger, S. (1998). *Ladybug's birthday*. New York: Scholastic.

Miranda, A. (1997). *To market, to market*. San Diego: Harcourt Brace.

Otto, C. B. (2001). *Shadows*. New York: Scholastic.

Peddicord, J. (2005). *Night wonders*. Watertown, MA: Charlesbridge.

Pfeffer, W. (1999). *Sounds all around*. New York: HarperTrophy.

Prima Games. (2004). *Yu-Gi-Oh!: Reshef of destruction*. Roseville, CA: Author.

Recorvits, H. (2003). *My name in Yoon*. New York: Farrar, Straus & Giroux.

Riley, L. A. (1997). *Mouse mess*. New York: Blue Sky Press.

Scotton, R. (2005). *Russell the sheep*. New York: HarperCollins.

Seuss, Dr. (1957). *The cat in the hat*. New York: Random House.

Silverstein, S. (1964). *The giving tree*. New York: Harper & Row.

Slobodkina, E. (1987). *Caps for sale*. New York: HarperTrophy.

Soto, G. (1993). *Too many tamales*. New York: Putnam.

Swamp, C. J. (1995). *Giving thanks*. New York: Lee & Low Books.

Terban, M. (1983). *In a pickle and other funny idioms*. New York: Clarion Books.

Trapani, I. (2001). *Baa baa black sheep*. Watertown, MA: Charlesbridge.

Walsh, E. S. (1989). *Mouse paint*. Orlando, FL: Harcourt Brace.

Walsh, E. S. (1994). *Pip's magic*. Orlando, FL: Harcourt Brace.

Yolen, J., Teague, M. (2006). *How do dinosaurs play with their friends?/¿Cómo juegan los dinosaurios con sus amigos?* New York: Scholastic.

Index

274